LITERATE LIVES IN THE INFORMATION AGE

Narratives of Literacy
From the United States

LITERATE LIVES IN THE INFORMATION AGE

Narratives of Literacy From the United States

Cynthia L. Selfe
Michigan Technological University

Gail E. Hawisher
University of Illinois, Urbana-Champaign

 LAWRENCE ERLBAUM ASSOCIATES, PUBLISHERS
2004   Mahwah, New Jersey   London

Lawrence Erlbaum Associates, Inc., Publishers
10 Industrial Avenue
Mahwah, New Jersey 07430

Cover design by Kathryn Houghtaling Lacey

Library of Congress Cataloging-in-Publication Data

Literate Lives in the Information Age: Narratives of Literacy from the United States,
  by Cynthia L. Selfe and Gail E. Hawisher
    p.   cm.
    Includes bibliographical references and indexes.
    ISBN: 0-8058-4313-2 (cloth: alk. paper)—ISBN 0-8058-4314-0 (pbk : alk. paper).

Copyright information for this volume can be obtained by contacting
the Library of Congress.

Books published by Lawrence Erlbaum Associates are printed on acid-free paper,
and their bindings are chosen for strength and durability.

Printed in the United States of America
10 9 8 7 6 5 4 3 2 1

Contents

133121

Acknowledgments

During the more than six years that we have been working on this research, we have met and talked with a great number of people from all parts of the United States and abroad. All have contributed enormously to our project in suggesting stories to us that we may have overlooked; in giving alternate interpretations to the literacy narratives we have collected; in recommending additional studies we had not read; and, sometimes, in confirming for us our analysis of how people have taken up and incorporated the literacies of technology into their everyday lives. We have been privileged to share our work with them and have learned a great deal about research into literacy along the way.

Large-scale investigations of literacy, digital and print, are difficult to undertake. They require time, money, labor—support of all kinds. There are interviews to collect, digital recorders and computers to purchase, transcriptions to type, graduate students to involve, interviews to analyze. Each case study takes time to draft; to set in historical, cultural, and social contexts; to share with co-authors and colleagues; to revise and re-think. The stories in this book, in other words, are told only with the generosity of many people, groups, and organizations.

We owe a great deal to Teresa Bertram, the project's transcription specialist, and to the graduate students who helped conduct some of the interviews: Paula Boyd, Julie Estep, Nichole Brown, Joseph Johansen, among them. Their work and ours could not have been undertaken without the generous and longstanding support of colleagues and graduate students in the Center for Writing Studies and Department of English, University of Illinois, Urbana-Champaign; the Humanities Department at Michigan Technological University; and the Department of English at Clemson University. In addition, we owe thanks to the International Society of Technical Communication and to the National Council of Teachers of English. Both organizations supported this research project with grant funding that allowed us to do work we consider important.

We are also indebted to those editors and researchers who have published parts of our research in the pages of their journals and edited collections: Rebecca Burnett, editor of the *Journal of Business and Technical Communication*; Marilyn Cooper, editor of *College Communication and Composition*; Don Daiker, Ed White, and Lynn Z. Bloom, editors of *Composition Studies in the New Millennium*; Nancy Barron, Nancy Grimm, and Sibylle Gruber, editors of *Taking on the Touchy Subjects of Race, Class, and Ethnicity*; and Beth Daniell and Peter Mortensen, editors of *Women and Literacy*. Our research is the better for their insightful editorial suggestions. Linda Bathgate and Eileen Meehan, our editors at Erlbaum, have at all times lent their professional expertise to making sure that the book on our research was every bit as good as the research that went into the study itself.

We are extraordinarily grateful as well to those colleagues and departments who invited us to share our work on their campuses and who provided a forum for productive discussions. These include those at Temple University; the American University of Cairo; University of Arizona; University of Oslo; University of Massachusetts, Amherst; University of Louisville; University of Tokyo; Dakota State University; Rutgers University; Pennsylvania State University; and Aristotle University, among them.

Special thanks also go out to our partners and family without whom it is unlikely that any of this work would have been accomplished.

Gail E. Hawisher
Urbana, Illinois

Cynthia L. Selfe
Louisville, Kentucky

February 2004

INTRODUCTION

Literate Lives in the Information Age

Gail E. Hawisher
Cynthia L. Selfe

The increasing presence of personal computers in homes, workplaces, communities, and schools has brought about dramatic changes in the ways people across the world create and respond to information. In the United States, for example, the ability to read, compose, and communicate in computer environments—called variously technological, digital, or electronic literacy[1]—has acquired immense importance not only as a basic

---

[1]We couple the concept of literacy with technology although recognizing the unease with which some scholars view the proliferation of terms like *visual literacy, digital literacy, media literacy,* and so forth. Anne Wysocki and Johndan Johnson-Eilola (1999), for example, argue that "when we speak ... of [alphabetic] 'literacy' as though it were a basic, neutral, contextless set of skills, the word keeps us hoping ... that there could be an easy cure for economic and social and political pain, that only a lack of literacy keeps people poor or oppressed" (p. 355). Increasingly, of course, this same kind of thinking is applied to online literacy practices: If only we could teach everyone to be technologically literate and give all easy access to computers, the world would rise above its poverty and ignorance. Gunther Kress (2003) also suggests that literacy is an inappropriate word to link with terms not specifically aimed at "[making] messages using letters as the means for recording that message" (p. 23). For Kress, not only is the move imperialistic (many cultures don't use the concept of literacy, and still others don't even use letters or an alphabet), but it's also confusing. According to Kress, it allows us to conflate too simply the competencies required to make meaning in multimodal contexts. As the title of our book attests, however, we endorse linking literacy with words, such as *technological, digital, electronic,* as well as the all encompassing *literacies of technology.* We believe that by naming these abilities *literacies,* we signal the enormous importance they hold for functioning in today's literate world. James Gee (2003) would seem to agree. By emphasizing "the idea of different sorts of multimodal literacy" (p. 14)

1

job skill,[2] but also, every bit as significant, as an essential component of literate activity.[3] Today, if U.S. students cannot write to the screen—if they cannot design, author, analyze, and interpret material on the Web and in other digital environments—they will have difficulty functioning effectively as literate human beings in a growing number of social spheres. Today, the ability to write well—and to write well with computers and within digital environments—plays an enormous role in determining whether students can participate and succeed in the life of school, work, and community. Despite their growing importance, however, we really know very little about how and why people have acquired and developed, or failed to acquire and develop, the literacies of technology during the past 25 years or so. Nor do we know how historical, cultural, economic, political, or ideological factors have affected, or been affected by, peoples' acquisition and development of these technological literacies.[4]

This paucity of information, unfortunately, has not stopped educators and policymakers from framing important national standards and policies designed to increase in the United States the level of technological literacy, nor from spending millions of dollars on programs that provide

---

and by asserting that "both modes and multimodality go far beyond images and words to include sounds, music, movement, bodily sensations, and smells" (p. 14), he extends the reach of literacy. For Gee, "in the modern world, print literacy is not enough. People need to be literate in a great variety of different semiotic domains" (p. 19). We agree.

[2]Evidence of the increasing importance placed on computing as a prerequisite for many available jobs is not difficult to come by. For various takes on this pattern, consult the Hudson Institute's *Workforce 2020* (Judy & D'Amico, 1997), and the *Falling through the Net* series (1995, 1998, 1999, 2000) issued by the National Telecommunications and Information Administration, *The Digital Workforce* report issued by the Office of Technology Policy (Meares & Sargent, 1999), and *Futurework,* issued by the U.S. Department of Labor (1999).

[3]See Paul Prior's (1998) *Writing/Disciplinarity* for a particularly apt discussion of literate activity. He writes, in part, that "writers and readers are inescapably situated in particular places and in the moment-to-moment flow of lived time. . . . Literate activity . . . is not located *in* acts of reading and writing, but *as* cultural forms of life saturated with textuality, that is strongly motivated and mediated by texts" (p. 138, emphasis in original).

[4]By *technological literacy,* or *literacies,* we mean the practices involved in reading, writing, and exchanging information in online environments, as well as the values associated with such practices—cultural, social, political, and educational. For us, the term differs from *computer literacy* in that it focuses primarily on the word *literacy*—thus, on communication skills and values—rather than on the skills required to use a computer. To distinguish technological literacy from computer literacy, literacy scholars have also used the related terms *electronic literacy* (Selfe & Hawisher, 2002; Sullivan & Dautermann, 1996); *digital literacy* (Tyner); and the *literacies of technology* (Hawisher & Selfe). We use the last term, literacies of technology, as an all-encompassing phrase to connect social practices, people, technology, values, and literate activity, which, in turn, are embedded in a larger cultural ecology. All these terms are synonymous with our use of technological literacy, and we use them in this book interchangeably. In all cases, they focus on literacy practices and values in online environments rather than on the skills required to use computers themselves.

training in this area, nor from designing curricula that teach the literacies of technology in schools.[5] Such ill-informed efforts are especially ironic in a time when computer-based communication has achieved increasing significance in both national and global arenas, and in all areas of political, economic, and governmental relations.

Perhaps most germane to this particular book, educators and policy-makers have continued to base important local and national decisions on a minimal amount of information about how students acquire, or don't, the literacies of technology. Before we can hope to do a better, more informed job of making decisions about these literacies as they are taught in classrooms, homes, community centers, and workplaces across the United States, we need to learn much more about how various social, cultural, political, ideological, and economic factors have operated dynamically, in relation to each other, at various levels of influence, and over time, to shape the acquisition and development of digital literacies within peoples' lives. Equally important, we need to learn much more about how people, individually and collectively, have shaped the nature of technological literacy as it continues to be defined and practiced.

The goal of this book is to begin such a process—to begin tracing technological literacy as it has emerged over the last few decades within the United States. In the following pages, we describe our long-term project, and we focus on the case studies of a group of people in the United States who have become proficient, to lesser and greater extents, with the literacies of technology during the last 25 years or so. For the book, we have selected 20 case studies from the larger corpus of over 350 people who participated in interviews or completed a technological literacy questionnaire during the past five or six years.[6] We recruited the participants in this study primarily through school settings, calling first on colleagues

---

[5]Efforts to develop standards for the literacies of technology have occurred both within and across academic disciplines. In 1996, for instance, the National Council of Teachers of English and the International Reading Association published a standards document for teachers of English and the language arts that describes skills and understandings students should acquire about reading, writing, and communicating in electronic contexts (*Standards for the English Language Arts*, 1996). Similarly, in 2000, the National Council of Teachers of Mathematics published the most recent version of *Principles and Standards for School Mathematics*, a document that identifies students' ability to communicate effectively about mathematics—in electronic contexts as well as in other situations—as a key principle in enabling individuals to "fulfill personal ambitions and career goals in an ever-changing world" (http://standards.nctm.org/). More broadly, across disciplines, The International Society for Technology in Education published educational standards in 1999 that are designed to "prepare our students for adult citizenship in the Information Age" ("Standards Projects," *National Educational Technology Standards for Students*, http://www.iste.org/standards/index.cfm).

[6]See Appendix for the interview protocol, which includes the questions to which participants responded in both the face-to-face interviews and online submissions.

and students we knew from around the United States. We also identified participants through the recommendations of these initial volunteers. As a result, the brothers, sisters, relatives, and friends of people we contacted also became part of our informant pool—secretaries, former domestic workers, graphic artists, technical communicators, program directors, and managers, among just a few of their current and former occupations.

Drawn from this larger group, the 20 individuals who contributed their stories to this book ranged at the time of the interviews from 14 to 60 years old and were brought up, or lived in, for extended periods, a wide array of states across the United States, with two spending some time in parts of Europe as members of military families. Among the various places in which the 20 grew up, just about every region of the United States is represented (Northeast, Midwest, Southeast, Southwest, and the West), primarily because most of the participants, like many other people in the United States during the latter half of the 20th century, moved frequently from one area to another. Although today the participants make their homes in California, Georgia, Illinois, Michigan, New Jersey, Ohio, South Carolina, Utah, and Virginia, many are likely in the future, as in the past, to move to other areas of the United States during their lifetimes. Several of the participants grew up in relatively rural areas, some in good-size towns, and others came of age and attended schools in the nation's largest cities, Chicago, Detroit, and Miami among them. Of the 20 in the group, 13 claim a European American heritage; 4 African American; 1 bi-racial; 1 Latino; and another American Indian. Fifteen of the 20 participants represented in our book are women and five are men. Sixteen of the 20 have earned high school diplomas, two were attending secondary school when they were interviewed, and one was attending the eighth grade. Several of the participants hold master's degrees, and five hold doctoral degrees, often in English and our own fields of writing studies and technical communication.

We have chosen to feature these particular stories for several reasons. First, we think they provide an interesting set of cultural tracings—albeit fragmentary and incomplete—of how personal computers found their way into the lives, homes, schools, communities, and workplaces of some people within the United States during the period we are studying. For these 20 people, the introduction of personal computers, a relatively cheap and durable example of technology, was associated with a period of major social, educational, and technological change, one in which peoples' lives, and literacies, were altered in fundamental ways.[7]

---

[7]For an extensive explanation of the role that networked computers have played in bringing about change and ensuring certain political phenomena an extended global impact—among them, international terrorism, religious fundamentalism, the Green movement, and feminism—see Manuel Castells' three volume series, collectively entitled *The Information*

Second, because many of these people grew up under markedly different circumstances, we believe their cases will help readers further appreciate the importance of situating technological literacy in specific cultural, material, educational, and familial contexts—in particular, contexts characterized by varied levels of support (social, economic, educational, technological) for electronic literacy efforts. In this sense, the case studies provide some clues about the constellation of factors that can affect—and can be affected by—electronic literacy acquisition and development. We call this interrelated set of factors the *cultural ecology* of literacy. With this term, we hope to suggest how literacy is related in complex ways to existing cultural milieu; educational practices and values; social formations like race, class, and gender; political and economic trends and events; family practices and experiences; and material conditions—among many other factors. As the work of Brian Street (1995), James Gee (1996), Harvey Graff (1987), and Deborah Brandt (1995, 1998, 1999, 2001) reminds us, we can understand literacy as a set of practices and values only when we properly situate our studies within the context of a particular historical period, a particular cultural milieu, and a specific cluster of material conditions.

Third, because these people grew up, attended school, and learned to use computers over a period of some 60 years, the oldest having been born in 1942 and the youngest in 1987, their cases can provide some valuable temporal and historical perspectives on literacy. Within a particular cultural ecology, we believe, various forms of literacy have their own particular life spans. As Deborah Brandt has argued, they emerge, accumulate, and compete with other literacies, and, we add, they also fade, according to what Ronald Deibert (1997) might call their general "fitness" (p. 31) with other key social, cultural, and historical phenomena. Thus, we have chosen these case studies for the temporal and historical perspectives they provide on both print and electronic literacies.

Finally, we feature these stories because they resonate with parts of our own stories: the ways in which these people's lives are situated historically and culturally; their economic backgrounds; the ways in which they have learned to use and cope with technology; the schools they have attended and in which they teach; their experiences as students and instructors; the mentoring they have experienced and provided; their relationships with family and friends; and the literacies they share with us. The stories of the participants speak to us, and we hope they will to readers as well.

Age: Economy, Society and Culture (Castells, 1996, 1997, 1998). The New London Group, in their book *Multiliteracies: Literacy Learning and the Design of Social Futures* (Cope & Kalantzis, 2000), explores the role that computer networks and technological communications systems have played in multiplying and transforming people's "lifeworlds."

Some Notes on Background and Method

In 1998, inspired by an outstanding talk Deborah Brandt gave at the University of Louisville's Thomas R. Watson Conference on her oral-history literacy project, we began a relatively large-scale study to identify how and why people in the United States acquired and developed (or, for various reasons, failed to acquire and develop) electronic literacy between the years of 1978 and 2003. During that period, as relatively cheap and durable, mass-produced and mass-marketed machines became commercially available for the first time to many families, personal computers entered composition classrooms across the nation in large numbers and were broadly accepted by many school-age children as the composing tool of choice. Since that time, these machines have become so ubiquitous that their many effects are becoming increasingly invisible.[8] Before our cultural memory of this important time faded entirely, we wanted to document the period during which these machines first wove their way into, and altered, the fabric of our culture.

Given this context, we also felt it would be important to analyze the information we collected within the larger contexts of the historic, political, economic, and ideological movements that occurred during this period. In addition, we wanted to reconcile, to register, to bring into intellectual correspondence this series of perspectives—the macro-, medial, and micro-levels—in the interest of obtaining a more robust, multidimensional image of technological literacy acquisition and development. We thought such a study would make important contributions to what we now know about how and why people develop or fail to develop the literacies of technology and that the results would be of interest to educators, employers, and parents. We also hoped that what we learned from the study would help make us more effective teachers and educators.

The project that we finally settled on, like Deborah Brandt's (2001) work, was grounded in oral-history and life-history research (Bertaux, 1981; Bertaux & Thompson, 1993, 1997; Lummis, 1987; Thompson, 1988). Our work attempts to investigate people's technological literacy experiences through a standard set of interview questions that participants respond to orally, in face-to-face interviews, or in writing, via some digital context (e.g., on a disk, on the Web, or in a word processing file residing

---

[8]See Bertram C. Bruce and Maureen Hogan's (1998) chapter for a fascinating discussion on "The Disappearance of Technology." They argue that "[a]s technologies embed themselves in everyday discourse and activity, a curious thing happens. The more we look, the more they slip into the background. Despite our attention, we lose sight of the way they give shape to our daily lives. This disappearance effect is evident when we consider whether a technology empowers people to do things that would be difficult, or even impossible otherwise" (p. 270).

on a computer network). The prompting questions ask for demographic data and for information about family history, stories about literacy practices and values, memories of schooling environments and workplace experiences, and descriptions of technology use and avoidance (see Appendix). Our goal was (and continues to be)[9] to collect what we call technological literacy autobiographies from a wide range of people of differing ages, genders, ethnic and racial groups, and geographical backgrounds, using face-to-face interviews and online submissions. After seeking and obtaining approval to conduct human-subjects research from our respective universities, we collected over 350 such autobiographies in oral interviews, conducted face to face, and in written interviews, conducted online. Over the years that the project has been under way, advances in computing, and the increasing number of people connected to the Internet have enabled us to do a great deal more of the research through e-mail and over the Web.

Brandt's (2001) oral-history and life-history methodology is congruent with the ecological model of electronic literacy studies outlined by Bertram Bruce and Maureen Hogan (1998). As these researchers point out, electronic literacy practices and values can be understood only as

> constituent parts of life, elements of an ecological system . . . that gives us a basis for understanding the interpenetration between machines, humans, and the natural world. . . . [L]iteracies, and the technologies of literacy, can only be understood in relation to larger systems of practice. Most technologies become so enmeshed in daily experience that they disappear. (p. 272)

For this project, we also tried to extend this ecological understanding in ways suggested to us by other literacy or media scholars, such as Marilyn Cooper (1986), Ronald Deibert, (1997), and Daniel White (1998)—exploring the social and cultural ecology that forms the context of literacy practices. In describing the cultural ecology of digital literacies, then, we focused on the "existing stock of social forces and ideas" (Deibert, p. 31), political and economic formations, and available communication environments within which individuals acquired electronic literacy. In using this term and this approach, we hope to emphasize the importance of context—how particular historical periods, cultural milieus, and material conditions affected people's acquisition of the literacies of technology.

---

[9]Our study is ongoing in that we continue to conduct in-depth interviews with new participants and to collect technological literacy autobiographies online. Most recently, we have turned to colleagues and students from different parts of the world in an effort to document their experiences in acquiring the literacies of technology. As information technology continues to change, through e-mail we also persist in asking many of the current participants additional questions regarding their acquisition of emerging digital literacies.

At the beginning of this project, our basic approach was to read transcripts carefully several times and to take notes on them in an attempt to
extract the outlines of the case study. From these efforts, we began to identify a list of the basic kinds of factors that seemed to shape digital literacy
(e.g., economic factors, business/workplace factors, sociocultural factors)
and the various levels at which these effects seemed operative (e.g., at the
level of the individual, family, local community, or nation).

Eventually, to increase the systematic nature of our examinations and
to gain a more systematic sense of how and where specific effects shaped
the literacies and lives of people, we created a matrix that allowed us to
represent data visually. We present the draft matrix in Table I.1 as an aid
to readers, but with some appropriate cautions. First, because the matrix
represents specific categories of factors, levels of effects, and discrete cells
of data, it gives an erroneous impression of tidiness. The data we collected
from the transcripts were (and continue to be) much less discrete, much
messier and more complex within people's lived experiences. Second, although we think all the major factors identified by the draft schema have
some organizing and structuring effects on people's lives (usually in some
complex relationship or interactive dynamic), particular factors or clusters
of factors may have only minimal, or invisible, effects on an individual's
acquisition and development of technological literacy—or, if they have a
greater effect, neither we nor the people who contributed their technological literacy autobiographies were conscious of the fact. Third, we know
that this matrix is only a start—there are many factors that affect the
literacies of technology that we have not yet observed and many ways in
which these factors interact to shape, and be shaped by, the lived experiences of people. We see this matrix, then, as a newly developed tool that
may be useful, in revised forms, to other researchers who want to describe
and talk about literacy.

The left-hand column of the matrix lists the different categories of factors, trends, and situations that we identified as affecting (and being affected by) people's technological literacy practices in the interviews and
surveys we collected (e.g., literacy, business/workplace, sociocultural,
political, economic/material, educational). The bottom row of the matrix
identifies the levels at which these factors seemed to be located (e.g., individual, peer group, family, community/local, regional, national, global).
The cells formed by the intersection of these axes are filled with gray ge-
neric descriptions that guided our thinking in noting data. After we read
and studied the transcripts, and as we prepared to write about the cases,
we correlated the guidelines in the cells with specific data from the cases,
listing the corresponding data as we did so.

Because voice was clearly an important part of these case studies, we
tried to maintain as much as possible of the contributors' responses, tell-

ing people's stories using their own words and language. Thus, in our writing, we feature participants' own voices as frequently as possible and try to keep intact their words and their phrasing, their grammatical structures and their distinctive word choices, even the oral markers of their speech (for people who completed oral interviews). This approach, we believe, has helped us retain the personality of contributors' language, along with important markers of class and age and geographical idioms. Because the questions asked within the autobiography protocol were not strictly chronological and because we wanted to provide readers with a concise and coherent discussion, we have excerpted and sometimes reordered the comments taken from these autobiographies. Ellipses in the texts that follow mark the removal of some redundant conversational markers, interruptions, and asides (in the case of face-to-face interviews), as well as obvious digressions and backtracking. Brackets indicate explanatory additions by the researchers.

Following Brandt, we have also relied in part on a kind of birth cohort analysis. By collecting stories from participants in different age groups, we have been able to examine their experiences through what Norman Ryder (1965) calls "their unique location in the stream of history" (quoted in Brandt, 2001, p. 11). We found this method particularly useful when looking at digital literacies, in part, because the rapid changes in the technology occasioned very different literacy experiences over relatively short expanses of time. For example, those individuals who came to computers in the 1970s and early 1980s were likely to have considerable exposure to various programming languages (e.g., Cobol, Fortran, Pascal, Basic), whereas those who followed sometimes ten or even five years later defined computer literacy by their knowledge of various software applications (e.g., WordPerfect, PageMaker, HyperCard). Through all these years, there was an increased emphasis on computer-based reading and writing as the sophistication of the software and the number and kinds of software programs changed over short periods of time. As Brandt (2001) notes, "what people are able to do with their writing or reading in any time and place—as well as what others do to them with writing and reading—contribute to their sense of identity, normality, and possibility" (p. 11). We would agree and, at the same time, add that the possibilities and effects of people's writing or reading are shaped, in part, by the information technologies to which people have access at any point in time.

Although the case studies we present here are set in the frames of large-scale social, historical, and cultural trends that have exerted shaping influences on people's electronic literacies, we want to avoid suggesting that these large-scale trends had a one-way structuring effect on people's experiences, literacies, and lives. Humans themselves, we believe, shape the circumstances of their lives in countless important ways. Moreover, we

TABLE I.1

Factors and Trends That Affect

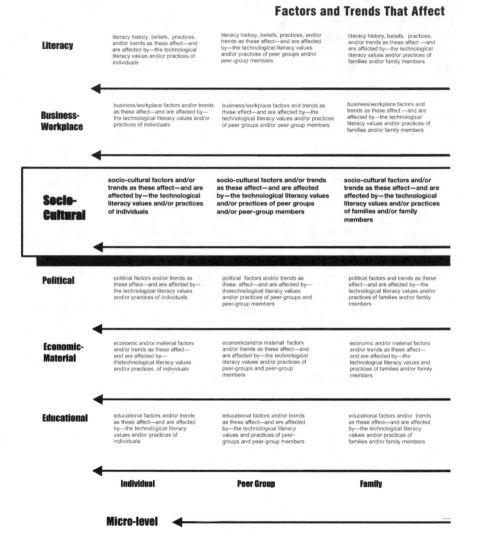

	Individual	Peer Group	Family
Literacy	literacy history, beliefs, practices, and/or trends as these affect—and are affected by—the technological literacy values and/or practices of individuals	literacy history, beliefs, practices, and/or trends as these affect—and are affected by—the technological literacy values and/or practices of peer groups and/or peer-group members	literacy history, beliefs, practices, and/or trends as these affect —and are affected by—the technological literacy values and/or practices of families and/or family members
Business-Workplace	business/workplace factors and/or trends as these affect—and are affected by—the technological literacy values and/or practices of individuals	business/workplace factors and trends as these affect—and are affected by—the technological literacy values and/or practices of peer groups and/or peer-group members	business/workplace factors and trends as these affect —and are affected by—the technological literacy values and/or practices of families and/or family members
Socio-Cultural	socio-cultural factors and/or trends as these affect—and are affected by—the technological literacy values and/or practices of individuals	socio-cultural factors and/or trends as these affect—and are affected by—the technological literacy values and/or practices of peer groups and/or peer-group members	socio-cultural factors and/or trends as these affect—and are affected by—the technological literacy values and/or practices of families and/or family members
Political	political factors and/or trends as these affect—and are affected by— the technological literacy values and/or practices of individuals	political factors and/or trends as these affect—and are affected by— thetechnological literacy values and/or practices of peer-groups and peer-group members	political factors and trends as these affect—and are affected by—the technological literacy values and/or practices of families and/or family members
Economic-Material	economic and/or material factors and/or trends as these affect— and are affected by— thetechnological literacy values and/or practices of individuals	economicand/or material factors and/or trends as these affect—and are affected by—the technological literacy values and/or practices of peer-groups and peer-group members	economic and/or material factors and/or trends as these affect— and are affected by—the technological literacy values and practices of families and/or family members
Educational	educational factors and/or trends as these affect—and are affected by—the technological literacy values and/or practices of individuals	educational factors and/or trends as these affect—and are affected by—the technological literacy values and practices of peer-groups and peer-group members	educational factors and/or trends as these affect—and are affected by—the technological literacy values and/or practices of families and/or family members

Individual   **Peer Group**   **Family**

Micro-level

TABLE I.1   *(Cont.)*

—and Are Affected by—Technological Literacy

Community/Local	Regional	National	Global
literacy history, beliefs, practices, and/or trends as these affect —and are affected by—the technological literacy values and/or practices of localities and/or communities	literacy history, beliefs, practices, and/or trends as these affect—and are affected by—the technological literacy values and/or practices of regions	literacy history, beliefs, practices, and/or trends as these affect— and are affected by—technological literacy values and/or practices across the nation	literacy history, beliefs, trends, and/or contexts as these affect—and are affected by— technological literacy values and/or practices around the world
business/workplace beliefs, practices, and/or contexts of as these affect —and are affected by— the technological literacy values and/or practices of localities and/or communities	business/worklace beliefs, practices, and/or contexts as theseaffect —and are affected by—the technological literacy values and/or practices of regions	business/workplace factors and/or trends as these affect— and are affected by—technological literacy values and/or practices acrossthe nation	business/workplace factors and/or trends as these affect—and are affected by—technological literacy values and/orpractices around the world
socio-cultural factors and/or trends as these affect— and are affected by—the technological literacy values and/or practices of localities and/or communities	**socio-cultural factors and/or trends as these affect—and are affected by—the technological literacy values and/or practices of regions**	**socio-cultural factors and/or trends as these affect—and are affected by—technological literacy values and/or practices across the nation**	**socio-cultural factors and/or trends as these affect—and are affected by—technological literacy values and/or practices around the world**
political beliefs and/or practices as these affect—and are affected by—the technological literacy values and/or practices of localities and/or communities	political beliefs and/or practices as these affect—and are affected by—the technological literacy values and/or practices of regions	political factors and/or trends asthese affect—and are affected by— technological literacy values and/or practices across the nation	politicalfactors and/or trends as these affect—and are affected by—technological literacy values and/or practices around the world
economic and/or material factors and trends as these affect by—the technological literacy values and/or practices of localities and communities	economic and/or material factors and/or trends as these affect—and are affected by—the technological literacy values and/or practices of regions	economic and/or material factors and/or trends as these affect and are affected by— technological literacy values and/or practices across the nation	economic and/or material factors and/or trends as these affect—and are affected by— technological literacy values and/or practices around the world
educational factors and/or trends as these affect—and are affected by— the technological literacy practices and/or values of localities and communities	educational factors and/or trends as these affect—and are affected by—the technological literacy practices and /or values of regions	educational factors and/ortrends as these affect— and are affected by—the technological literacy practices and/or values across the nation	educational factors and/or trends as these affect— and are affected by—the technological literacy practices and/or values around the world
Community/Local	**Regional**	**National**	**Global**

duality of structuring (Giddens, 1979)   **Macro-Level**

know that large-scale social or cultural patterns are created by the ac-
tions—and the divergent experiences—of people living out their lives.
Thus, our project is also based on the work of scholars such as Anthony
Giddens (1979), Michel DeCerteau (1984), and Ernesto Laclau and Chantal
Mouffe (1985), who suggest that human agents both shape and are shaped
by the cultural, educational, economic, and social contexts they inhabit.

Given this understanding, our work in this book attempts to demonstrate the active agency of the participants with whom we worked. For example, all of the case-study participants have been asked to co-author
their chapter with us. We were influenced in this decision by Caroline
Brettell's (1996) collection *When They Read What We Write*, which presents
a series of perspectives on studies like ours—anthropological projects,
ethnographies, and life histories—and talks about the ways in which
modernist approaches to such writing has often suffered from the limited
perspectives of academics and professional scholars who, as Schoen
(1983) notes, still cling to an understanding of "the superior academic
value of 'pure knowledge' inherited from the 'model of technical rational-
ity' that has been influential in all American social sciences" (p. 27). As
Alexandra Jaffe (1996) points out in this same collection, such an approach
to research claims a "distance between observer and observed" that is, to a
great extent, an "ethnographic fiction," one that scholars have employed
to "maintain control over . . . 'subjects' " (p. 51). As a corrective to this
modernist approach, Brettell and others in her collection suggest the alternative method of having subjects "talk back" (p. 9), comment on, modify,
change, and correct scholars' interpretations of what they said. Talking
back, as Jaffe goes on to say, helps to "undermine" professional
ethnographers' "ability to construct an unproblematic other, and hence,
an unproblematic self" (p. 52). In our experience, the reflexivity established by this dialogue is not only a positive and productive characteristic
of postmodern anthropology, but, as Jaffe points out, a realistic and "essential condition of interaction with the people we study" (p. 51).

Other feminist researchers who question their abilities to represent accurately the stories of research participants also shaped our thinking.
From Deborah Britzman (2000), for instance, we learned that although,
like her, we desired to tell "good stories filled with the stuff of rising and
falling action . . . that there is a contradictory point of no return, of having
to abandon the impossible desire to portray the study's subjects as they
would portray themselves" (p. 32). We recognized this dilemma and decided that co-authorship, as a refinement in method, would give the participants more say in the politics of interpretation. We looked, too, to experimental sociologist Laurel Richardson (2000) who asks "what practices
[can] support our writing and develop a care for the self" (p. 153), ourselves in this case, at the same time honoring "the ethical subject's relation

to [our] research practices" (p. 153). How would, in Richardson's words, "the theoretical concepts of feminist poststructuralism—reflexivity, authority, authorship, subjectivity, power, language, ethics, representation"—play out in our study? And we turned to Patti Lather (2000) and her decision to situate her research on women living with HIV/AIDS in a "feminist poststructural problematic of accountability to stories that belong to others," all the while attending to "the crisis of representation" (p. 285). In other words, we asked how we could change our actual ways of working—of writing and interpreting—to learn more from the participants we studied rather than just about them (Reinharz, 1992). To our minds, co-authorship seemed a viable, practical, and ethical resolution.

In thinking through our decision, we also slowly came to the realization that the project we had undertaken was no longer our own. It belonged, as well, to the people we interviewed and surveyed—their words and their stories were continual reminders that they had claimed the intellectual ground of the project as their own. When we turned to the participants, finally, and asked if they would be willing to co-author their chapters, the great majority of those whom we approached accepted, only a few preferring to maintain their anonymity and privacy.[10] In the pages that follow, then, co-authors include Damon Davis, an undergraduate at Michigan Technological University, who found a calling in designing Web sites for Black social organizations; Sally Osborne and Jill Van Wormer, who both serve today as technical communicators in the corporate sector; Paula Boyd, now Director of the Learning Center at Parkland College, a community college in Champaign, Illinois; Mary Sheridan-Rabideau, an assistant professor at Rutgers University; Karen Lunsford, an assistant professor at the University of California, Santa Barbara; Dean Woodbeck, a university public relations manager; Melissa Pearson, faculty member at Midlands Tech, a two-year school in Columbia, South Carolina; Tom Lugo, writing instructor at the University of Illinois; Nichole Brown, a technical communicator in the public sector; Jená Burges, colleague at Longwood College; Jane Blakelock, colleague at Wright State University; Janice Walker, colleague at Georgia Southern University; Dànielle DeVoss, colleague at Michigan State University; Joseph Johansen, a professional graphic artist and communication designer; Brittney Moraski, a high school student in rural Michigan; and Charles Jackson, a high school student in Greenville, South Carolina.

In addition to the reasons given earlier, we chose to foreground these participants within the larger study because as we read, reread, and analyzed the interview data, these particular interviews resonated with our

---

[10]Three of the participants featured in the book chose not to take on the role of co-authors. To them we have assigned pseudonyms.

own experiences and with the themes we understood as emerging from the larger corpus of data. Our selection also enabled us to make use of the birth cohort analysis we mentioned earlier. In other words, by comparing the age groups and generations of these case-study participants, we were able to situate our study within a larger cultural ecology.

Responses and Observations of Co-Authors

After we began to engage in our collaborations with participants, we came to realize how much they enriched the reports of the project. We also began to wonder how our co-authors had perceived the collaborations, how they felt about the process of speaking back to the investigators who had initially asked them to tell their stories. Their responses, we believe, add dimension to the stories presented throughout the book and may be of help to readers engaged in similar case study research projects.

Brittney Moraski, for instance, interviewed first as a 15-year-old high school student in Escanaba, Michigan, was pleasantly surprised at our invitation:

> To be asked to be a co-author surprised me. . . . While I thought that my answers to the questions you gave me were a relatively important part of the chapter, I never-in-a-million-years thought that my answers merited a "co-author" status. When I did learn of this, I was pretty excited! . . . [R]eading the first draft of the chapter was the most exciting part. It was really neat to see my sentences, and more than that, my thoughts, turned into a book form.

Tom Lugo, writing instructor and PhD candidate at the time of the interview, expressed similar surprise about the importance with which his words seemed invested:

> I liked reading my own little, tiny, insignificant tales, but I'd not recommend my stories as "must-read" material for others. There doesn't seem to be much helpful, insightful stuff in my experience. My own enjoyment in reading these stories stems mainly from a self-indulgent pleasure, which I'd find strange if someone else experienced—if they gained the same kind of enjoyment from reading about a stranger, in this case, me.

Along with several of the participants, Paula Boyd, director of a community college learning center and 30 years old when interviewed, echoed Tom's concern that people's experiences, in this case hers, seemed rather insignificant when considered in isolation. She explained:

I liked being able to add more or respond to the original analysis of my experience and therefore I felt less like an object of research. But it was really difficult to think about my own experiences as meaningful, too. I had to work hard to add things that my mind automatically labeled insignificant, but that my co-authors might see differently.

And Dànielle DeVoss, who participated in the study as both a graduate student at Michigan Tech and a faculty member at Michigan State University, described the process like this:

[T]he approach to co-authoring this chapter delighted me. Drafts were exchanged, comments shared, and I believe we maintained an open and honest dialogue throughout the process. At no point did I feel as if I was being represented, or being spoken for. At no point did I feel silenced. I do believe that one author . . . did the majority of the work—drafting the chapter based on a conference presentation. From this framework, I feel it was quite easy for myself and the other authors to contribute, tweak, add, et cetera. But I've found that in most successful collaborations, someone has to take the lead—create the first draft, send out an outline, suggest deadlines and priorities.

Jill Van Wormer—interviewed as a 23-year-old undergraduate—concurred on this generally positive assessment of the method, and added that the experience prompted what was for her an unusual, and not unpleasant reflection on her life, her past experiences, and the way in which she had related her own stories:

My stories were mostly represented in large chunks of the things I literally wrote. . . . I had to think back to a long time ago. It was hard to recall facts, and I was worried I wasn't going to have enough information. . . . It did seem kind of odd when I saw them [my stories] in written form, because though I did originally put them in written form, it was as if I was hearing myself talk. I did enjoy reading them though; they brought back memories.

Although this comment of Jill's was gratifying in one sense, it also encouraged us to recall Sally McBeth's (1993) caution about the "major weaknesses" of life-history methodology, specifically "its subjective nature," which depends, at least in part, on the "accuracy of the informant's memory" (p. 150); which, McBeth notes, "selects, emphasizes, rearranges, and even alters past episodes" (p. 151). Karen Lunsford, a participant interviewed while a doctoral student at the University of Illinois, also spoke of the importance of participants' memory, suggesting ways in which our method might be refined. When asked what she'd say to other scholars considering this co-authoring approach, she replied:

Repeat parts of the interview in a later session. In this case, I was finding that as I thought about the history of my computer literacy more, I was remembering more and more things. Also given some time to search the Internet, I could probably turn up examples of what I was talking about in the interview—copies of the images I remember, computer program emulators that replicate the games I used to play, and so on. I know that a scholar would not want to skew the memories, but it would be interesting to compare what was initially remembered and what was found or recovered later . . . and whether or not the interviewee agrees with today's representations of past technologies. What do those representations emphasize and what do they leave out?

Kamala Visweswaran (1994), in *Fictions of Feminist Ethnography*, problematizes this complicated issue of memory, especially as it relates to identity. She asks, "how are the identities of self related to the mechanics of memory, and the relevance of the past? Or, more specifically, what are the identity-defining functions of memory?" (p. 68). In addition, we ask, what might the sharpening of memory, through strategies such as those Karen outlined, contribute to identity formation as it relates to the literacies of technology? In other words, does memory always index loss or can it reveal, despite distortions and errors, people's cultural attitudes and their relationship to their lived experiences as evidenced through their literate practices? Although Jill Van Wormer noted the limitations of memory, she was also concerned about her own powers of expression. As she stated,

I guess if I'd have known that I was going to be taken word for word, maybe I would have tried to write better. . . . [M]ost of my writing was used word for word. Sometimes I worry that I didn't express myself clearly enough and came off sounding like an idiot.

This last comment also helped us come to a second understanding about the process of involving subjects as co-authors of their own stories. In particular, we became aware of the ways in which the narratives we composed were collaborative fictions as well as postmodern life histories, interested representations constructed—at various levels and at times—by both the researcher and the subjects.

As we considered, then, what it might mean to take a poststructural feminist approach to our research and the stories of the participants, we listened to Elizabeth St. Pierre and Wanda Pillow (2000), who foreground in their introduction to *Working the Ruins* the importance of stressing process and becoming rather than constructing categorical static representations (p. 9). Although we knew that our participants should in no way bear the responsibility of representing a cultural group or birth cohort, we also hoped that their first-person narratives could indeed evoke a larger community. Thus, as we continued in our research and sought out co-authors, we also developed a feminist sensibility in our attempts to do justice to the participants' responses to co-authoring.

Jená Burges, a 47-year-old writing program director at Longwood College in Virginia when interviewed, described for us the rich process in which she engaged as co-author. She tells of:

> . . . the paths of thought that the process led me along. Questions-answers-reading-questions-reflecting-writing-questions-answers. In a way, it was kind of a call-and-response procedure, kind of like an African Methodist service—or an extended therapy session—with the products being greater than the sum of the parts.

Karen Lunsford described a technological variable that got added to the process. She explains:

> Here's something interesting—I've been finding that [after the oral interview] I've been using follow-up e-mail a lot to expand on things I said in the interview, or to provide more accurate details. In part, I'm trying to be as helpful as possible. But I suspect that there are different control issues here as well. E-mail is still informal, but it is often more crafted than speech is, and more accurate than transcripts. At the same time, I enjoy talking with people face-to-face because I'm interested in the follow-up questions to a response, and I can often tell from facial expressions or body language whether someone is understanding what I am saying. That, too, is a way of trying to control the interaction.

It matters, in other words, on several different levels whether the communications between researcher and researched are face-to-face or in writing. For us, in working on this project, e-mail has introduced a whole new dimension to the process of open-ended interviewing.

The comments of other participants also shed additional light on the realization that our narratives were, to some degree, collaborative fictions. Several of the co-authors, for instance, mentioned how their stories—especially when set within the larger contexts of social, historical, and economic trends; or, more importantly, when they were represented in print—seemed to assume increased significance and, in ways they didn't anticipate, spoke back to them about the accumulated events in their lives. Nichole Brown wrote:

> It was especially insightful to see [myself and my family] in a historical perspective. Reading the story made me realize that my experiences are what have gotten me where I am in life, academically and professionally. I rarely

stop to think about how my experiences in such areas as technology, literacy were shaped by family and environment. It was an eye-opening experience.

Working [on this project] gave me such motivation and a sense of self-worth, importance. . . . [It] has allowed me to grow professionally and to believe in myself and in my abilities.

Damon Davis—an undergraduate student in Michigan Tech's technical communication program—reflected on the importance of his own story as a message to other young Black people in his situation:

What surprised me the most was the detail given to the information on our former lives. . . . Getting to explain the tribulations I have surpassed to get to college is what I liked the most. I hope that this will reach someone some day to let them know that they are the master of their own fate, and that anything is possible if they believe they can do it. . . . I enjoyed telling my story and for some of it to be printed is a great honor for me. As a child I was told I would not make it. This is just hard evidence that I will and have made it. . . . Sitting down and reading my own stories was lovely.

Another participant, Jane Blakelock, who, with Jená Burges, is central to the chapter on the literacies of technology as they relate to women born during the middle of the 20th century, had this to say:

I most liked viewing a relaying of Jená's and my narratives against a backdrop of sociological and historical perspectives: the blend of feminist and technological influences. The only way in which I'd say [the representation is] unfaithful is the unavoidable difference between a tale selectively told and a more complete rendering. Still, the representative truths seem in order. I cannot overemphasize that your interpretation of second-wave feminism being at work in my life seems accurate. The model holds up to the experience. My brothers, especially, did not fare so well, and it is true also of my first cousins' family: daughters fared better than sons. Divine neglect perhaps—and some second-wave feminism. Thank you for asking me; I actually found your recasting of information, grounded in theories of interest, to be a good fit. I thought your perspective was proven valid, that my perspectives are enhanced by yours. That's always fun.

Jená also seemed to regard more seriously her own experiences when set in the larger cultural ecology. She writes:

It was very odd to read about myself in "third person disguised" and to have my stories framed in particular ways that gave them more substance than I would have thought possible. The role of reading and writing in my early life, for example, was not something I'd thought much about, and it was slightly uncomfortable to read about it academically. Also, I certainly do not consider myself to be particularly savvy, technology-wise. . . . I'm not exactly an early adopter, and I don't consider myself to have "kept up" with advances to the degree that I would like. This all made me feel uncomfortable with any indication that I was a "technological leader."

Janice Walker, who figures prominently in that same chapter, added:

I enjoyed the reading (I guess we all like reading about ourselves!), but I also felt [the experiences] again, which is sometimes (often) painful. Of course, it is impossible to include all of the story of my life here—and not necessary for what you are trying to present—but I do feel there's so much more to tell. Reading this chapter, I actually, for the first time, saw my life's events as something that might have value for others to read!

Many of the participants in the project not only began to think about their stories and experiences within particular historical and political contexts but were also eager to add their perspectives to our interpretations. Following Gesa Kirsch's (1993) method of turning the interview and analysis process into "a cycle of conversation" (p. 35), our exchanges helped us to elaborate upon and enhance initial provisional interpretations as we e-mailed back and forth with the participants.

From our perspective, these reflections indicate that the co-authors' stories about literacy were shaped bilaterally—both by us, as researchers, and by our collaborators, as informants—and in multiple ways and times. Such stories were, for example, actively constructed by us, through the original prompts we provided to individuals, and by our informants, through the responses to these prompts. These stories were shaped, in addition, by the ways in which we contextualized them within larger social, historical, and economic narratives—by our decision, for instance, to set Nichole's family story within the historical narrative of racism in the Jim Crow South; by our decision to frame Jane, Jená, and Janice's stories with the larger narrative of the 1960s and second-wave feminism; by our decision to set Melissa's, Tom's, and Damon's stories within a historical and contemporary narrative about race, ethnicity, class, and literacy as these formations intersect in the U.S. educational system; by our decision to frame Brittney's story in a cultural narrative about the emergence of electronic literacies and the increasing importance of visual communication. The co-authors' stories (and our own interpretations of them), moreover, were reinterpreted through the informants' rereading and reflection, and by the ways in which these individuals chose to understand the stories within the larger narratives of their lives. Finally, there is little doubt that, as our book is published and read, these stories will be shaped and interpreted and, thus, in a sense recomposed by every reader who eventually comes in contact with them. As McBeth (1993) observes:

Memory, then, is central to the life history, since the events of a life are reinterpreted over and over. The fascination and frustration of this approach are
revealed in this reinterpretation, for not only are events and remembrances
of the past discovered, interpreted, and reinterpreted by the individual who
has lived them, but they are also interpreted and reinterpreted in recording
them, and later by the reader of the documented life. (p. 151)

Even though we asked the participants to reflect on what surprised
them about the process of co-authoring, we ourselves were surprised to
find that their thoughts often coincided in interesting ways with our own.
Jane, for example, touched upon her experience of watching her story unfold:

It is somewhat surprising to watch a story go from interview base to anonymous case study to documentary with feminist critique. I had never thought
of my experiences—my story—going through genre and point of view shifts
and that the genre switching would become a kind of shape-shifting experience.

This "tangling of genres" (Visweswaran, 1994, p. 6) represented a second major challenge uncovered through the process of asking co-authors
to reflect on the process of collaboration. We have, for instance collected
what some might call *literacy autobiographies* and others might call *life histories;* we have interpreted these autobiographies and reported our observations of the informants, their lives, and the contexts within which they
live as some ethnographers might do; we have described specific cultural,
economic, and social eras in a way that some might call *history* or *historiography.* If, at times, we have wondered what genre we were shaping in our
project, we have also discovered that we are not alone. In her collection
about feminist ethnographies, Visweswaran refers—at various times and
quoting various other ethnographers and critics of ethnographic methodology—to studies with elements like those incorporated into our project
as "conjectural historiography" (p. 71), "individual history" (p. 70), "life
history" (p. 6), "first-person narratives" (p. 21), "telling stories" (p. 2),
"window(s) open on life" (p. 6), "autobiographic" (p. 6), "experimental"
(p. 32), "postmodern" (p. 80), "interpretive" (p. 78), "deconstructive" (p.
78), "feminist" (p. 17), "reflexive" (p. 78), or "auto-" (p. 4) ethnographies;
and our favorites, "authorized fictions" (p. 2), "local legitimations" (p. 91)
that resist universalization, "discursive hijacking" (p. 81), and "fables of
imperfect rapport" (p. 29).

We also identified other challenges to the collaborative configurations
we had orchestrated. We agreed, for example, with Elizabeth Chiseri-
Strater (1996), that we were "in a situation to construct a polyvocal text by
folding our informant's voices into our own" (p. 128) and we acknowl-

edged, with Shulamit Reinharz (1992), that in choosing—indeed in crafting—a particular method, we also chose "a certain type of control over [the] subject matter and a certain type of focus" (p. 132). We acknowledged too, as Reinharz also noted, that in choosing a form of oral history we needed to "contend with the difficulties (and enjoy the delights) of writing about a living person in a way that satisfies both parties" (p. 132). How could our attempts to co-author, then, in some sense to create a polyvocal text, satisfy the participants and ourselves, and also meet the requirements of publishing? In this context, a third major challenge of the co-authoring methodology was that the act of co-authoring meant different things to different people.

Each of the case study participants with whom we worked, for instance, had ideas about how such a process should proceed and who should be doing what work and when. Dànielle DeVoss, for example, observed the following:

> Because I am a control freak, there were moments in the process—and I do mean mere moments—where I felt that the "project" was out of my hands, out of my control. This is, however, a good feeling, a good experience for me. Learning to deal with true collaboration and cooperation is important, as I enjoy co-authoring and want to continue working on shared projects with others.
>
> [W]e . . . need to develop methodological frameworks and approaches for these sort of collaborative approaches. We need to do so for a variety of reasons, many of which I'm sure you're aware of already: human-subjects issues, for example. What I'd really like to see is an article or set of articles both reflecting on this process and providing for theoretical and practical justification and rationales for this sort of research—I think this would be an incredible base for future research, and a huge contribution to research methodologies in the humanities.

Yet, predictably perhaps, not only did some of the participants disagree on definitions of co-authorship, but they also questioned whether the process in which they engaged was truly co-authorship. When asked about what most surprised her about co-authoring the chapter, Janice Walker had this to say:

> I am most surprised by the form of the process itself, beginning with the oral interview, readings of the transcript, both my own and in the context of others, and the opportunity to respond to specific questions. It both does and does not "feel" like co-authoring!

And Mary Sheridan-Rabideau, too, contemplated her role in the study:

I guess I didn't really feel like a co-author. To me, the "co" part implies more of a shared inquiry either from the get-go or from the point where both parties hopped on board. Rather, I felt as if I was supporting a project that I valued, but I didn't shape the guiding questions or really much of the analysis. Instead, I felt more involved as a verifier. I don't underestimate this role—it is an important one as too often juicy data (or data that can be made to be juicy) serve the researchers' aims, at almost any cost. I definitely did not feel this was the case. But so, too, I did not feel myself as a co-author.

This is interesting, as it questions who is an author of a story. I guess just the mere fact of the frame of the larger project, the frame of the interview, and the frame of the draft where I first encountered the analysis made me feel that this story (a version of my story if not my story itself) was really in service of another story—the story of the book. The way my story was elicited and situated as part of the book project made it feel less like my story. Again, I feel this is the nature of this type of research and I fully support your research project. It's just the term co-authoring feels like something else to me.

We wondered if Mary wouldn't be more comfortable with the term "collaboration" rather than "co-authorship." When asked this question, she replied:

I've been thinking about your comments, and it's taken me a while to determine I don't know what to call my role in [the] book. I think we (researchers, especially feminist ones) want to think that our participants are involved in our research. Of course, in many, quite varied ways, they are. But I'm still unsure if I'd call my role collaboration. I never thought of me having the possibility of saying, "no, that's just not right" unless there were a factual error. Indeed, the story itself seemed surprisingly distant (though factually quite accurate) from me. I guess I thought of myself as more of an active participant, but I never felt a sense of ownership nor the ability to direct the project. . . . However, I never thought I should have that responsibility either, soooo. What I liked most is supporting the project; I'm happy to be an anonymous part, but also enjoy being a named part. Similarly, I value being valued.

For Mary, co-authorship and collaboration signaled a kind of involvement in our study that she would dispute or at least question having had. And in these questions, we find further complications of the relationship between the role of author and research participant. Mary considered herself an acknowledged and valued supporter of research in which she was invested and that she respected, but not an author of the study itself.

What conclusions might we draw from the comments presented here? What strengths and limitations tend to characterize the research methodology we have stitched together? First, we have come to understand that our method provides no panacea for dealing with the thorny issues entailed in the politics of representation. As hard as we have tried to represent the participants' stories in ways that would do justice to them and to the research, we have stumbled along the way. Jane Blakelock told us she was "a wee bit" uncomfortable with the characterization of her family; Paula Boyd thought maybe she'd do the "class thing" differently; and Mary Sheridan-Rabideau felt more like "reality-checker" than co-author although she thought the research faithful to the facts and agreed with the analysis. But the participants, despite experiencing some uneasiness, also gave us their full-fledged support for the interpretations we drew from the transcripts and secondary sources.

We come back, then, to Caroline Brettell's caution. In discussing a more active role for participants, Brettell (1996) writes of the possibility of the "coproduction of texts" (p. 21), in which the researcher and the researched engage in an ongoing dialogue. Elsewhere (1993) she notes, however, that this solution to getting things straight "really works best when a single individual or only a few are the subject of ethnographic research" (p. 21). She goes on to note that the method seems more amenable to those who are working with life histories. Yet it is likely that, even having culled from the 350 or so stories the 20 case studies we chose to people our book, the number of stories is simply too great for the coproduction of texts. Or, as Mary Sheridan-Rabideau said,

> Having all the participants . . . actually "co-author" as I define it (hash out the project to solve a problem, negotiate analysis decisions, determine which stories are told and which aren't) doesn't seem feasible in a project of this size.

And there are other cautions to consider. Delmos Jones (1979), for example, an African American anthropologist, mentions a methodological danger when he notes that the interested nature of each party's insights in such a process may well magnify, with a force increased by accumulation, the distortion of the stories we have collected:

> The outsider may enter into the social situation armed with a battery of assumptions which he does not question and which guide him to certain types of conclusions, and the insider may depend too much on his own background, his own sentiments, his desires for what is good for his people. The insider . . . may distort the "truth" as much as the outsider. (p. 256)

Thus our method is fraught with difficulties but is also enriched by the different perspectives the informants brought to the project regardless of, or perhaps because of, the ambivalent feelings they had about their contri-

butions and the often conflicting subject positions they perceived themselves as occupying within the larger study.

A Final Note on Method and Organization

The strengths of this combination of qualitative methodological approaches lie, we believe, in their ability to capture the ongoing life stories
of people living in a particular period of history—in great detail and in
personal terms. Also importantly, this approach does not purport to identify generalizable results. Although we began our project with the intent
to sample a representative group of people within the United States, we
quickly realized that only a limited number of people were willing to
share detailed, and revealing, life-history narratives—especially in connection with technology use. Like Deborah Brandt (2001), however, we
also found that the richness of information contained within the individual stories outweighed the limitations of our sample.

Even so, we recognize, and hope readers will as well, that the stories
told by participants in this project constitute only a small portion of some
larger national narratives: stories of how individuals and families have
adapted their literacy values and practices to computer-supported environments; how individuals' access to computers has varied, in part, along
the axes of race, class, and gender; how and why technological literacy has
thrived within the cultural ecology existing within the United States from
1978–2003; how and why people have struggled to acquire computer-
based literacies; how children have shared computer-based literacies with
adults and how adults have shared with children. Far too many stories remain uncollected, unheard, and unappreciated for such larger narratives
to be considered completely or, even, accurately rendered.

This recognition, however, does nothing to diminish the value of the
first-hand accounts told to us. On the contrary, each of the literacy histories in this project is richly sown with information that can help those of us
in composition and writing studies situate the processes of acquiring the
literacies of technology in specific cultural, material, educational, and familial contexts. We hope, in this sense, that these case studies will provide
some initial clues about combinations of factors that affect—and are affected by—technological literacy acquisition and development. For us, the
value of the first-hand accounts told here is that they present, in abundant
detail, everyday literacy experiences that can help educators, parents,
policymakers, and writing teachers respond to today's students in more
informed ways.

The book is organized into seven chapters that follow the 20 participants in their efforts to acquire varying degrees of technological literacy,
along with this introduction and a conclusion sandwiching the case stud-

ies. Each of the chapters also attempts to situate the participants' life-history accounts in the cultural ecology of the time, tracing major political, economic, social, and educational events, factors, and trends that may have influenced, and been influenced by, literacy practices and values.

Chapter 1, Cultural Ecologies and the Literacies of Technology, takes on the stories of Damon Davis, Sally Osborne, and Jill Van Wormer, all born during the late 1970s when personal computers first entered schools and homes. With these initial case studies, the chapter defines and exemplifies the definition of a cultural ecology and the role such a concept assumes in relation to people's lives and their acquisition of digital literacies. The three stories present an important counterpoint to one another, contrasting as they do the struggles of Damon, an African American undergraduate who grew up poor in inner-city Detroit, with those of Sally and Jill, White undergraduates who grew up in more privileged environments, technological and otherwise. Despite their different beginnings, however, all three students today are highly proficient in computer-based literacies. This chapter not only provides important information about the specific acquisition and development of electronic literacies but also demonstrates how literacy practices accumulate, compete, and fade in people's lives. It also highlights the contested nature of the literacy landscape that people may inhabit.

Chapter 2, Privileging—or Not—the Literacies of Technology, looks at the experiences of three White women all born in the last years of the 1960s and attempts to relate notions of class, gender, and identity with the prevalent cultural ecology of the times. Paula Boyd calls herself working class and spent much of her young life moving with her mother, sister, and brother from one place to another in the same town to avoid eviction. Her town, however, was also headquarters for IBM, where her father worked, and which may have made all the difference in her acquisition of digital literacies. Mary Sheridan-Rabideau, on the other hand, came from a privileged family in which her father was a lawyer and her mother a homemaker who could afford to stay home and look after her four children. There were few deprivations that Mary experienced growing up in that largest of midwestern metropolitan cities, Chicago. The third, Karen Lunsford, spent her life as a daughter of a military officer whose career took her mother, sister, and herself from one part of the United States to another, as well as to Germany and England. When we consider the acquisition of electronic literacies, we find that Paula and Karen came to them most easily. Whether such proclivity to the technological has to do with their fathers' technological expertise; the girls' penchant to play computer games; their ability to define themselves outside common understandings of middle class femininity; or, most likely, with some combination of social, cultural, and economic factors that overlap and intersect, we are not entirely sure. We do know, however, that growing up in the late 1960s, unlike those in our study who were born earlier or a decade later, presented very different challenges for these three women. It is with this group that we see the greatest divergence among those who count themselves as electronically literate—or not. We suspect that with this generation, for the first time in our history, literacy practices became inextricably and irrevocably tied to computers and one's ability to make them work. This chapter analyzes the importance of gender and class in shaping literacy values but also considers the critical choices people make in departing from common cultural expectations.

Chapter 3, Complicating Access: Gateways to the Literacies of Technology, tells the stories of two people born during the mid 1950s—Dean Woodbeck, born into a White, middle class family, and Carmen Vincent, born into a poor, Native American family. Our goal in this chapter is to complicate the whole notion of access, in part, by introducing the concept of *technological gateways*. For us, technological gateways offer sites and occasions for acquiring digital literacies but vary across people's experiences and the times and circumstances in which they grow up. These gateways constitute the places and situations in which people typically gain access to computers for the purpose of practicing digital literacy and are typically accessed through schools, homes, communities, and workplaces. The chapter attempts to go beyond simplistic definitions of access to show also how factors like race and class, interest and motivation, timing and opportunity, support, overlap, and interact with each other to affect access—and, thus, to affect the ways in which people acquire and develop electronic literacies through various gateways. By focusing on the lives of Dean Woodbeck and Carmen Vincent[11] as they unfolded from 1955 to 2000—the chapter takes up the issue of access at a more specific level within the lived experiences of real people. The chapter provides an understanding of access that is both more complex and more accurate, we believe, than that which is currently available. These two life histories, as well as others in the study, indicate that issues of access exist within, shape, and are shaped by, a complex network of social formations—operating continually at many different levels—that form a cultural ecology.

Chapter 4, Shaping Cultures: Prizing the Literacies of Technology, relates the stories of two writing instructors who were brought up in very different kinds of local cultures—an African American woman and a Latino, both born in 1964. Melissa, an African American, was a military child and moved with great regularity from school to school, often attending schools in Europe for dependent military children. Although personal

---

[11]Carmen Vincent is a pseudonym, which we have chosen in the interest of protecting the participant's confidentiality.

computers had not entered mainstream society when she was growing up, over the years, first through her work and then through graduate school and her own teaching, she became extremely competent when it came to the literacies of technology. In contrast, Tom Lugo, a Mexican-American, who hails from Los Angeles and identifies himself as an "Angeleno Chicano," moved only slightly east of the city growing up, attending local schools in the area until he transferred from a two-year college to a university. Like Melissa, he came to prize print and alphabetic literacies early on, and today values technological literacies far less, despite computers becoming regularly available to him when he was an undergraduate. Although Tom in his everyday work engages in the literacies of technology, he believes strongly that face-to-face communication and print reading is to be preferred over computer-mediated venues. In this chapter, then, we foreground the effects of local cultures in shaping communities' and people's attitudes regarding computer-based literacies, all the while examining those cultural experiences and beliefs that finally encourage, or not, their acquisition.

Chapter 5, Those Who Share: Three Generations of Black Women, explores the role that families play in both changing and sustaining generational patterns of literacy practices and values. In it, we trace three generations of Black women who grew up and acquired literacy in the rural South during the last six decades. Sheila, who grew up in South Carolina during the 1940s, graduated from the tenth grade, went to work in a sewing factory near her home, and never felt the need to develop electronic literacies. When personal computers became prevalent in the United States, she was already 40 years old. In 1971, Sheila's sister became the mother of Nichole Brown, who grew up in Greenville during the 1970s and 1980s, and inherited many of the literacy values that both her mother and aunt had acquired from their family. Nichole, however, also grew up in a national culture that was coming to place a high value on electronic literacy, and she first acquired basic computing skills in high school. She became so adept at computer-based communication that she enrolled in a Master's level technical communication program at Clemson University. Yolanda, Nichole's cousin, born in 1987 and educated in the technological culture of the 1990s, began using computers in elementary school. Although both Yolanda and her mother recognize the importance of the computing skills she acquires, Nichole Brown, the most technologically sophisticated member of the family, worries that her young cousin's teachers are not providing her with sufficient electronic literacy skills and that the school she attends does not have the funding to change this situation. Our goal for this chapter is to begin to trace the familial and generational changes that occurred in the South as a result of desegregation and the civil rights movement with an eye toward discerning what, if any, effects the social, political, and cultural milieu might have had on these women's technological literacy acquisition.

Chapter 6, Inspiring Women: Social Movements and the Literacies of Technology, examines how second-wave feminism—and other calls for societal change—influenced the lived experiences of three women who came of age in the late 1960s. During these years and those that followed in quick succession, women protested their unequal treatment in a society that proclaimed itself a democracy and demanded changes that would enlarge their educational opportunities and their roles in society. These were the same years in which the U.S. military supported the development of a decentralized communication network, a system that would later become the Internet. The three women whom we highlight in the stories in this chapter turned 18 and graduated from high school during these turbulent years. Our goal for this chapter is to demonstrate how three 50-something female writing instructors—all of the same counterculture generation—have been able to use information technologies successfully in carving out places for themselves in the digital age. In their life stories, we begin to glimpse not only the tremendous changes that have occurred in our ways of living during the late 20th and early 21st centuries but also the resourcefulness and persistence of these particular women in acquiring the requisite electronic literacies.

Chapter 7, The Future of Literacy, offers what we hope is a glimpse into the future of new kinds of literacy practices that will mark the 21st century. Here we present two professionals, a woman and man, both 28, who recently completed advanced degrees, and two youngsters, a female and male, ages 15 and 16 at the time of their interviews, who are currently making their way through public high school in two different towns and states. These individuals, along with many others like them, form a vector for literacy in the coming decades. Tracing this vector, considering its direction and pace, can help us anticipate the future and speculate on the kinds of expertise writing instructors will need to recognize and support. For these students, composing takes place not only with words but also with digitized bits of video, sound, photographs, still images, words, and animations to support communications across conventional linguistic, cultural, and geopolitical borders.

Finally, the concluding chapter examines the findings of all the chapters and pulls together the insights of the volume to suggest different and increasingly accurate ways for understanding the new information technologies and their relationship to people's literate lives. In particular, the conclusion describes eight themes that grew out of our research and that acknowledge the complex cultural ecology within which these information technologies exist and within which people have acquired and developed the literacies of technology over the past 25 years or so. By illuminating the relationships between computers and literacy, people, and the cultural ecologies within which they practice and learn literate activity, this chapter provides individuals, scholars, and educators—in homes, writing programs, online classes, public literacy programs, and workplace settings—guidance in thinking about and dealing with critical issues that digital literacy raises in our lives.

1

Cultural Ecologies and the Literacies of Technology

Damon J. Davis
Gail E. Hawisher
Sally A. Osborne
Cynthia L. Selfe
Jill R. Van Wormer

> *Awareness of how technologies merge with daily practices leads us to view technology and literacy as constituent parts of life, elements of an ecological system.... This viewpoint gives us a basis for understanding the interpenetration among machines, humans, and the natural world.*
> (Bertram C. Bruce and Maureen Hogan, 1998, p. 272)

In this chapter, we present three case studies with the hope that they help readers appreciate the importance of situating literacies of technology in specific cultural ecologies. These cases help us begin to see the connections between the acquisition of literacy, technological and otherwise, and the specific cultural, material, educational, and familial contexts that influence the acquisition and development of literacy. In foregrounding the significance of multiple contexts (historic, social, economic, educational, technological) for electronic literacy efforts, we hint at the many related factors that influence people's adoption of computers as literacy tools and environments. As mentioned in the introduction, we refer to these related contexts as the cultural ecology of literacy and, with this metaphor, attempt to signal the complex web of social forces, historical events, economic patterns, material conditions, and cultural expectations within which both humans and computer technologies coexist.[1]

---

[1]Our understanding of cultural ecologies is based on a long history of work by exemplary scholars who have come at the phenomenon from different directions. We mention only three of the most salient figures in our own readings here. In 1986, Marilyn Cooper helped us

   This chapter also introduces the basic methodologies and concepts that characterize all the investigations in the book. As explained in the introduction, our methodology relies on a combination of autobiographical and ethnographic approaches. We believe, with Deborah Brandt (1999), that interviews with individuals about their lives, practices, and values can provide a richly textured understanding of literacy at a particular period of time, especially when the multiple life stories of people "who have experienced the same set of structural relations and have lived through the same events" (p. 375) are assembled and compared in various ways.[2] In addition, by asking individuals to co-author their stories with us, we hope to enrich possibilities for interpretation and to acknowledge the tremendous contribution of the participants to this project. Finally, this chapter points to Anthony Giddens' (1979) concept of the "duality of structure" to explain how people's actions are not only shaped by the society within which they live and the technological systems they inhabit, but also how the people themselves help constitute these environments.[3] With an eye toward tracing the acquisition of technological literacy as it has emerged in recent decades, we now turn to the case studies of three U.S. citizens—Jill Van Wormer, born on December 12, 1977; Sally Osborne, born on June 9, 1978; and Damon Davis born on December 15, 1978.

Three Case Studies

Why begin with these three particular cases? In part, we do so because the education histories of these people are essentially contemporaneous

---

understand that language and literacy practices are "essentially social activities, dependent on social structures and processes not only in their interpretive but also in their constructive phases" (p. 366). More recently, Ronald Deibert (1997) enriched our understanding of mediated communication with a discussion of ecological holism (pp. 37–93) that brought an additional dimension to our study of computer-based literacies. Still more recently, Bertram Bruce and Maureen Hogan (1998) reminded us that computer technologies and the literacy activities they mediate are best understood through a study of the social systems and settings within which machines, and the humans who use them, exist.

   [2]For a more elaborated discussion of Brandt's (2001) methodology, see *Literacy in American Lives*, pp. 2–24. Our tremendous debt to Brandt's fine work should be evident in every page of this book.

   [3]We borrowed the concept of the "duality of structure" from Anthony Giddens (1979), although we applied the term somewhat more narrowly within the intersection of literacy and technology issues. Readers may want to consult Andrew Feenberg's book *Questioning Technology* (1999) for a more elaborated understanding of how this concept is played out in technological cultures. Feenberg argues that although technology clearly shapes the world humans inhabit, and is, indeed, the "medium of daily life" (p. vii), humans also shape the design and use of technologies, and could do so more effectively and productively through "democratic interventions" that "open up new possibilities" for living with technology (p. xv).

with the invention and mass production of microcomputers in 1977. The period during which Jill, Sally, and Damon first attended public schools—entering first grade in 1983 and 1984—witnessed some of the first significant efforts to integrate personal computers into public education settings. In this sense, the cases are of interest because they provide specific cultural tracings of how and when personal computers came to shape the literacy practices and values of three different young people and their families; and, in turn, how the literacy values and practices of these individuals—and others who lived and worked in similar circumstances—contributed to the cultural transformations associated with the information age.[4]

These cases are also intriguing because they trace a period in which the definition of literacy changed significantly. From 1978 to 2000, literacy and computer technology became so inextricably linked in the minds of most people that, by the end of the century, many considered students no longer fully literate unless they could communicate within electronic environments.[5]

Given this historical context, the cases remind us that we can understand literacy fully—as a complex set of cultural practices and values—only when we examine this phenomenon within the context of a particular period, cultural milieu, and cluster of material and economic conditions. Within any given cultural ecology, moreover, particular forms of literacy have life spans. They emerge, accumulate, and compete with other literacies, and fade according to their general fit with other key social, cultural, historical, and material phenomena.[6] These three cases support this understanding, and they suggest, in addition, that literacies accumulate

---

[4]For a thorough examination of the rise of the information age and the global transformations that accompanied it, see Manuel Castells' three volume series: *The Rise of the Network Society* (1996), *The Power of Identity* (1997), and *End of the Millennium* (1998).

[5]One explanation of the historical processes and social dynamic that resulted in this emerging redefinition of literacy in the United States (and its increasingly close connection with computer technology) can be found in *Technology and Literacy in the Twenty-First Century: The Importance of Paying Attention* (Selfe, 1999). This book looked at the roles that the U.S. government and educational system played in this transformation, as well as the ways in which parents became invested in the national project. The book also explores the ideological bases that helped secure the investment of people living in the United States in technological literacy.

[6]In *Parchment, Printing, and Hypermedia: Communication in World Order Transformation*, Ronald Deibert (1997) provides a valuable exploration of how and why communication technologies that "fit" (pp. 30–31) well within a given cultural context tend to prosper. In his book, Deibert gives two extended historical examples of this process: one focused on the printing press and the other on hypermedia.

faster and sometimes compete more vigorously when cultures undergo periods of particularly dramatic or radical transition.[7]

Readers may benefit from a preview of how this chapter is structured. We begin by describing the cultural ecology within which microcomputer technology emerged in the 1980s in the United States—the period during which Jill, Sally, and Damon attended elementary school and secondary school, and when they first used computers as literacy environments at home. In the second major section, to ground our work in the lived experiences of individuals, we look at the three case studies themselves, relying primarily on Jill, Sally, and Damon to tell in their own words how they learned to read and compose on computers. We follow with a third major section that characterizes the cultural ecology of the 1990s, the period during which all three individuals attended college and chose the computer-intensive/communication-intensive career paths they wanted to pursue. We conclude this chapter by identifying three important themes running through the case studies: how computers became so tightly linked to literacy instruction in the United States at the end of the 20th century that they transformed our collective cultural understanding of what it now means to be literate, how this transformation was differentially enacted in the lives of these three young people along the axes of race and poverty, and how their electronic literacy acquisition both shaped the cultural ecologies in which they lived and were shaped by them.

The Cultural Ecology of the 1980s: Setting the Stage for Electronic Literacy

Because the three individuals on whom we focus were born in 1977 and 1978 and entered first grade between 1983 and 1985, the 1980s provide a convenient historical framework for an initial exploration of their stories. That decade marked the beginning of the Reagan presidency on January 20, 1981.

At that point in history, the United States was deeply mired in a stubborn recession at home. Abroad, it was occupied with fighting a troublesome, multifront Cold War and confronting a perceived loss of economic sovereignty.[8] Domestically, as Ronald Reagan had learned, the economic picture was bleak. Within the context of the recession,

---

[7]Literacies, we maintain throughout this book, have life spans: They emerge, compete, and fade depending on a complex combination of historical, material, and cultural factors. Literacies may compete more vigorously, moreover, in times of rapid cultural and technological change. For two excellent explanations of this phenomenon, see Deborah Brandt's (2001) *Literacy in American Lives* and Miles Myers' (1996) *Changing Our Minds: Negotiating English and Literacy.*

[8]For an extended explanation of the U.S. economy in the late 1970s and early 1980s, see the Hudson Institute's landmark report, *Workforce 2000: Work and Workers for the 21st Century* (Johnston & Packer, 1987).

. . . labor productivity in the nonfarm business sector in 1980 was 2.2 percent below its 1978 level; the total unemployment rate had risen to 7.4 percent from a low of 5.5 percent in mid-1979; the 12-month inflation rate as measured by the consumer price index (CPI) was 11.7 percent, compared with only 4.8 percent in 1976; and the 13-week Treasury bill rate was 15.0 percent, up from a 1976 average of 5.0 percent.[9]

But these domestic economic woes represented only part of Reagan's concerns in the 1980s. Internationally, the political battles of the Cold War raged on and provided a focus for U.S. global efforts. Although Iran had released 52 hostages on January 20, 1981, the day of Reagan's inauguration, the United States continued to smart from the insult of the hostage-taking. It seemed as if countries around the world were bent on challenging U.S. resolve, and people watched warily as old and new international tensions seemed to flare up on an almost daily basis. In 1981 alone, for example, the United States closed the Libyan embassy in Washington, D.C., on the 6th of May; shot down two Libyan planes on the 19th of August; and announced, on the 2nd of December, that terrorist squads trained in Libya had infiltrated the United States. The relations were no better with other countries that year. Although Reagan lifted the grain embargo against the Soviet Union in April of 1981, in November, he accused that nation of using chemical warfare in Asia; and, in December, he announced new sanctions against the Soviet Union in retaliation for their invasion of Poland. The situation improved little over the next few years. In 1982, Brigadier General James L. Dozier was kidnapped by the Red Brigade in Italy, and the Polish government defaulted on loans from nine U.S. banks. In 1983, the United States cut the Nicaraguan sugar quota to put pressure on the Sandinista government, saw its embassy in Beirut bombed with lethal consequences, and participated in an invasion of Grenada at the invitation of Margaret Thatcher.[10]

These Cold War political struggles were mirrored by, and actually related to, international economic battles the United States found itself waging around the world. After World War II, as industrial Japan and Germany recovered and began to flex their political and economic muscles, the global scene became increasingly populated by nations who had their own opinions about U.S. politics and financial policies, and, moreover, felt justified in challenging the United States in both areas. By the end of

---

[9]This description of the early 1980s economy comes from the Council of Economic Advisors (1985, p. 21).

[10]For a snapshot of the United States during this decade, and for detailed timelines of the events that helped to make up the decade's character, see *Annals of America, Volume 21* (1987, pp. xxx–xxxvi). The events mentioned in this chapter are contained in the detailed historical timelines of events provided by this resource.

the 1970s, then, the increasingly competitive global economic picture had become at least as disturbing to many citizens as the contested political landscape: the U.S. standard of living was threatened; the competitive status of the domestic steel, automobile, textiles, consumer electronics, and other manufacturing industries had begun to erode; and U.S. citizens had begun to express a "growing crescendo of support for trade restrictions" (Johnston & Packer, 1987, p. 13).

By the end of the 1980s, the effects of these international wrestling matches were being felt more directly. The oil cut-offs by OPEC, for example, convinced many that these struggles were serious, indeed, and that the United States' former influence over global economic matters was severely diminished. By 1987, when the landmark Hudson Institute report, *Workforce 2000* (Johnston & Packer, 1987), was published, a disturbing picture of economic decline had begun to dominate the U.S. consciousness:

> Between 1975 and 1980, [productivity] output per hour in U.S. manufacturing rose by an average of 1.7 percent per year, compared to 3.8 percent in West Germany and 8.6 percent in Japan. . . . U.S. steel production dropped by more than one-fourth between 1975 and 1983, and the U.S. share of the world steel production declined from 16 percent to 12 percent; for autos, the drop in volume was 22 percent, as the U.S. share of world production fell from 27 to 17 percent. (p. 13)

Domestic growth in the United States was now "inextricably intertwined with world growth" (Johnston & Packer, 1987, p. 3), and this linkage was not going the way the United States desired:

> Between 1960 and 1985, the world economy grew at an average rate of 3.9 percent per year, while U.S. growth averaged 3.1 percent annually. As a result of this lower growth, the U.S. share of the world economy . . . dropped from 35 percent in 1960 to 28 percent in 1985. . . . The U.S. share of the economy will fall further by the year 2000. (p. 6)

Given this political and economic environment, the national mood in the United States was increasingly tense and defensive. On the 23rd of March, in 1983, Ronald Reagan delivered a televised address in which he described a space-based, missile-defense system that the media called Star Wars. Although many scientists remain skeptical about whether or not such a system could succeed, the first and second voyages of the space shuttle *Challenger*—concluded on April 9 and June 24 respectively— helped convince many that the Star Wars project might actually work (*Annals of America*, 1987, pp. xxxiv–xxxvi).

This combination of macro-level historical, political, economic, and social factors—the global struggles of the Cold War and the diminished economic status of the United States, the domestic recession, and the ongoing race for the domination of space—converged to fuel U.S. national investment in technology and the resultant explosion in technological innovation that was to characterize the 1980s and the 1990s. As the thinking went, such an investment could help revitalize a flagging domestic economy and stop the downward spiral of the United States in global political and economic arenas (Johnston & Packer, 1987). This investment was enacted, on a practical level, by a range of social agents: among only a few of these, members of the military-industrial complex, medical researchers, industry leaders, and educators in public schools.

Technology was certainly a primary focus of the nation's military-industrial complex during the Reagan presidency.[11] In particular, the military's need for increasingly sophisticated technological weaponry and the domestic industrial sector's need for lucrative contracts proved an extremely potent combination. By 1983, for instance, the military and the private sector—represented by large research universities and major technology companies—had begun collaborating on the Defense Department's Advance Research Projects Agency's (DARPA) Strategic Computing Initiative, a "major program for research in microelectronics, computer architecture, and AI [artificial intelligence]" (Kurzweil, 1990, p. 480). In Michigan, Sally's, Jill's, and Damon's home state, the DARPA effort inspired a related statewide project, the Michigan Educational Research Information Triad (MERIT), which would link major universities conducting technology research to both the National Science Foundation and corporate sponsors such as IBM and MCI. In 1983, the year that Jill entered first grade, the NSF provided initial funding to begin linking the MERIT network with the DARPA network, then called ARPANET ("Merit's History," 1998).

By 1987, when Damon was entering second grade and Sally third, similar collaborations between military, industrial, and educational partners were under way on AI vision systems for military aircraft and AI support for remotely piloted aircraft (Kurzweil, 1990, p. 480). These projects exploited the U.S. Cold War concerns about foreign aggression and increased willingness to fund military efforts. During the two terms of the Reagan presidency, from 1981 to 1989, national defense spending increased from $167.5 billion to $303.4 billion (*Economic Report of the Presi-*

---

[11]For additional perspective on the connection between the military-industrial context and computer technology, see Les Levidow's and Kevin Robins' (1989) *Cyborg Worlds: The Military Information Society.*

dent, 1990, p. 295). With such resources available to support military projects, private industries and public universities participated willingly and vigorously in defense-based research and development efforts, many of which involved technology (Noble, 1989).

The needs of medical and health researchers also fueled the demand for increasingly sophisticated technologies and a workforce capable of both using and manufacturing such technologies. By the early 1980s, for example, the medical research team that had worked on an early diagnosis project named MYCIN had also produced two more expert systems for disease diagnosis: NeoMYCIN and ONCOCIN, both of which used newly designed hierarchical database structures. By 1982, CADUCEUS, a computer program based on the expert knowledge of internists, was able to make thousands of associations between symptoms and diseases and to cover 70% of that field's knowledge. By 1986, the development of computer-based imaging systems allowed doctors to see "inside our bodies and brains" (Kurzweil, 1990, pp. 479–481). *Workforce 2000* (Johnston & Packer, 1987) summarized the medical establishment's stake in computer technology for the next decade and a half:

> [Biotechnologies] . . . will have large impacts on health care. . . . For example, the task of mapping the human genome is well under way. As this knowledge advances, not only will genetic birth defects become uncommon, but it will become feasible to treat many chronic and degenerative diseases such as heart disease. As the interaction of genetics and environment is better understood, advances will also be rapid against some acute diseases, with the prospect that many of today's killers will be contained by the year 2000. Although AIDS and many cancers are unlikely to be conquered within this short time frame, the knowledge gained in research on these diseases is likely to have wide-ranging impacts on the practice of medicine generally. (p. 35)

The Reagan administration hoped that the increasing numbers of industries undertaking such technology-rich projects would need to hire large numbers of technologically savvy workers, thus creating an employment trend that would reduce high unemployment figures and boost the United States out of the current recession. To grease the skids for this recovery dynamic, Reagan began a program of industry deregulation (Council of Economic Advisors, 1985, pp. 119–126), an approach that, along with other factors, contributed to the rapid growth of the computer industry during the 1980s and 1990s.

By mid-decade, the expansion of the technology industry was well under way, and people in the United States had begun to recognize its value as a key to both domestic and global difficulties. If the United

States could develop advanced technologies faster than other countries, the thinking went, it could recapture its share of global and economic power, but to accomplish this task, the United States had to continue down a high-tech path. Thus, when Japan formed a consortium to develop a new "Fifth Generation" of computers in 1982 and funded it with a billion dollars of government and private monies, the United States undertook, in short order, a similar project. By 1984, Ronald Reagan had signed legislation paving the way for the Microelectronics and Computer Corporation (MCC), a U.S.-based consortium of more than 20 companies that shared a goal of developing intelligent computers and a budget of $65 million a year. By 1986, the revenue of the AI industry in the United States alone reached $1 billion, growing to $1.4 billion by 1987 (Kurzweil, 1990, pp. 479–480).

The vigor of all these converging trends led to astonishing growth in the computer industry during the 1980s, and not only in the manufacturing of large mainframe computers for advanced research and development. In the late 1970s, the invention of integrated microcircuit technologies—such as Motorola's 68000 16-bit microprocessor containing 68,0000 transistors (*Timeline of Computing History*, 1996)—fed into the rapid and far-reaching development of personal computers, and the invention of these handy, relatively affordable machines transformed many aspects of life in the United States.

In 1981, for example, the IBM PC was launched (*Timeline of Computing History*, 1996), and its open architecture system, in turn, invited additional industry collaborations and partnerships. Among the first of these, in 1982, was Microsoft's release of *DOS 1.1* and WordPerfect Corporation's release of *WordPerfect 1.0* (*Timeline of Computing History*, 1996). Indeed, within a year of the IBM PC's release, IBM was supporting 12 new Microsoft products, and 30 other companies had announced the development of DOS based programs (Hawisher, LeBlanc, Moran, & Selfe, 1996, p. 41). Also in 1982, the word *Internet* was used for the first time (*PBS Life on the Internet*, 1997), *Time* magazine named the computer "Man of the Year," and the first commercial e-mail service linked 25 cities. In 1983, the Apple Lisa was launched; and, in 1984, the Apple Macintosh followed. By the end of 1984, computers were so much a part of the national consciousness that William Gibson invented the term "cyberspace" in his novel *Neuromancer*. The software industry also continued to grow in tandem with the personal-computer hardware industry: The 300 software companies in existence in 1970 skyrocketed to over 2,000 companies in 1983; sales in this industry went from $750 million in 1977 to $475 billion in 1983 (Hawisher, LeBlanc; Moran, & Selfe, 1996, pp. 95–96).

The U.S. educational system was quick to understand the implications of these national trends, especially for new, technologically rich curricula. A successful global superpower needed increasingly sophisticated technologies—to manufacture goods more efficiently, to wage war more effectively, or to conduct medical research on new and threatening viruses. And to invent and operate these new technological systems, increasing numbers of technologically prepared people were needed.

The Condition of Education (National Center for Education Statistics, 1980) described the new national dynamic as it was to affect U.S. education during the coming decade:

> The 1980's are expected to be a period of new assessments of our scientific capabilities, as National concerns shift to such areas as energy, the environment, and health. . . . Our Nation's continued advancement in technology is dependent to a large extent upon its supply of science and engineering personnel. The persons who can make up this manpower base conduct basic research to advance the understanding of nature, perform applied research and development in a variety of areas such as health, energy, and the environment, and train the nation's future scientists and engineers. (p. 6)

In support of this project to expand technology use—and technological education—in schools, as Hawisher, LeBlanc, Moran, and Selfe (1996) note, a powerful coalition of social forces aligned themselves:

> Computer industry giants like IBM, Control Data Corporation, and Mitre Corporation were rushing to explore the educational marketplace [for computer applications]. Government agencies like the National Science Foundation, the U.S. Office of Education, and the Defense Advance Research Projects Agency (DARPA) were seeking to inform and enlist American education in response to Cold War politics (Thurston, 1994). Private foundations like the Carnegie Corporation and the Annenberg/CPB Project were funding new answers to old educational questions. (p. 34)

Within this milieu, the newly invented personal computer promised to be an exceptionally powerful educational ally. These small, affordable machines offered a cost-effective way of helping educators produce a technologically informed citizenry, and the comparative ease of programming personal computers appealed to teachers outside of computer science. These machines made it relatively easy for faculty to create their own computer-assisted instruction (CAI) packages for mathematics, social studies, and, more importantly, English, where personal computers quickly became popular environments for reading and writing instruction. It was within this period of educational innovation—framed by a growing investment in technology as a response to some of the challenges posed by the Cold War, raging economic battles at home and around the globe, the need for new energy sources, and the call for medical and health innovations—that the early educational experiences of Jill, Sally, and Damon were structured and organized.

The Case Studies of Jill Van Wormer and Sally Osborne

Jill and Sally first encountered computers and began to acquire technological literacy in their elementary school years, specifically in the third grade when they were eight years old. Educational computer games were their very first experiences with technology in elementary school.

> [Jill] [I]n the third grade . . . we would use a computer program on Apple computers to help learn math facts, such as the multiplication tables. It would ask us problems, and we'd have to type in the answers. . . . I first learned to use the computer in the fourth grade, we started playing games such as the Oregon Trail, and we also began typing in word processing programs . . . I was probably about nine years old. . . . We had maybe two hours a week access to the computers. It was usually in the afternoon . . . and the other students and the teacher were there. I never used a computer by myself. . . . We were allowed to talk, but it wasn't rowdy.
>
> [Sally] When we first used computers at school, we used them to play easy learning games. The class got to go once every other week to the computer room and play with the computer games. You only could go if you were good that week and we worked in groups of two. We had a volunteer that came and helped us. They really didn't know much more than we did. This was during my elementary school years. We didn't have computers in the individual classroom. . . . As we went on, fewer and fewer people had access to computers.

Sally and Jill both recalled enjoying educational computer games and remembered what they had to do to play the games in terms of shaping school-appropriate behavior:

> [Sally] Only if your teacher thought you were responsible and deserved to play with . . . computer[s] could you use them. . . . They were fun. We didn't mind doing work on the computer because it was made into a game. It was so neat to use the computer, it didn't matter what we had to do on it or if we understood what we were doing. I don't really think that we thought we were learning stuff, we just thought we were playing games.
>
> [Jill] [I]f we finished our homework early, and had free time, we were allowed to play games on computers. . . . I did play the Oregon Trail quite frequently.

The early game playing led, in relatively short order, to other technological literacy practices, as well:

> [Jill] [I]n fourth grade, we started playing games . . . and we also began typing in word processing programs. This was all done on the Apple IIe computers with the green screens. With this [word processing], we started to have to learn to turn on and off the machines, and be able to get to the program we wanted by typing various commands.

The instruction Sally and Jill received in school was only one factor affecting their acquisition and development of technological literacy. Both Jill's and Sally's parents were also personally invested in literacy, generally, and in the process of formal education, more specifically. Both sets of parents had finished high school, and at least one parent in each family had attended college. Sally's mother had finished high school before becoming a homemaker, and her father had completed high school, technical school, and approximately one year of college before becoming a technician and salesperson for a company that manufactured hospital emergency equipment. Jill's mother had graduated from college with a B.S. degree in Business Management, and her father obtained an Associate degree in Construction Management before becoming the Vice President of Transportation for a landscaping company.

Within their home environments, the parents of both girls inculcated literacy values in their children as well, encouraging most particularly those literacy practices they knew their children would later encounter as students in more formal instructional situations. Jill, for instance, one of three siblings, remembers her parents reading books, magazines, newspapers, and fiction on a regular basis and encouraging her to do so as well. Within this environment, reading instruction was built into the informal practices characterizing day-to-day parent–child interaction. Importantly, this informal literacy instruction and modeling was designed to ready Jill for later success in school. As she noted,

> [Jill] I learned to read on my own. My parents would read stories to me, and one day they said I just started reading the words on my own. This was when I was four years old. They had me read to my preschool teachers.

Sally's home literacy values and practices were also similar to those she would later encounter at school:

> [Sally] [My] parents greatly valued literacy for children; [they] made it a point to help us learn to read/write, encourage trips to the library, reading

for fun, always felt reading to us when we were young was very important, encouraged us to write stories and use imagination.

The economic situation of these two families—middle class for Jill and upper middle class for Sally—meant that both households could afford to purchase books, newspapers, magazines, pens, pencils, paper, and, later, computers. The mothers of both girls worked inside the home and devoted considerable time to instructing the children in their early reading and writing practices, as well as modeling these practices themselves.

As Jill's and Sally's elementary schools began to integrate computers into various curricula—and as computers were becoming increasingly important in the world of business and increasingly visible in the culture at large—the parents of both families eventually began to perceive the value of having a computer in the home. Sally's and Jill's families were not alone in this perception. From 1988 to 1994, the home PC market flourished, driven, at least in part, by the production of high-quality, low-price machines and a ready market. As Freeman (1996) notes, the sales of home computers grew by approximately 2.7% each year until 1992–1993, when 30% of all the computers sold in the United States were destined for home use:

> Among the social reasons for the market change in home-based computer systems is the desire of parents to expose children to computers at younger ages. Also, parents are buying computers for their college-bound students who are, in turn, teaching parents about home computing . . . 38.3 percent of first-time buyers want a computer at home for their children's schoolwork. (p. 47)

As part of this national trend, although neither set of parents originally knew much about using computers themselves, both decided it was important to purchase a home computer when their daughters were in public school. Both sets of parents, influenced by the rapid expansion of the information society, embraced computers as powerful tools that they could exploit for the benefit of their families. Jill's and Sally's parents considered the purchase of a computer an important investment for their children's future success, and these values fed back into the cycle of consumerism and technology innovation that characterized the rapid growth of technology in the United States during the 1980s and 1990s.

Within this cultural context, Sally's parents were relatively early adopters of computer technology, purchasing a home computer in 1986:

> [Sally] [My] parents bought an Apple IIC when I was about nine. [My] parents set up the computer in [the] dining room and we all watched in awe as

we turned it on and watched the tutorial. . . . From what I can remember, my father ordered it. . . . It was confusing for us that our parents couldn't tell us exactly how the computer worked, because they didn't know how to use it either. My father bought it to do some word processing and to play games.

Although both Sally's mother and father were eventually involved in the use of the computer, the family's early-adopter profile was driven primarily by her father. As Sally noted in her interview:

[Sally] My father has always been a technology buff. He was very excited that we were using computers, and encouraged me to use ours at home. My mom thought that computers were too complicated for her, but she did encourage me to use them. My parents always bought learning games for me, not regular play games. . . . We had to have all our homework done before we could use the computer. They also stressed that we were lucky that we had a computer, and that it was a learning tool.

The values that Sally's parents placed on technology and technological literacy at home matched closely with those her teachers and school promulgated—computers were valuable tools that represented a larger program of progress in the United States; these machines could be used to enhance learning, literacy, and educational performance; computers were fun to use; and children would benefit from knowledge about technology. These values encouraged Sally to continue associating computers with privilege, a sense of accomplishment, and fun. Even at home, educational games remained a key focus of her computer use as a child, and her parents underscored the school's treatment of computers as a source of privilege—one that was accessible only through good behavior.

Sally's parents, it is clear, took an active role in teaching those technological literacy practices officially sanctioned within the school system—not simply encouraging their children to understand computers as valuable learning tools, but also actively monitoring the childrens' computer use at home to ensure that the appropriate values prevailed. Although game playing was encouraged on the computer in Sally's home, for example, the games were primarily "learning games." Later, when their home computer was linked to the Internet, as Sally noted, her parents' active involvement continued in the same vein with her younger sister:

[Sally] The computer my parents have has rules. It is treated as a privilege and it can be taken away at any time. My parents monitor what my sisters do with the computer. They would be present if my nine-year-old sister is using the Web.

In these ways, Sally's parents influenced her own and her siblings' sense of appropriate technological literacy, although it is also clear that the views of the children and the parents were never exactly congruent. Through their literacy practices and values, Sally's parents also influenced both micro-level environments and larger macro-level trends during this period. Their views on the positive value of computer-based education, for example, was communicated in multiple ways to the local school system: through the expectations that Sally brought with her to school, in parent-teacher conferences, and through comments to school board members. And, when their views and consumer habits aligned themselves with the views and habits of other parents in the community, this influence was amplified in proportion, thus encouraging continued uses of computers in local schools. This same dynamic worked, as well, with regard to the parents' influence on national-level trends. The consumer habits of Sally's parents, for example, who tended to purchase educational computer games rather than non-educational computer games—when magnified by similar habits of other parents across the United States— generated a cumulative shaping effect on products, product development, and product marketing in the U.S. computer industry.

Sally's peers also played a role in reinforcing the positive value she placed on computers and the literacies of technology. Her friends, for instance, often came to her house to play with the computer, especially in 1986 before many other families in her neighborhood had purchased home computers. As she explained,

> [Sally] When I was young, my family was the first one out of all my friends' [families] to have a computer. I became really cool. Everyone wanted to come play with the computer. The only values we placed on it was that it was new and fun.

This richly textured network of positive associations was fostered over time, and it continued to define the family's relationship with technology and technological literacy. And as the rapid pace of technological innovation continued in the United States, Sally's family—along with many others who could afford to do so—continued to invest in the latest forms of computer technology, thus helping to drive the pace of change and innovation in the computer market, as well as deriving some benefits from it:

> [Sally] In the years that followed [the purchase of our first home computer], we bought another Apple, this time a II GS and later an IBM compatible when I was in high school. Since I have been in college, my parents have had

two new computers, both IBM compatibles. They are now also buying more "extras," such as a scanner and a writable CD-ROM.

[Sally] After a while [the computer] became something we used as a tool. We wrote papers, and my father used it to track financial transactions. It became almost a part of our family, and we couldn't live with out it.

A similar pattern existed in Jill's home, although the family was not characterized by a profile of early adoption. It wasn't until 1989, in fact, when Jill was in junior high school, that her parents brought a computer into their home. When they did, they were directly supported in their decision by other family members:

[Jill] What happened is that my aunt and uncle had an Apple IIe and then they upgraded to a PC. We took their old computer. . . . We gave it back when we eventually bought an Aptiva [in 1993]. But the reason we got the computer in the first place is because us kids wanted to play games and, and, also so we could type things in a word processor.

The sponsoring influence of Jill's uncle and aunt, however, was not limited solely to their material contribution of a computer. Neither of Jill's parents used the family computer when it was first purchased, and so her uncle and aunt also provided Jill with important role models of adults who used computers frequently and expertly in their own lives:

[Jill] No one else in my family had a computer, except for that uncle and aunt. And they did a lot of stuff on the computer, like . . . [keeping] all their finances and photography club files on the computer.

Although Jill's parents adopted computers later than Sally's, the patterns of support and use in both houses were similar:

[Jill] At first, we just played games on the computer. It was something to occupy all the cousins when we had family functions. And eventually, we typed a lot of things, especially for school papers. As we continued to learn, we would make spreadsheets and databases, but it was still primarily used for school. The kids used the computer the most. I don't think my dad ever used it, and my mom used it if she wanted to have something typed. Then I started to learn Basic in school [7th grade], and sometimes, I would fool around with various programs.

[Jill] . . . my brothers now use it to type things up as well, and now that we have the Internet, everyone uses that. My youngest brother knows his way around the computer. He can fix a lot of problems that I can too. For example, if the rest of my family can't get anything to print, he and I can solve that problem.

Jill's friends, too, played a role in establishing support for technological literacy:

> [Jill] The more adept I became at typing, the more I used the computer, because it was faster for me to write at the computer than [to] write on paper. I loved using the PC we had because it had more things on it like better games, and then we got the Internet, which was just addicting. I remember before we got Internet access at my house, I'd go to my friend's house, and we'd play on her computer in the chat rooms on the Internet. Those things are evil.

Both kinds of interaction—the games and chat rooms, as well as the more academic uses such as word processing—helped construct the framework of Jill's technology use and technological literacy values. Like Sally, by the time Jill reached high school, she knew from experience that computers were fun and that they were useful both at home and in school; she also knew that parents and teachers and peers valued computers and the ability to work with them, especially in support of officially sanctioned literacy activities. In addition, the two girls' use of computers at home shaped their expectations for computer use at school, as well as their understanding of what it meant to be fully literate at the end of the 20th century in the United States.

As the pace of innovation and growth continued in the computer industry, as schools and workplaces placed an increasingly heavy premium on computer skills, and as the culture became increasingly dependent on computers, Sally's and Jill's families continued their investment in technology and technological literacy. Their dependence on computers as literacy environments became a habit in the lives of both families and a sustained influence on the lives of both young women:

> [Jill] My mom bought [the family's latest computer] off the TV on QVC last year (1998) for Christmas. She just felt that we needed a newer, better computer. I think she was right.
>
> [Jill] Yes, it is fantastic. I'm not sure of the brand name, but it is a PC. It is equipped with a fast modem, a sound card, a movie player, a CD-ROM, and a large monitor. I just love it. We have Internet access, as well as telnet access, and we are able to play multimedia things, like minimovies. I can play songs off the Internet. We have the Corel series for our office products . . . and a database program, et cetera. We also have a flat-bed scanner and some programs similar to Photoshop.
>
> [Sally] [The family's latest computer] is an IBM compatible, has a writable CD-ROM, a printer, and a scanner.
>
> [Sally] My family uses it for browsing the Internet, writing papers, making greeting cards, playing games, e-mail, and financial stuff. They basically taught themselves.

Raised within rich systems of technological support and class-based expectations, eventually, the two girls were bound for college. Not surprisingly, when the time came to choose the college they would attend, both Sally and Jill sought out institutions and academic majors that took advantage of their technological literacy practices and strengths. Both became Scientific and Technical Communication (STC) majors at Michigan Technological University, a mid size midwestern university that emphasized technology in most of its major areas of study.

As STC majors, Sally and Jill recognized that students were expected to have considerable knowledge of computers and to be proficient in literacy practices within digital environments. Students were also required to maintain a certain level of material investment in their technological literacy, not only in the form of tuition payments but also in the form of computer lab fees:

> [Sally] We are expected to know how to use the computer to do papers and other homework. We are expected to check our e-mail for classes.
> [Sally] I use both Mac and IBM compatibles . . . I know many programs . . . various web browsers, word processors, Photoshop, e-mail programs, video-editing programs, page-layout programs, drawing programs, math software, the list goes on.
> [Jill] I use the Web for a lot of research type things. I also use it to find images and graphics I need. I use the Web to buy tickets for concerts, to buy CDs and books and other shopping things, and I use the Web to get free e-mail when I'm home. I also use the Web to put up my web page to show off my resume to employers. Just recently, I used the Web to research a Web site I made about backcountry downhill skiing.
> [Jill] I use the computer to type papers and memos, I use the computer for e-mail, the Internet, and creating various desktop publishing things (posters, table tents, etc.), and I use the scanner and software like Photoshop, and Macromedia, [and] Freehand/Adobe Illustrator to create graphics for various things like papers, projects, and Web sites.

By the time these two young women were preparing to graduate from college, they had become habituated to communicating in electronic environments. They had also become consumers who continued to purchase technology for their own use at home, thus exerting an ongoing influence on U.S. marketing and manufacturing practices. As members of a high-tech communication profession, they planned to participate in and influence computer uses within the companies that employed them and to bring their personal expectations to bear on the larger national context of technological innovation. In these ways, among others, Sally and Jill helped structure and order the role of technology and technological literacy in their world, just as their own lives and literacies had been structured by technology.

Finally, it is important to note that the influence that these two women exerted within the culture was complex—certainly not straight down a party line of "more and better technology, faster." Growing up with computers had, among other things, given both a clear understanding of what they liked and disliked about these machines, what they considered appropriate and not so appropriate uses of technology. As Jill explained:

> I think there is a relationship between what I like to do on computers and what I'd like to do with my major. . . . I'm not too computer intensive (I've never taken a multimedia class, and I'm not interested in taking any); I really like using the computer to be creative in page layout and [using] Illustrator software, which is why I want to go into the graphic design field. But I don't want to program, so I don't really want to go into web design or multimedia fields, because I see them as too much work on the computer . . . I like STC because I can use the computer and learn things, but the field is broad enough that I can stay away from some things on the computer if I want to.

Jill's ongoing immersion in a technology-rich program has prepared her to assess her future career desires with what is, we would argue, an uncommon degree of sophistication.

The Case Study of Damon Davis

Damon Davis was born in a Detroit hospital. An African American, Damon reported his religious denomination as "reality," and his family's income situation when he was growing up as "broke . . . broken home, no money, moving from place to place." Damon never knew his father. His mother, a high school graduate, moved the family to Florida when Damon was two and began classes in beauty school before falling prey to a drug habit that eventually broke up the family. As Damon explained:

> She took classes at the beginning. . . . Tried, but I don't think that's actually the word. . . . You either do it or you don't, so . . . she started but she didn't finish.

His mother, Damon continued,

> . . . couldn't care for me as she should have at first when I lived in Florida, I moved with my neighbors and they were OK people but they were older people and then I moved back with my mom, then I moved with some lady,

I haven't the slightest idea what the lady's name is and she was a nice person. Then I was able to move back with my mom and then we moved back to Michigan and I bounced from house to house since.

But Detroit, Michigan, proved no better for the family than Florida, and Damon's life for the next few years was turbulent:

Now between 9 and 10, I moved from Detroit to Toledo, back to Detroit, back to Toledo, then back to Detroit. I stayed in Detroit from that point on until I was 11, got incarcerated, by, when I was 13 . . . no 12 . . . moved to California. I had moved to California once before too but I can't remember the exact dates of that.

. . . I moved back to Michigan three weeks before my mom passed, then my mom passed, then me and my sister's situation got rocky and they put me in a foster home. . . . So I stayed there until I graduated high school.

Despite his ongoing family troubles, however, Damon enjoyed school and often found himself motivated best by individual teachers whom he remembered as upholding high standards. In elementary school, for instance, Damon recalled,

I started [to read] when . . . I was living in Pensacola, Florida . . . I still believe that their school systems are beyond the Michigan school systems. . . . I had a teacher . . . she was a second-grade teacher that was turned into a kindergarten teacher. . . . And at first, I thought, "why is she teaching kindergarten?" But she had us so excelled, I mean we got computers in our classroom, I learned to count to 100 within like the first week.

I didn't read too much before school, but, I mean, we were in our class and it was like everybody is dying to catch up and then probably about midway through that year it was, everybody was just excited to go to school. I've never seen that many people, I mean my whole class was just happy to be there.

Damon was also influenced by his mother's habit of reading. As he remembered,

[T]here was never a lack of . . . books at the house . . . she was a novel reader, that's all she read was novels . . . stuff like what John Grisham writes now. She wasn't too much into the romance novels nor mystery. . . . [S]he just read all the time. . . . Her and my sister are just alike. . . . [I]f they get engrossed in a book then they'll sit there and they will read it all day and I can't do that.

[I]t was a habit. My whole family has picked up on it. I don't know if it started with my great-grandmother, my grandmother, but my whole family does it, my brother will sit up and he'll read all day . . . I'm in college now . . . but, I used to, when I did learn how to read, *Encyclopedia Brown,* oh, I sat there and read *Encyclopedia Brown* all day.

I lived on Barcelona Street in Pensacola and about four or five blocks down was the library. . . . I'd read them at the library, grab and bring them home. It didn't matter. I have them in school, on the bus on the way home since it takes me about a half hour to get to where I stay, so wherever I can read, I was there.

His love of language, Damon recollected, was also connected directly to a growing interest in music:

[S]ince I was about probably seven or eight, I was not necessarily dealing with music but just picking up on words that people are using in music and I started trying to use [them] myself and more and more I just started getting into the English thing. I was like, well, I know all these big words and you see that I know it so I just want to use them in sentences and use them in paragraphs and my papers are coming out great. I'm like, oh, it fits. I'd come out of class and I'd be struggling and I was like, why do I have to take all the English for? And, . . . I guess that was the main attraction.

By high school, however, his unsettled family life had taken its toll on Damon's school performance:

I had a 1.5 [grade point average] when I started high school . . . my cousin told me, well my cousin and his friends, since we all lived in the neighborhood in the projects, they said, "Well if you don't have a 3.0, you can't hang around us." And, they had all the ladies with them, so, I decided to pick it up and I said, "OK, well, OK." I got a 3.0, then it became addictive. . . . I don't think Detroit public schools actually prepare you for college. I'm a strong believer in that.

I was like, "Why go to school? It ain't no fun!" But they started showing me things about school, why not go to school? It's boring if you ain't in school all day and when you are there, I mean, you've got your friends there, you crack jokes, and they were showing me things where you can crack jokes in class, but as long as you are getting your work done, you are pretty much doing OK . . .

Although Damon first encountered computers in elementary school, he remembered using them only to play games when the regular work of the class was done. And in junior high school and high school, although computers were present, they were not central to his life, nor were they integrated into the curriculum of his school or the work of his classes:

From where I'm from, computers was not the big thing. . . . No computer at home, actually nobody I knew in the neighborhood had one.

After I came back from California [in ninth grade], I had a business course and I had to write a 10-page paper so I don't like using typewriters so I had to sit, so I sat in there and did the majority of the stuff in the library on the computer. . . .

[In high school], I had, I had one of the hardest teachers they thought they had for English, so I had her and, she was hard enough so I wasn't too knowledgeable about the computers or what not. . . . [S]o I would just go [to the library to use the computers] . . . they did have them, my last year there. . . . I got to use them once or something like that but I wasn't even sure what I was exactly using them for.

During his last year of high school, however, Damon took a computer literacy course, and, after that experience, he began to see technology in a different light:

Late in high school, it was like, wow, computers are cool and that's where all the money is going to be so I want to do it. . . . My counselor, she had a list on her, her door of the, like, the top-paying jobs. . . . I was like, "Wow, you know, computers, all the stuff with the computers is up at the top of the list!" Now that I've went back, I look on the back of the door [and say], "Yeah, that's one of the most stressful jobs in the world, too, ain't it?"

But it was an athletic scholarship to Michigan Technological University, ultimately, and not his late-blooming interest in technology, that launched Damon into college. After several false starts in computer engineering and computer science courses, which he didn't like because they contained too much math or programming, he settled on a course of study in Scientific and Technical Communication—not because that major involved the use of computers. Rather, he chose the program because of its emphasis on communication skills and language play, which he saw as feeding into his love of rap music.

And, listening to it, I mean, I go back and listen to the stuff that we had from there. Just listening to it and some of the words . . . in the word play and where it was placed and using, um, basically using things that normal people might not catch. Yeah, it was like, it is always an underlying meaning. Underlying meaning to, everything. . . . And I was like, "I like that!" So, it was like, OK, I need to stay . . . here so I can learn how to do that. . . .

It was in 1999, after joining a Black fraternity on campus, that Damon began spending more time on the Internet and, later, developed a strong interest in web design.

I learned a little bit about them [the fraternity] through the Internet first, but I already knew a little bit, but they are just the reason why I use the Internet so much because I just create everything for them. I just like to put out information and . . . I created Chi Alpha Phi's [Web site], well we are Omega Chi Beta Chapter as of Valentine's Day and I created the Web site for this chapter.

I've also created the Web site for the Society of African-American men on this campus. I'm starting a Web site for Phi Beta Sigma Fraternity, Incorporated, which I am not a part of on this campus, but a couple of my friends are, and they asked me if I would do it since one of their members isn't here to do it. Um, I'm also the web master for the Kappa Alpha Fraternity, Incorporated, alumni chapter near Detroit.

Like most students, Damon learned his web-design skills on his own, using tactics that many teachers might associate with plagiarism.

I was like, oh, this [Web site] looks cools. I want to do this. And somebody told us [the fraternity] we had a Web site. I didn't know everyone actually had a Web site. So after I found out . . . [they] had a Web site, it was like, well, so how do I create one like these?

And someone told me that they couldn't teach me how to do it but they suggested that I take, I just steal someone's code, plant it into my page, and go back and just mess with stuff. And the more stuff that you mess with certain things will change and you go, "OK, I think I want to put that back" or "I think I want to delete this," or something like that. So that's, that's how I started with the Web, with the whole Web site there.

By March of 2000, Damon had taken courses in computer applications and web design, and was planning to take two courses in multimedia. He had begun to communicate so much and so consistently through e-mail that he turned off his telephone to save money and learned how to telnet so he could check his mail from remote sites. By this time, Damon was confident in using several word processing packages like Microsoft Word to compose documents; WebChat to speak with others synchronously on the World Wide Web; Poser, Bryce, and Photoshop to create various kinds of representations; and HTML, Java, and Shockwave to design web documents. Most recently, he reported downloading and learning Flash. He was now also receiving payment for his web work by some of the Black fraternities and social organizations he served.

Although Damon's development of digital literacy was extraordinary, the rest of his academic situation was less promising. Working within a cultural context of rapidly accumulating literacies (Brandt, 1995), his teachers in the Humanities Department required proficiency not only in emerging literacies but also in fading literacies. These teachers became increasingly concerned about the amount of attention Damon devoted to organizing and writing formal essays, his lack of concern about the conventional standards of grammatical correctness and spelling, and the logical argumentation strategies he could bring to bear on the essays he wrote. Faculty noted that Damon spent a great deal of time on his online design work, and many weekends traveling to consult with his web-design fraternity clients or writing and producing homemade rap CDs using departmental computers. But they were concerned that Damon might fail to complete the requirements of his bachelor's degree program in technical communication because he did not devote enough attention to the more traditional forms of written communication.

Damon's response to the cultural ecology of the late 20th century, however, cannot be sketched quite so simply. Like Sally and Jill, he was influenced by the explosive growth of the computer industry and by the expectations associated with the technology–literacy linkage. Unlike Sally and Jill, who were both raised in middle class White families, Damon was Black and was raised in poverty. He had not, in addition, had the opportunity to build skills in standard written English to the same degree Sally and Jill had by the time he was ready to begin his final year of college.

Within this cultural ecology, Damon—partially because of the value he came to place on digital literacy—voted differently on his literacy allegiances than did Sally and Jill. Damon chose not to subscribe, at least in the same way as the two women did, to the conventional print literacy values and practices that many faculty at his university held up as standards. He found these standards, frankly, of limited relevance to his life, in his attempts to gain an education and to enter a sphere of economic success and personal fulfillment. Damon did not see these more conventional standards, these practices of print literacy, as the only effective or efficient means of resisting a life of poverty or unskilled labor or of maintaining the social identity he had chosen for himself.

In rejecting these standards—or renegotiating their importance in his life—Damon also re-appropriated, at least in part, the currency of the academy and the material realities of the multimillion dollar university computing system, applying this currency to his own project of identity politics. At a university that was 95% White and characterized by a solidly conservative political cast, Damon established an active online identity—through his digital literacy practices—that linked him to other Blacks who had created their own micropolitical organizations. These organizations, and their social projects built around identity politics, were represented and functioned partially online; were devoted to the support and success of their members; and were anchored, at least in part, in a system of racial identity and a shared social values and codes.

The Cultural Ecology of the 1990s:
Coming to Terms with the Literacies of Technology

If the explosive growth of the computer industry during the late 1970s and the 1980s, informed by the United States' general transformation from a manufacturing society to an information society, provided a context for Jill's, Sally's, and Damon's early education in elementary and secondary school, the subsequent emergence and global expansion of the Internet and the World Wide Web in the 1990s helped shape the context of their later college education and their choices of computer-intensive careers.

The historical backdrop for this period of technological growth in the United States included a substantial budget deficit, pressing unemployment in certain sectors of the economy, and continuing inflationary pressures (Council of Economic Advisors, 1997, p. 3). And the international economic situation was little better from the U.S. point of view. The waning of the Cold War and the failing health of communism had led to the global expansion of international economies, the increasing industrialization of developing countries in East Asia and Latin America, and the opening of increasingly competitive global markets. Although recognized as positive developments globally, these factors were also recognized by U.S. leaders as potentially threatening to the economic and political primacy that the United States had enjoyed in the years immediately following World War II (Council of Economic Advisors, 1997, pp. 235–257).

Facing this global context, the Clinton Administration recognized the need to "position the United States to benefit from the global changes" (p. 248) through a policy of liberalized international trade, which was seen as an essential foundation for the continued growth of post-war global markets—especially markets that could sustain and enhance an increased standard of living for members of the industrialized world, while at the same time supporting the spread of democratic market capitalism (Council of Economic Advisors, 1997). To take full advantage of the liberalized trading system, however, the Clinton Administration needed to define a primary area of specialization in the world marketplace, one that could be exploited in order to secure the continued economic success of the United States in the changing global climate. In the end, there was little doubt of what that area should be: computer technology, both goods and services.

Although the ultimate effort was a global one, the domestic arena proved itself a key venue for the Clinton Administration's project. Without a vital computer industry at home, a technologically adept workforce that knew how to use and appreciate computers, and strong research and development support, the engine of technology might sputter and die. With these key components in place, however, technological growth would be, to a great extent, self-fueling.

As the Administration's reasoning went, growth in the domestic computer industry required the involvement of a population heavily dependent on computer-based environments for its own literacy practices. Given the increasing pace of technological change, such a population would be continual technology consumers. Such a population would also develop an increased appetite for powerful and sophisticated technology products produced by the U.S. computing industry. To keep pace with the demand, this industry would need to create increasing numbers of high-tech and high-paying jobs, and hire highly trained employees, who, in turn, would contribute additional momentum to the domestic economy. Further, the increased demands of such a technologically savvy population for new products and new capabilities would also pressure that industry to increase the pace of innovation even more dramatically than it already had. The entire force of this dynamic would result in expanded exporting of technology goods and services, and a revitalization of the domestic sectors that produced these goods, resulting in a system of imports and exports that fed on its own momentum.

Recognizing that computers had to become not only the business of the public school system, but also part of the "new basics" of a public school education in the United States, the Clinton Administration, on February 15, 1996, announced the Technological Literacy Challenge—a literacy project that would use the U.S. school system to prepare students for the technological challenges of the 21st century. This national literacy project had the goal of creating a citizenry comfortable in using computers not only for the purposes of calculating, programming, and designing, but also for the purposes of reading, writing, and communicating. According to its sponsors, this project was to provide all people equal access to an education rich in opportunities to use and learn about technology. With such an education, the project's sponsors claimed further, graduates would gain the qualifications needed for high tech, high-paying jobs, and thus, the means of achieving upward social mobility and economic prosperity within the increasingly technological culture.

To achieve this goal, U.S. schools were to help "all children to become technologically literate" by providing them an understanding of, and the ability to use, communication technologies, specifically computers, in the practice of reading and writing effectively (*Getting American Students Ready*, 1996, p. 3). The deadline for creating such a citizenry—one that understood literacy practices primarily in terms of technological contexts—was "early in the 21st century" (*Getting America's Students Ready*, p. 3).

The Technological Literacy Challenge—its effects amplified by the rapid expansion of computer-based environments for communication, the U.S. investment in the computer manufacturing and service sectors, and a fundamental belief in science and technology as progressive social forces—helped to link literacy and technology in increasingly direct ways. By the end of 1996, for instance, the National Council of Teachers of English and the International Reading Association published their first set of joint national standards for the teaching of English and language arts, noting that U.S. students should be able to use "an array of technologies, from computers and computer networks to electronic mail, interactive video, and CD-ROMs" to prepare for the "demands that will face them in the future" (*Standards for the English Language Arts*, 1996, pp. 39–40).

But, if the project to expand technological literacy was justified in 1996 as a means of achieving positive social changes and new opportunities, actually achieving such goals proved more difficult than anticipated. Indeed, for the remainder of the 20th century, in U.S. schools and in the cultural ecology in which these schools existed, computers continued to be distributed differentially along the related axes of race and socioeconomic status. Moreover, this distribution continued to contribute to intergenerational patterns of racism, poverty, and illiteracy. Through 1997, for instance, schools primarily serving students of color and poor students continued to have less access to computers, and access to less sophisticated computer equipment than did schools primarily serving more affluent students or White students. In addition, schools primarily serving students of color and poor students continued to have less access to the Internet, less access to multimedia equipment, less access to CD-ROM equipment, less access to local area networks, and less access to videodisc technology than did schools primarily serving the more affluent (Coley, Crandler, & Engle, 1997, p. 3).

These data, which were profoundly disturbing, became all the more problematic when traced into U.S. workplaces and homes. There, too, as census figures indicated, the distribution of computer technology, and hence digital literacy, was strongly correlated to both race and socioeconomic status. Black employees, for example, were less likely than White employees to use a range of computer applications in their workplace environments.[12] As late as 2000, 14.1% of White workers had access to the Internet at work whereas only 8.6% of Black workers and 5.6% of Hispan-

---

[12]See, for example, table 430 in chapter 7 of the *Digest of Education Statistics 1999* (National Center for Educational Statistics, 2000).

ics had similar access (*Falling through the Net,* 2000, p. 47). Moreover, families of color and families with low incomes, like Damon's family, were less likely to own and use computers than were White families and families with higher incomes.

In other words, in the United States at the end of the 20th century, the poorer and less educated people were (both conditions closely correlated with race), the less likely they were to have access to computers at home and to high-paying, high-tech jobs in the U.S. workplace. The young lives of Sally, Jill, and Damon, and their determination to acquire the literacies of technology, all point to a recognition of the importance information technologies would continue to assume in the 21st century.

The Uneven Development of Digital Literacy in the Cultural Ecology of the 1980s and 1990s

The rise of the networked society and the beginning of the information age in the United States, which dates roughly from the mid-1970s and the invention of microcomputers to the end of the 20th century, represented a cultural transformation of astounding proportions. As we have noted, during this time literacy expectations in the United States became inextricably tied to computer use. As these three case studies indicate, in the 1980s and 1990s the emergence of computers and computer networks as transformative media for literacy and communication shaped a converging set of social, political, ideological, and economic forces, as well as people's lives and literacies. In turn, the literacy values and activities of these people and their families contributed to the vigorous growth and expansion of computers, computer networks, and the computer sector in the United States. These factors, in turn, contributed to a cultural ecology that supported technological expansion at many different levels and in many different social spheres.

In emphasizing the importance of cultural ecologies as defining concepts for understanding literate activity, this chapter has undertaken three key tasks. First, we have attempted to trace the ways in which literacy and computer technology became increasingly and inextricably linked in the United States at the close of the 20th century and how this linkage affected the lived experiences of three young people and their families, in homes, schools, and, to a lesser degree, workplaces. The chapter has summarized how the early integration of personal computers into U.S. schools shaped the elementary- and secondary-school educations of Sally, Jill, and Damon, and how the investment in computer technology in the 1990s contributed to their high school and college experiences as well. The chapter has also indicated how the digital literacy practices and values of these three young people, in turn, helped constitute the social, economic, and cultural ecology of the late 20th century.[13]

Second, the chapter has argued that computers, even though they transformed the U.S. culture and its definition of literacy both broadly and deeply in the 1980s and 1990s, continued to be distributed differentially along the related axes of class and race in schools and homes. As a result, many of the same intergenerational patterns of illiteracy that characterized the age of print[14] also continued to characterize the rise of digital literacy in the United States at the end of the 20th century. Thus, at the end of the 20th century, the national project to expand technological literacy had not necessarily resulted in a better life or more democratic opportunities or enriched educational experiences for all people in the United States. Instead, within the national educational system, especially at the elementary and secondary levels, poor students and students of color, like Damon Davis, continued to have limited access to technology support and to suffer from higher incidences of educational dropout rates and failure than did students, like Sally Van Wormer and Jill Osborne, who are White and middle class.

Finally, this chapter has introduced a number of the methodological approaches used throughout this book. These approaches are informed primarily by the life-history scholarship of Deborah Brandt (1995, 1998, 1999, 2001) and by the work of other literacy scholars, such as David Barton and Mary Hamilton (1998) who build on the oral history foundations laid by Daniel Bertaux (1981), Paul Thompson (1988), and Trevor Lummis (1987). The chapter has also discussed the concept of cultural ecologies—the metaphor we employ to describe the interaction of a multi-

---

[13]British sociologist Anthony Giddens (1979) identifies this kind of social dynamic by the "duality of structure" (p. 5) that characterizes it, noting that social structures both shape people's lives and are shaped by the ways in which people live their lives. As he explains this concept, "the structural properties of social systems are both the medium and the outcome of the practices that constitute those systems. . . . [S]tructure is both enabling and constraining" (p. 69). The recognition of the duality of structure, Giddens goes on to say, provides people with a basis for understanding and enacting their own agency. Because "every competent member of every society knows a great deal about the institutions of that society" (p. 71), humans draw on their understanding of "structure, rules and resources" (p. 71) as they live their lives. They are, however, also constrained by such factors, and their actions generate unintended consequences (p. 56).

[14]For extended descriptions of these persistent patterns, see Elspeth Stuckey's (1991) *The Violence of Literacy*; Shirley Brice Heath's (1983) *Ways with Words: Language, Life, and Work in Communities and Classrooms*; Harvey Graff's (1987) *The Legacies of Literacy*; James Gee's (1996) *Social Linguistics and Literacies: Ideology in Discourses*; and Mike Rose's (1989) *Lives on the Boundary: The Struggles and Achievements of America's Underprepared*.

tude of social forces, material conditions, and cultural expectations that mark particular periods of history. Finally, the chapter introduces Anthony Giddens' (1979) concept of the "duality of structure" to explain how the actions of people are not only shaped by the society within which they live and the technological systems they inhabit but also how they themselves help constitute these environments.

2

Privileging—or Not—the Literacies of Technology

Paula Boyd
Gail E. Hawisher
Karen Lunsford
Mary Sheridan-Rabideau
Cynthia L. Selfe

> *Identity is constructed relationally through difference from the other; identification with a group based on gender, race or sexuality, for example, depends mostly on binary systems of "us" versus "them," where difference from the other defines the group to which one belongs. Conversely,* identity *also suggests sameness . . . some shared ground. (Susan Friedman, 1998, p. 19)*

> *A good deal of what we do with language, throughout history, is create and act out different "types of people"—including multiple types of selves for ourselves—by putting words, deeds, values, other people, and things together in integral combinations for specific times and places. (James Gee, 1996, p. viii)*

For some women in this study, especially those who came of age at times and in cultural ecologies that favored conventionally determined social roles, gender and the related timing of key technology developments played an important role in shaping the acquisition and development of electronic literacy. To understand more precisely why some women considered this combination of social and historical factors so influential, this chapter features the stories of three women—Paula Boyd, Mary Sheridan-Rabideau, and Karen Lunsford—and underscores their birth dates in the late 1960s as a time of great social unrest in the United States and as the dawn of second-wave feminism.

By 1967, although many of the political and social issues associated with this time had already become clearly established in the public arena, the range of acceptable social roles available to women had changed only slightly since the 1950s.[1] Nor had technological changes opened up the digital world for women, as it would for Sally Osborne and Jill Van Wormer born a decade later (see chapter 1). The first personal computers entered schools when Mary, Paula, and Karen were just becoming teenagers, and, thus, their school experiences often differed markedly from those born in the late 1970s, especially as far as information technologies are concerned. When Mary, Paula, and Karen began schooling in the early 1970s, no fully assembled personal computers were available to the general populace. It is not surprising, then, that except for an isolated computer here or there, none of the three has memories of encountering computers in her elementary school years. By 1980 when the girls had reached junior high school, video games and computer games had become part of the social ecology, but personal computers still remained relatively scarce commodities.

Within this context, despite the political upheaval of the late 1960s and 1970s, literacy practices tended to remain conventional, with Mary, Paula, and Karen relying primarily on pens, typewriters, books, and other print materials for their writing and learning. None of the three learned or used word processing with any regularity until college; none—unlike Sally, Jill, or Damon in the last chapter—learned programs, such as Pagemaker or Photoshop, even in college although the programs were available at the time. E-mail, similarly, was not part of their repertoires as undergraduates.

The similarities in these women's school lives and literacy practices support Deborah Brandt's (2001) contention that people born within a particular timeframe often share with their age cohort[2]—and we would add, their gender cohort—specific kinds of literacy education, reflecting

---

[1]For a discussion of women's lives in the United States during the 1950s, see Marty Jezer's (1982) *The Dark Ages: Life in the United States 1945–1960*. For discussions on women's emerging roles during the late 1960s, see Alice Echols' (1989) landmark *Daring to Be Bad: Radical Feminism in America 1967–1975*, and Howard Zinn's (1998) *The Twentieth Century: A People's History*, pp. 255–269.

[2]Brandt (2001) uses the work of Trevor Lummis (1987) and Norman Ryder (1965) to undergird the methods she employs in conducting and analyzing life history interviews. She includes, for example, this statement from Lummis (1987):

> . . . people live their lives within the material and cultural boundaries of their time span, and so life histories are exceptionally effective historical sources because through the totality of lived experience they reveal relations between individuals and social forces which are rarely apparent in other sources. Above all, the information is historical and dynamic in that it reveals changes of experience through time. (p. 108)

the values and material practices of a given culture at a particular point in history. The life history interviews of these women also indicate that they shared similar experiences and followed a similar trajectory to other members of their age cohort when they did have an opportunity to learn the new information technologies. The stories of Mary, Paula, and Karen indicate that this pattern can hold true despite considerable differences in people's life circumstances.

In this chapter, we describe the tenor of the times and the cultural ecology in which these women grew up, and then move to a description of their own particular experiences with digital literacies. Throughout the chapter, we concern ourselves with gender and identity formation, agreeing with Susan Friedman (1998) that identity is constructed through difference and sameness, and, with James Gee (1996), that literate practices—electronic and print—are crucial to one's sense of identity and, in fact, to one's sense of multiple identities.

The Cultural Ecology of the Late 1960s and 1970s: Tumultuous Times

The Women's Movement in the United States dates itself as re-emerging in a second wave of feminism in 1967,[3] the same year, Howard Zinn (1998) notes, that the United States experienced "the greatest urban riots of American history."[4] Within the Civil Rights Movement of the late 1960s, issues of women's inequality were identified as especially pressing. Unfortunately, although many women participated actively in the Civil Rights Movement, more often than not they were not in positions of leadership and had little influence over the direction the Movement should take. Instead, they found themselves regularly filling subordinate roles in campus organizations where more visible male leaders directed much of the early activism that took place. In political organizations, such as Students for a Democratic Society (SDS), men customarily defined the issues and set the goals while women served as typists, clerks, errand runners, and the like.[5] Women desired more opportunities for activism in these tu-

---

In explaining birth cohort analysis and its advantages for looking at social change, she includes these words from Norman Ryder (1965): "Each new cohort makes fresh contact with the contemporary social heritage and carries the impress of the encounter through life" (quoted in Brandt, p. 11).

[3]Alice Echols (1989) dates radical feminism as beginning in 1967 and documents its influence on both cultural and liberal feminism, even as radical feminism itself came primarily to inhabit universities.

[4]For additional discussion on the underlying causes of civil rights protests and uprisings in U.S. cities at this time, see Howard Zinn (1998), p. 203 ff.

[5]See especially Echols (1989) pp. 3–50 for a look at women's experiences within the Civil Rights Movement.

multuous times. If they were to participate in a social movement that demanded social justice and equal rights for all, they too should be counted
as equal partners—or so the thinking went.

These same years of political and social upheaval in the United States
saw the assassinations of Martin Luther King Jr. and then Robert Kennedy; the civil rights protests and riots; the massacre of villagers at My
Lai; draft card burning and the anti-war movement; prison rebellions; uprisings of Native Americans; anti-nuclear protests; and the first stirrings of
state legislative acts to legalize abortion. School desegregation was ostensibly in the process of being implemented, and busing was becoming increasingly common. Demonstrations on college campuses continued to
protest the U.S. involvement in Vietnam, and, tragically, at one such protest in 1970, four Kent State students were killed by National Guardsmen.[6]
Although some would later attribute these uprisings to the coming of age
of that large demographic phenomenon called the baby boomers, others
would recognize the deep changes taking place in everyday life within the
United States.[7] As Howard Zinn (1998) observed, never before were there
so many movements for change concentrated in so short a stretch of time.[8]
What was surprising, during much of this period, young children continued to attend their first years of school immersed in the same kinds of
early learning environments that their parents had experienced. Whereas
their older sisters and brothers were already considered part of a problem
called "the generation gap," this cohort born in the late 1960s went
through its paces in schools that seemed to be characterized by "unchanging continuity."[9] Yet the times into which these women were born witnessed spectacular societal changes.

---

[6]See Kent State University's Web site at http://www.library.kent.edu/exhibits/
4may95/ for a collection of exhibits and archives marking the tragedy.

[7]See Margaret Mead's (1970) *Culture and Commitment: The New Relationships Between the
Generations in the 1970s* for a prophetic view of the future and the kinds of learning that
would characterize it. Writing in 1970, for example, she notes:

> Today, suddenly, because all the peoples of the world are part of one electronically
> based, intercommunicating network, young people everywhere share a kind of expe-
> rience that none of the elders ever have had or will have. Conversely, the older gener-
> ation will never see repeated in the lives of young people their own unprecedented
> experience of sequentially emerging change. This break between generations is
> wholly new: it is planetary and universal (p. 64).

[8]For a more detailed discussion of these events, see Zinn (1998), pp. 255–300.

[9]See Mead (1970), p. 14. See also pp. 13–38 for Mead's discussion of the postfigurative
"cultural style" (p. 13). In societies that demonstrate a postfigurative cultural style, the main
channel for learning consists of adults handing down knowledge to children.

Because Mary, Karen, and Paula all entered kindergarten and elementary school in the early 1970s, it seems appropriate to explore in greater detail the historical events of that decade. Economically, it was a time in which people continued to do well. Throughout the 1970s, the United States maintained a rising standard of living.[10] Disposable income from 1970 to 1985 grew approximately at 1.7% per year, one of the best indications of the steady economic prosperity in the United States (Johnston & Packer, 1987, p. xix), and a growing number of people entered the workforce. These were also the years when the United States continued to compete with the Soviet Union in the race to space, and throughout these years, successive waves of baby boomers, who belong to the large population group born between 1946 and 1964, continued to come of age.

In the years that accompanied the three girls' entrance into schooling, some of the results of the clamoring for social justice began to be felt. The 1970s marked significantly the years in which the United States ended its war in Vietnam, a development that was likely a direct result of the activist dissidence at home protesting the war.[11] Despite Richard Nixon's announcing sometime after his presidential election in 1968 that he would not be influenced by the antiwar activity, 1973 witnessed the withdrawal of U.S. troops from Vietnam. Just as citizens felt relief that the war was finally coming to an end, the newly documented Watergate scandal, as it came to be called, entered the news. During the 1972 presidential campaign, five men with wiretapping equipment broke into offices of the Democratic National Committee, men who it was later learned had connections to the Nixon campaign. This event and the scandals that followed—everything from Nixon's using public funds inappropriately for his Florida and California homes to the United States military, unbeknownst to Congress or citizens, carrying out massive bombing raids on Cambodia during 1969 and 1970—eventually led to the resignation of Richard Nixon as President of the United States. In 1974, Richard Nixon became the first and only United States president to resign from office.[12]

Yet even during these difficult years, women's issues moved steadily to the forefront, and as early as 1972 Title IX was passed. An educational amendment that prohibited discrimination, Title IX stated that "No person in the United States shall, on the basis of sex, be excluded from participation in, be denied the benefits of, or be subjected to discrimination under any education program or activity receiving Federal financial assis-

---

[10]See Johnston and Packer (1987) and their *Workforce 2000*, pp. xvii–xviii for further discussion.

[11]Zinn (1998), see especially pp. 213–254 for a discussion of the Vietnam conflict.

[12]For more discussion of the Watergate scandal and Nixon's resignation, see Zinn (1998), pp. 301–311.

tance . . ." (U.S. Department of Labor, 1972). Although not specifically naming women, Title IX had the effect of allowing women to participate in sports and other activities from which they had previously been barred and also encouraged schools to develop team sports for women. Today it's difficult to fathom that women born before the 1960s had few school athletic activities in which they could participate, but it was so. Before 1972, these privileges or rights had not been part of the culture in which most young women were brought up and had been effectively denied girls and women as they made their way through school. The year 1973 also marked the decision of *Roe v. Wade,* which ruled that states "could prohibit abortions only in the last three months of pregnancy, could regulate abortion for health purposes during the second three months of pregnancy, and during the first three months, a woman and her doctor had the right to decide" (Zinn, 1998, p. 264). Illegal abortions had claimed the lives of many, especially poor women who couldn't afford abortions that the more affluent in the United States managed to obtain under safe conditions. "A woman's right to choose" became—and continues to be—a critical refrain for proponents of women's rights in the United States and in many countries worldwide.[13]

The 1970s was also the decade of school desegregation. Although *Brown v. the Board of Education* had been ruled on in 1954, it took the social unrest and civil rights uprisings of the times to finally bring Black and White children together in schools, most noticeably in the South. Living in several different places in the North, the women of this chapter were less affected than they might have been by attempts to open the doors to all children regardless of race. That's not to say that segregation wasn't prevalent in the North, but only that residential segregation was often sufficient to keep children of different races and ethnicities divided. Neighborhood schools of the North also tended to keep the races separated through a method of tracking, in which children were placed in different classrooms based on test scores that favored mainstream culture. Busing became commonplace as a court-dictated method to achieve equality in schools, with large numbers of Black and White students alike being taken out of nearby schools and transported sometimes long distances to even out the demographics of particular schools. However disruptive Whites and sometimes Blacks may have viewed these strategies of desegregation, Blacks were often able to attend better schools with better resources and achieve a higher level of education than had previously been available to

---

[13]For a discussion of abortion rights worldwide in 2000, see "Nations Worldwide Support a Woman's Right to Choose Abortion" at the Web site hosting the Center for Reproductive Rights, http://www.crlp.org/pub_fac_atkwwsup.html.

them. In higher education, desegregation had already made important strides during the previous decade with Charlene Hunter-Gault and James Meredith admitted among the first Black students to the University of Georgia in 1961 and the University of Mississippi in 1962, respectively. Thus, the United States and its schools were poised to experience a sea change in access to educational opportunities, or so it seemed at the time.

If 1975 is regarded as the year that officially saw the end of the Vietnam War, it also is the year in which Steve Jobs and Stephen Wozniak worked at home in Jobs' garage constructing what has come to be known as the first fully assembled personal computer, the Apple I. Completing their work on the machine the following year, Jobs and Wozniak, then 20 and 25 years old, respectively, founded what eventually grew into Apple Corporation, but not before trying to sell the Apple I and Apple II unsuccessfully to corporations such as Hewlett-Packard and Commodore. By 1979, the Apple IIe was selling for $1,195, and work on the Lisa Apple (named after Jobs' baby daughter) and the soon-to-be-born Macintosh had already begun. It was this same year, 1979, that Apple began awarding hundreds of thousands of dollars in grants to schools and hence established itself as the computer of choice in the educational community.[14]

Although the success story of the Apple and its introduction into schools constitutes the best known information technology story associated with these times, other important developments in computer technology also occurred during the decade. In 1970, Murray Turoff developed the first system of computer-mediated communication. He and Roxanne Hiltz (1978) in their landmark book, *The Network Nation*, speculated on this new development:

> In place of thinking of a nation or a society as a collection of communities, we need to think of it as a complex set of overlapping networks of actual or potential communication or exchange. Unlike a group, not all of the members of a network are directly in communication with or even directly aware of, one another; but they are connected by communication and relationships through mutually known intermediates and thus, the *potential* for direct communication or exchange is there. (p. xxviii)

Thus, as Hiltz and Turoff went on to point out, these new systems were capable of "allow[ing] a person meaningful, frequent, and regular communication with five to ten times more people than is possible with current communication options" (p. xxviii). Created by the U.S. govern-

---

[14]M. A. C. Fallon (1993), "Apple Computer Corporation" (pp. 70–73). See also Hawisher, LeBlanc, Moran, and Selfe (1996), pp. 32–42.

ment's Advance Research Projects Agency (ARPA) in 1968, ARPANET was used increasingly during these years and served as a kind of all-encompassing network to connect thousands of smaller networks. Wide area networks or WANs, as they were called, were also increasingly used, and networks, such as USENET and later BITNET, became very popular, the latter especially among academics in the 1980s. Some form of these systems would also eventually make its way into schools and universities and radically change the everyday activities of schooling, especially at the college level. This decade also saw the rise of grammar and style checkers, which along with the growth of ubiquitous word processing and spell checkers, continue to be part of the computing environment in which people in the United States live, learn, and work.

The late 1960s and 1970s, then, saw the beginning of huge changes poised to transform life in the United States. Although for many, the Women's Movement and Civil Rights Movement failed to reach their potential, they did make a difference in the number of opportunities available for women and people of color in the years that followed. It is also interesting to note in this context, however, that during the years Mary, Karen, and Paula attended public school—from 1972 to 1986—these women have little memory of desegregation efforts, despite Karen's attending schools in many different geographic locations, including the southern United States. These years also saw the largest influx of young people attending universities in the United States, and graduate school education grew enormously.[15] In addition, as women's studies programs began to establish themselves in universities, many women, like Mary, would take advantage of them in their graduate programs and go on to earn a minor in women's studies. The rise of computing technology would also have an effect on education and work to change the literacy practices that the women of this chapter would develop over time. Spanning the girls' years through life and schooling, the space missions, beginning with the first lunar landing in 1969 and slowing dramatically with the Challenger disaster in 1986,[16] would also contribute to the miniturization of computing technology and thus increase the usefulness of information technologies to the commercial sector and eventually to the general public. Yet despite the great changes taking place in society and the tremendous advances in information technologies, early school activities changed little for the women we highlight in this chapter.

---

[15]For further discussion, see David Russell's (1991) landmark *Writing in the Academic Disciplines, 1870–1990: A Curricular History,* especially pp. 274 ff.

[16]See NASA, http://www.nasa.gov/, for a history of the various Apollo lunar landings and Challenger space missions. On January 28, 1986, the Challenger exploded into space taking the lives of its seven crew members. Christa McAuliffe, the first civilian, only teacher, and second U.S. woman in space was among them.

The Case Studies of Paula Boyd
and Mary Sheridan-Rabideau

It was into this cultural ecology, then, that Mary Sheridan-Rabideau, Karen Lunsford, and Paula Boyd were born in 1967, 1968, and 1969, respectively, all three women eventually choosing to attend graduate school in English and writing studies, although each followed very different paths into graduate education. In this chapter, we focus on how and why these three 30-something White women—one an assistant professor of English at Rutgers University, another a newly appointed assistant professor at the University of California, Santa Barbara, and the third a director of a learning lab at Parkland College, a premier midwestern two-year college, acquired, or not, the literacies of technology. We begin with Paula Boyd and Mary Sheridan-Rabideau, who on the surface seem to have a great deal in common. Mary and Paula, a little more than a year apart in age and of Irish or English/Irish descent, were born into a Chicago that was either anticipating, or recovering from, the reverberations of the 1968 Democratic convention. Both were born into fairly large extended families, and each remembers her early writing with her grandmother as one of the more meaningful experiences in her literate life. For all their similarities, however, there are decided differences in their life circumstances.

Paula speaks of her family as working class. When she was five, her family moved from Chicago to less of a metropolitan area in New York. There her parents divorced shortly after the move, with her father going to work in an IBM plant and her mother waiting tables while she attended a local community college. Paula remembers her mother as a reader—she was always reading novels, as well as books and articles for her classes—and indeed Paula's mother, for many years a practicing social worker in Hawaii, eventually went to graduate school and earned her master's degree. But it was Paula's older sister and brother who directly supported Paula's early literacy efforts. She would dictate letters to them and then copy what they had written on a separate sheet of paper and have them sent off to her grandmother back in Chicago. Her older sister even went so far as to teach her how to read using the daily newspaper. Paula looked up to her siblings who were four and five years older than she. She explains:

> [My older sister and brother] were just enough older than me that they were always wanting to show me stuff, you know. I can remember reading things way above my head because of wanting to read the things my sister and brother were reading. Like the first full-length book, like grown-up book I remember reading and this probably says a lot about my current personality. [laughing] I was probably seven years old or eight years old. They had just read the *Amityville Horror* and so I read that—the first full-length, grown-up book I ever read.

Extraordinarily bright, Paula did well in school, although she attended several different schools, moving from one small town to another in a relatively restricted geographical area as her mother tried to make a living, support her family, and get through college. But soon Paula faltered. She says:

> I was actually through most of school a pretty good student. I was kind of a star and, um, not that I worked that hard at it but I just was and then in high school I got more interested in juvenile delinquency myself and that sort of thing and, and so, you know, I was partying and doing a lot of stuff and, that was a lot of it and then I think, and I just, you know, wasn't interested. I don't know, I mean, a lot of people have speculated maybe I was bored or whatever, I don't know if I was. But I certainly didn't like to be there. I mean I liked to be at school, I just didn't like actually going into the building. That's the joke I always tell. I liked hanging around the back smoking cigarettes and talking to people.

All through her young life, she was especially close to her sister, who in many ways was the success story of the family, first going on to the university and then eventually to medical school. (Paula's brother, like Paula, dropped out of high school and earned his GED. He then went into the Navy and today is a taxi cab driver in New York.) But, in 1986, as Paula was about to enter her senior year in high school, Paula's sister, living in Pittsburgh and in her second year of medical school, was murdered by her in-house lover. The police called it a suicide and refused to investigate the killing any further. The death affected Paula profoundly, and she views it as being immediately responsible for her dropping out of high school.

When we turn to these years in the life of Mary, we see a different picture, but one similarly marked by strong family ties. Mary classifies her childhood circumstances as middle class, although with two older, college-educated parents—her father a lawyer, her mother a high school teacher—we might well say upper middle class. Like Paula, Mary has two older siblings, both brothers, and a younger sister who today practices law. Unlike Paula, Mary remained in the Midwest and attended Catholic schools, one a magnet school for the very bright in the heart of the city. When asked about the valuing of literacy in her home and her early literacy learning, Mary replied:

> My parents definitely valued literacy. I guess the story—I don't have many stories because I was so normed—but college was expected, certainly expected, as opposed to a discussion. It was which college as opposed to going to college. My dad was a lawyer, is a lawyer and a judge, so he has a law degree and my mom is a teacher. My grandmother was a teacher, and we would spend our summers at a lake—both my grandmothers were up

there—and our games would be either cards or we would be learning our numbers or writing things. You know, my grandmother always, I remember there would be those brown papers with the dotted lines to practice writing on and that sort of stuff.

During those summer outings, Mary also remembered her oldest brother's reading to her and her cousins a chapter every night out of the *Trojan Horse*. Her oldest brother today works at the Chicago Board of Trade, and her other brother, like her sister (and father), went on to become a lawyer. Mary entered high school in 1981, the same year in which the first IBM personal computers appeared on the market and during the same year, as mentioned in the last chapter, that Ronald Reagan took office, and that Iran released 52 U.S. hostages. Paula followed a year later before finally dropping out of high school in 1985 as Mary prepared for her first year as an undergraduate. Mary graduated from high school in June of 1985 and proceeded immediately to Notre Dame, the private Catholic university that her father and all her siblings also chose to attend. Like many private universities in the United States, Notre Dame did not admit women as undergraduates until 1972, granting them admission during those heady years when the Women's Movement was palpable and strong. Thirteen years later, Mary was able to take advantage of the revised policies regarding women's admissions.

As far as other opportunities for women were concerned during the years in which this chapter's participants came of age, the United Nations declared the 1980s the Decade of the Woman. And in 1984, perhaps in keeping with the spirit of the decade, Europe's last bastion of male supremacy, Liechtenstein, gave women the right to vote; a year earlier New York's Columbia University enrolled women for the first time in its 229 year history (Feminist Majority Foundation, 1995). However, despite being the Decade of the Woman, the 1980s also saw increasingly in North America what Susan Faludi (1992) termed a "backlash." In 1982, the U.S. Congress defeated the Equal Rights Amendment once and for all (by three states); and in 1986, only 11.4% of all professors on U.S. campuses were women (Feminist Majority Foundation, 1995). Nineteen eighty-six was the year that General Mills gave a sixth makeover to Betty Crocker, transforming her from a traditional homemaker to a well-dressed, 30-ish, career woman and the year that the *New York Times* finally adopted usage of the title "Ms." (Feminist Majority Foundation, 1995). It was into these times that Mary and Paula sallied forth, one continuing her education, the other deciding she had had enough.

During their high school years, Paula's and Mary's experiences with computers differed dramatically. Although attending excellent schools, Mary maintains that the first time she came to really use a computer was in college—the schools, she related, were more interested in Latin than machines. In fact, it wasn't until her sophomore year, 1987 to 1988, that she put her electronic typewriter aside and learned from a woman in her dorm how to write her papers using word processing. Although she had an honors math class on computers in high school, she found the class, in her words, "a gendered thing," with far more boys in the class than girls. Paula, on the other hand, had many more opportunities for working with computers in high school. She signed up for two computer courses, one in Basic during her junior year and another in Pascal, which she never got to take when she dropped out of school. Although she loved the Basic class, Paula maintains that she was more enraptured with the video games she'd play at the local mall. When asked about her early contact with computers, Paula replied:

> This is actually sort of odd, too. I mean, it's all, it's always odd or maybe I just perceive myself as odd. I was thinking about it on the way here and I think one of the things that I was always fascinated by were computerized things like video games, which for a 13- or 14-year-old girl my age was different—like I always wanted to be in the video arcade. That was just when that all started getting popular and my other girlfriends did not, but I did. I spent tons of time in them. I mean I just hung out. I lived a couple blocks from the mall so I was in there all the time.

PacMan, Zaczon, and Tempest were her top favorites.[17]

The town that Paula, her mother, father, and siblings lived in was very much an IBM company town. Paula describes it as having "10 square city blocks of IBM buildings." Her high school also distinguished itself in 1982 as having both an Apple and an IBM computer lab, which was very unusual for 1982. Although Paula describes her father as working within the plant only as an "IBM service technician," at various times he played a key role in supporting Paula's technological literacy efforts. It was he, for example, whom she convinced when a teenager to buy a computer through a special discount employee program at IBM. Although it remained at his and her stepmother's house, Paula would use it to program and to participate on one of the early Prodigy bulletin boards. She explains:

---

[17]In his recent book, *What Video Games Have to Teach Us About Learning and Literacy,* James Gee (2003) makes the overarching argument that "when people learn to play video games, they are learning a new *literacy*" (p. 13, emphasis in original). For Gee, video games "build into their designs and encourage . . . good principles of learning, principles that are better than those in many of our [U.S.] skill-and-drill, back-to basics, test-them-until-they-drop schools" (p. 205). During her adolescence and beyond, Paula—through playing video and computer games—became an expert at reading and manipulating multimodal texts. As she grew older, these abilities would become increasingly important to her in acquiring the literacies of technology.

The computer was at my dad's and I didn't live there and so it was, you know, I would spend my quality computer time doing programming stuff and didn't want to waste it doing writing stuff because it seemed like something you could do without the computer.

Always a techie at heart, she did not regard word processing as serious, hard-core computer work. According to Paula, she was really "some kind of a computer geek in a weird way."

Thus Paula and Mary came to computers along competing trajectories: Mary, through word processing used for school writing, like many women at the time, and Paula through video games and then programming, probably a less common route for girls her age. But, as Paula repeatedly says throughout the interview, she regards herself as a little odd, a little weird. We would argue that Paula's so-called weirdness served her very well as far as the literacies of technology are concerned. Her "oddities," again her word, allowed her to participate in the kinds of computer activities that society typically assigns to boys—to depart from dominant notions of femininity associated with middle class women in the United States. Given the material conditions of her life, she could step outside the common subject positions available to young females in the cultural ecology of the times.

As mentioned earlier, the middle 1980s were a boom time for the growth of the new information technologies. Not only did the Macintosh appear in 1983 with its graphical user interface (GUI), the prototype for Microsoft's Windows 1985 operating system,[18] and whose later versions revolutionized personal computing, but also network technology continued to develop. Bulletin boards, listservs, chat groups, and e-mail became established and introduced new forms of communication. Early hypertext programs also appeared on the scene in these years (e.g., HyperCard, StorySpace), although they seemed to have little impact on the educational environments in which these women participated.

During her years in college, 1985 through 1989, Mary made great strides in working with the new information technologies, but she continued to compartmentalize her work with computers in ways that Paula was never able to do. Whereas Mary tried to make sure that she restricted computers entirely to her work life, Paula allocated the largest room in her house to her computer paraphernalia; whereas Mary refused to do e-mail at home, Paula was one of the first in her community to sign up for cable modem service; and whereas Mary at times fits the description she assigned to her parents—"very pro-education but very not-technology"— Paula herself pushed her father to acquire technology that he might otherwise have passed on.

---

[18]See Hawisher, LeBlanc, Moran, and Selfe (1996), pp. 74–78 and pp. 131–134.

Yet, lest some may think from our description that Mary is a technophobe, let us hasten to explain more. Mary, in important ways, has served as the key sponsor of her parents' and younger sister's technological literacy abilities.[19] She arranged for the buying of a computer for both her parents and sister and continues to this day to teach them the intricacies of word processing, e-mail, and a few computer games she thinks they might enjoy. She has also added web authoring most recently to her other literacy practices. Unsurprisingly, Paula, too, has been a sponsor not only of her mother's developing technological abilities but also of those of her brother, cousins, aunts, and other relatives. She says, laughing, that at the very least she had to get them all up on e-mail so that she'd have people to write to. Moreover, both women have taught—and continue to teach—their own students the many different kinds of writing that today rely on computers and the World Wide Web.

In the years that have passed since 1985, when each teenager took off from high school, each has acquired advanced degrees, Paula two master's degrees and Mary a PhD, both in writing studies and English. Along the way, Paula has worked as a factory worker, security guard, counselor at a group home, and aide at a rehabilitation center. Mary, too, has filled many different jobs: high school teacher, foundation and development associate for a Chicago zoo, and graduate teaching assistant, among them. But unlike some of the older people in our study, the workplace was not the primary gateway that provided opportunities and access to the new technologies. Mary, however, does see the workplace as confirming her idea of herself in relation to computer applications. She states:

> In many ways, the workplace did spark my involvement with computers. At the zoo, I was put on a technology committee. This fact was crazy because I knew next to nothing, but neither did most of the members of my department and since I was new I was stuck figuring this one out. I learned lots about creating databases, which confirmed my "need-to-know" attitude about technology; I could learn it if I truly needed it; but just playing around with computers was not pleasurable so it would take a "need-to-know" situation for me to sit down and do it.

---

[19]Mary even went so far as to color-key her parents' machine. She explained:

[My parents'] computer now is color coded. We have a little red sticky on the control button and a little yellow sticky on the off button and things like that. So, when I need to do things, we can just sometimes, we don't necessarily need to use the words because delete doesn't actually print it on there, it's just *del,* so saying delete would sometimes be confusing 'cause they would look for a delete button, so, you just say the red button. (Laughing) And things like that. So we, so that's how we do it there.

As with her parents, Mary stepped in to provide the necessary computer knowledge even though she saw herself as having less expertise than she might need to do the job well. As she herself learned, however, she could do it if she had to.

Overall, however, family and community stand out as contributing— or not—critical early resources to the women's literacy efforts, technological and otherwise. Family cohesiveness, family hardships, parents' occupations, childhood experiences, community values, attitudes toward school and education, material circumstances, personal motivation, class privilege, gender expectations, and their own everyday decisions all shaped profoundly the three women's developing practices with the literacies of technology. All played a role in influencing—and being influenced by—how, when, and why these women defined themselves as they did, and do, in relation to, and sometimes against, the new technologies.

The Case Study of Karen Lunsford

When we turn to Karen Lunsford, the third case study in this chapter, we see these same influences as crucial to contributing to a person's sense of identity in an increasingly information-rich world. We see also, however, these influences played out in subtly different ways with Karen's family and its military roots pivotal to her emerging sense of self, family, and her own literacy practices. Karen's father and mother are first generation college graduates, but just as important is the fact that her father is second generation military, his father an enlisted man but he himself an officer. Like Karen, he too was born into a military family.

Born in 1968, Karen spent her early childhood in Minot, North Dakota, where her father was an Air Force officer and where her most vivid memory occurred with the birth of her sister when Karen was three and a half years old. Like Mary and Paula, Karen as a young child well remembers her grandmother and especially her visit from Florida to take care of her as her mother tended to the new baby. During these years she remembers vividly seeing a field of little snowmen, arranged like an army of soldiers, in the aftermath of an Easter blizzard, the military always a part of her life. But she remembers too that her grandmother was so excited that Karen could read the letters of the car name on the car door that she immediately bought her a present. As with Mary and Paula, literacy activities were prominent in Karen's life at a very early age. Because during this time Karen's father's orders to Vietnam were canceled, the birth of her sister and her grandmother's visit made a greater impact on her than the Vietnam war, although she does have early memories of the war. She recalled:

I do remember early images of war protesters . . . because they were terrify-
ing. Now that I have much more context, today it's hard for me to imagine
. . . academics I know being so frightening. But the war continued to 1975,
and the war protests continued into the aftermath and merged with nuclear
protests, so I grew old enough for them to register. And both the national
and local news media selected the most lurid pictures to spice up the daily
news. I may not have known what the protests were all about, but I could
tell that the people around me were upset by these other angry, chanting
people. . . . I remember one group throwing rocks at us in our school bus.
My home was on the other side of the fence.

During these childhood years, Karen also began participating in hobbies
and games that would become, along with reading, primary family activities around which Karen built her life. The family's first five years in
North Dakota turned out to be her longest stay in any one place for the
next 20 years as she experienced life in a military family. When Karen was
five, her family was transferred from North Dakota to California; this initial move was only the first in military transfers that took her to Nebraska,
Alabama, to another base in California, and then back to another base in
North Dakota, before moving her to Arkansas, Louisiana, Germany, and
England. Her father retired from the Air Force in 1991 as Karen finished
her first year of graduate school at the University of Chicago.

When asked about her family economic circumstances, Karen replied
that upper middle class might be an accurate designation, but she noted
first that her father was a military officer, which changes things. Not only
did he probably earn less in the military than he would have in civilian
life, but the military marked her family's daily lifestyle in other ways as
well. Because they moved so frequently and because military children
were often labeled as "different" in schools, Karen found herself often on
the outside of everyday school activities despite being a star in the classroom. Although she would invariably be placed in an honors cohort with
each new move, first was always the assessment that she was terribly
wanting in an academic area that the new school prized. In describing her
six moves up through sixth grade, Karen explained:

> Fort Crook is the [elementary school] I remember [best]. That's Nebraska,
> Omaha, Nebraska. . . . And when I got to Nebraska, I couldn't add and sub-
> tract. And so they put me into the remedial math class and I got out of there
> as fast as I could. That's why I remember it, though—you know, the change
> of schools always meant that one school privileged something else and so I
> was always catching up every time I moved.

Perhaps her most serious disenchantment with a particular school system—if not, fortunately, with schooling itself—occurred with her prema-

ture entry into the ninth grade in Grand Forks, North Dakota. Here's how she described it:

> [Grand Forks] didn't have courses like those from where we were coming, California again. Spanish and stuff like that wasn't offered in the eighth grade . . . they said, well, why don't we send her downtown . . . so the eighth grader could take classes with the ninth graders there. And so I was absolutely isolated. . . . There was [also] a lot of friction between the base and the town there. We weren't allowed to be in orchestra and we weren't allowed to be in the band [or on sports teams]. The reasoning, they said, was because it was 14 miles between the base and town.

That none of these difficult experiences deterred Karen from excelling in school probably had everything to do with her passion for learning and the rich literacy environment her parents provided for her at home. The occasional isolation and frequent moves also encouraged her to be flexible and adaptable, qualities that help her adjust today to constant changes in technologies.

Along with books (Karen's mother was an avid reader of mysteries and her father of science and science fiction, a reading habit Karen continues to share with him), her home environment was filled with family activities: cross-stitching, crewel embroidering, and cooking she learned from her grandmother and mother; photography, woodwork, and astronomy from her father; piano lessons and crafts she shared with her sister; and gardening with the entire family. Add to this mixture the onset of computer games in the 1970s, and there emerges a picture of an active, closeknit family drawing on all sorts of resources to enrich their lives together.[20]

In 1976, the year of the U.S. Bicentennial celebration and well before even primitive computers became common household items, Karen's father bought the electronics consumer product Atari and hooked it up to their television. This set-up enabled the family to play *Pong* and to learn innumerable computer and video games over the next several years. Karen pointed out that many of these early games are today on the Web and that she and her sister occasionally still play them. Her first memory of what she calls "real computers," however, occurred when her father was stationed in Alabama from 1978 to 1979 when Karen was around 10 years old. Karen explained:

> One of the earliest real computers that I remember was in, um, we were in Alabama, we were there for one year from 1978 to 1979. . . . And he was tak-

---

[20]David Barton and Mary Hamilton (1998) point out that "[t]he resources people have access to can be seen in terms of technical skills and equipment, as well as sites and supports for learning. . . . Resources consist of physical resources as well as people" (p. 17).

ing courses of some sort, and he had a simulation computer that he brought home and it had a daisy wheel printer in it. It didn't have a screen. And I remember he brought it home, he linked it to the telephone and we were playing *Star Trek* on it. And it was so funny because the daisy wheel printer was printing out reams and reams as we were playing this game and I also remember the phone connection wasn't fast enough for the computer on the other end because we would be in the middle and they'd be saying the Klingons are coming and we'd say, Ok, fire phasers, fire photon torpedoes, do something and by the time the command went through the phone lines back to the computer, the Klingons had blown us up, you know. (Laughing) And it happened every time. We had totally lost out. But that's really my earliest image [of a computer]—butcher block kitchen table with this machine sitting on it, looked like a typewriter but it was a daisy wheel printer with a telephone cord attached to it.

Over the years, Karen and her family continued to enjoy and play the early Atari games (e.g., Adventure, Blackjack, Bowling, Backgammon, CanyonBomber, Battlezone, Defender, Hangman, and Space Invaders) and also moved on to other games after they bought the Commodore 64 for Christmas in 1984. Two of the family's favorites were M.U.L.E., a game in which the players competed to colonize a planet, and a pinball game with a World War II bomber on the screen that her mother, too, enjoyed.[21] Although Karen remembers taking a high school programming class in Cobol in Arkansas and doing geometry problems, her family computer games at home, along with her books, engrossed her in ways that her school participation on computers never did.

Karen's entry into college in January of 1986 coincided with the Challenger disaster and her family's move to Barksdale Air Force Base in Louisiana, where she attended Centenary College, graduating, unsurprisingly, with high honors. Like Mary, it was in college that she took on word processing for the first time, using the family's Commodore 64 at home, until they moved to England and she moved into a dormitory. At this point she learned Wordstar on the IBM for all her writing. Although she took a computer literacy class in college, which focused on learning the intricacies of CPUs (central processing units) and disk drives, Karen found this class totally extraneous to anything she wanted to do with computers and was much happier programming at home with Basic on the Commodore and creating flashcard programs for learning Spanish. In the fall of 1990, Karen left her family, now in England, to begin graduate school at the University of Chicago. That spring she bought a Mac-LC, the first computer that she

---

[21]Today many of the old Atari games and Commodore 64 games continue to be available on the Web. See, for example, http://www.atariage.com/, http://videogames.org/, and http://www.gamefaqs.com/ for just a sampling of the many Web sites. Accessed May 16, 2003.

acquired on her own with fellowship money. In the years that followed, Karen used her computer for "writing those dozens and dozens of papers that [she] had to write," learned citation programs like Endnote, and led the way in the program at Chicago in acquiring e-mail and joining listservs in the early 1990s. And as she progressed in her graduate career, finally settling in the doctoral writing studies program at the University of Illinois, Urbana Champaign, she learned an increasing number of programs for both her teaching and research. Especially important to her developing expertise and influential in exposing her to a wide range of communication technologies is the graduate position she assumed as project manager for two large technology-based research groups. Just as her father assumed larger and larger command posts as he worked his way up through the military, Karen has taken on greater responsibility for organizing research projects, sustaining, as she says, "both the social and technological networks." More important, Karen understands the new technologies not so much as independent tools but rather as technologies integrated into larger systems (e.g., family hobbies, research activities). Here her mother too, as an officer's wife overseeing many volunteer initiatives, provides Karen with a model. As part of her research assistantship, Karen organizes people, as well as all the other resources that are part of the research grants.

Today, like Mary and Paula, she is versed in a substantial number of computer technologies, our list barely touching upon the accumulating literacies that she continues to acquire. These literacies of technology include but are not limited to experiences with web design, HTML coding, video conferencing, listservs, MOOs, and the many application programs she uses for teaching, writing, and her work as research project manager. Despite her peripatetic journey through school, Karen has managed to position herself as a knowledgeable user, manager, and researcher of information technologies.

Thinking About Women and the Literacies of Technology in the Cultural Ecology of the 1970s, 1980s, and 1990s

What insights can we draw from Mary, Paula, and Karen's stories? Perhaps the most striking conclusion is that regardless of their personal inclinations or the opportunities these women enjoyed in relation to the literacies of technology, each today demonstrates a high degree of expertise. Especially striking is the marginal role that formal schooling played in introducing the three women to electronic literacies. Unlike Sally, Jill, and Damon, born 10 years later, public schools did not provide the kinds of technological literacy experiences that would inform these women's future learning. Schools in the early years of computers were a conservative force, stumbling toward the new information technologies, eventually reflecting changes in society rather than leading the way in efforts to teach young people computing.[22] It was really not until their years of graduate study in the 1990s that the three were able to use their schooling—their own teaching and research as graduate instructors—to become fully literate as technology users. During the last decade of the 20th century, women, as well as men, were expected to be technologically literate, and all three women felt and responded to these expectations.

Secondly, we note that, regardless of their traditional masculine associations, computer games played something of a role in Mary, Paula, and Karen's lives as far as introducing them to computers. But we should note at the same time that the contexts in which their participation occurred were far more important to them than the gaming itself. Mary, for example, played these games minimally but does remember actively participating in them when she and her cousins were all on vacation together, and Paula remembers being totally absorbed by them but often in a video arcade away from school where it was cool for all the "guys" to hang out. Playing computer games emphasized her fascination with technology and set her apart from other girls. For Karen, however, games were very much an activity of her immediate family. Her frequent moves and military housing often isolated her from other young people her age, and computer games, along with other hobbies, provided a wonderful space for playing and learning. Although the content of these games more often than not related to combat and war, Karen seldom cared; these trappings just came with the military. The fun of trying out something new and of playing the games with her father and sister, and sometimes with her mother, was what counted. Thus, although computer gaming is often thought to give boys an early advantage with computers, for these women and for the women in our last chapter, computer games provided a base, however tenuous, for future literate activity.[23]

Thirdly, issues of gender certainly shaped the women's attitudes toward computers but exerted a somewhat different influence in each of their lives. Paula prized computers from the start, understanding, as she states, "that there was a certain amount of status" connected with the new technologies. While Paula carved out for herself an identity that allowed her to prize "boys' toys," Mary took on the more available subject posi-

---

[22]For a more in-depth discussion on the conservatism of schools in relation to the new technologies, see Hawisher and Selfe, 1993.

[23]For several fascinating discussions on girls and computer games, see Justine Cassell and Henry Jenkins' (1998) *From Barbie to Mortal Combat*. See also James Gee's (2003) *What Video Games Have to Teach Us About Learning and Literacy*.

tions permitted middle class young women in the cultural ecology of the United States—honor student and "all-around girl." Karen, in identifying herself as a military daughter, was able to sidestep some of the issues of gender in civilian life that young women in the United States commonly face. Brought up in the military, surely the most patriarchal of institutions, she was expected to know about technologies, even as a girl. As she puts it, "technologies [were] everywhere and were being used by nearly everybody—they were part of my environment." Although Karen is competent with computer technologies, they lack the absolute fascination for her that Paula evidences for all electronic gadgets; they are just part of the terrain. Thus Paula's working-class background and Karen's military roots permitted them both more freedom in experimenting with electronic literacies than was available to Mary, in some respects the most privileged of the three. That Mary is in no way shortchanged in her expertise with technology today demonstrates the very complexity of literacy learning and identity formation in relation to a given cultural ecology. In other words, although she'd claim not to be as proficient in the literacies of technology as Paula or Karen, she has other strengths she developed in mainstream society that contribute to her overall success as a young professional in one of the nation's foremost public universities.

In focusing on gender and identity formation as key elements in understanding the three women's complicated and obstacle-laden pathways to technological literacy, we highlight the complexity of literacy learning. Paula's dropping out of school, her always-difficult economic circumstances, and her ability to laugh at herself and call herself weird did not deter her through adolescence and early adulthood from pursuing the life of a "techie" and from acquiring for herself those literacies of technology that increased—and continue to increase—her cultural capital significantly. In fact, she directly attributes her current job as Director of the Learning Lab at Parkland College to her technological expertise. Because of her considerable experience with information technologies, she is well qualified to oversee the instructional computer lab, manage her unit's web pages, and coordinate the unit's computer courses. Mary, too, relies on her background in instructional computing in her work as an assistant professor at Rutgers University, although, admittedly, unlike Paula, she does not exactly see herself as a pro. Her upper middle class background, her somewhat privileged economic circumstances, her ability to laugh at herself and call herself "normed," allowed her—indeed probably encouraged her—not to bother much with the literacies of technology through her adolescence and later teen years. Her family raised her to become an upwardly mobile, professional woman (and mother), which in the 1970s and 1980s did not necessarily include the mastering of technological literacies. Her upbringing, however, gave her the confidence to take up technology at critical junctures in her life. Today, these very circumstances provide her with the necessary support and wherewithal to achieve what Catherine Hobbs (1995) called "effective literacy"—and to which we add "effective electronic literacy," that is, "a level of literacy that enables one to effect change in her own life and society."[24] Karen, too, has accumulated the necessary electronic literacies to guarantee her success as an academic. Her organization skills—her ability to manage and adapt to several academic communities at once—enable her to balance competing interests and competing technologies. The military family in which she grew up also ensured that she was not only introduced to the new technologies at a very early age but also that she valued them regardless of her gender. The three women, then, each in very different ways, have achieved, and will continue to achieve as information technologies change, "effective electronic literacy."

The stories of Mary, Karen, and Paula, along with those cases in the previous chapter, are aimed at making sure that 20th and 21st century electronic literacies, especially those of women and people of color, are not neglected, for their stories underscore the human element in literacy studies and foreground human beings as agents of change within a complicated cultural ecology. If we define literacy as the power to enact change in the world, we cannot—must not—ignore the women, and men, who struggle to come to literacy in the information age.

---

[24]See Catherine Hobbs' (1995) introduction to her collection on 19th century women's learning to write for a fascinating discussion of gender and its historical relation to literacy. In writing of 19th century women in the United States, Hobbs, for example, notes that questions, such as how literacy affects women and how women affect literacy, have not been adequately addressed in current histories of education and the teaching of writing. She argues that "the various ways in which changing patterns in women's [19th century] lives helped construct modern life have been little studied and women's participation in transforming literacy has not yet been thoroughly explored" (p. 4). Hobbs also asks whether today the meaning of literacy has shifted to include "types of literacy bearing more cultural capital . . . leaving women again with less effective, lower-valued print literacy" (p. 2).

Complicating Access: Gateways to the Literacies of Technology

Cynthia L. Selfe
Gail E. Hawisher
Dean Woodbeck
Dennis Walikainen

> *I need more than a computer to have access to the real meaning of the new in-*
> *formation age. I need to connect myself and that computer to a network of*
> *people, organizations, software, and information programs. Some of that con-*
> *nection depends on financial resources, some on the vagaries of personal cir-*
> *cumstances—where I work or go to school, who my friends happen to be.*
> *Other aspects depend on the support of employers, teachers, parents, and oth-*
> *ers who set out to help me learn. (Bertram C. Bruce, 2003, p. 176)*

For more than 20 years, U.S. educators have known that access to computers plays a key role in when, how, if, and to what extent students acquire
and develop those skills and values associated with digital, or electronic,
literacy. Educators have also been aware that access to computers in this
nation has remained aligned, in persistent and embarrassing ways, along
the related axes of race and class. The statistical data documenting this
trend indicate that students of color and poor students have been much
less likely to have access to computer technology during the last two decades of the 20th century, both at home and at school, than have White
students or students from families of privilege.[1] Furthermore, the race-

---

[1] One of the best, and most consistent, sources of statistical data on this topic during the
last years of the 20th century was the *Falling through the Net* series sponsored by the National
Telecommunication and Information Agency. Between 1995 and 2000, three of these reports
were published: *Falling through the Net: A Survey of the "Have Nots" in Rural and Urban America,* published in July 1995; *Falling through the Net: Defining the Digital Divide,* published in July

based gap characterizing families' computer ownership in the United States increased, rather than decreased, from 1999 to 2000.[2]

Unfortunately for classroom teachers in the United States, these statistics, by themselves, provide little useful information about the real complexities of access as a social phenomenon. They indicate how many students lack access to computer technology, but not how to address this situation. Nor do they provide much useful information about how the lack of access to computers shapes the daily, lived experiences of individual young people and their families. Such statistics do not explain, for example, whether improved access to computers in the later grades of secondary school or in college can counteract the effects of limited access in the early grades of elementary school. Nor do the statistics help teachers determine which specific conditions of access are particularly salient, even necessary, for people who want to develop digital literacy at various times in their lives.

This chapter takes up the issue of access at a more specific level, with the goal of expanding the current understanding of this term. The following pages examine the particularized effects of access in the lives of two very different people from the United States—Dean Woodbeck and Carmen Vincent[3]—born in 1956 and 1955 respectively. It introduces the concept of *technology gateways* (places and situations in which individuals typically gain access to computers for the purpose of practicing digital literacy), and it identifies the specific *conditions of access* (among them, timing, motivation, fit, safety, resources, and appropriateness of equipment) that assume considerable importance in these two case studies. With the information presented in this chapter, we hope to formulate an increasingly useful and pragmatic understanding of access and its relation to digital literacy.

The Case Study of Dean Woodbeck

In 1956, as Republican Dwight D. Eisenhower was campaigning against Adlai Stevenson in their second head-to-head presidential race, and Elvis Presley was seducing teenagers with renditions of *Heartbreak Hotel* and

---

1999; and *Falling through the Net: Toward Digital Inclusion: A Report on Americans' Access to Technology Tools,* published in October 2000. See http://www.ntia.doc.gov/ntiahome/ digitaldivide/. For additional statistical data and discussions of access trends related to race and socioeconomic status, compare Selfe (1999); Coley, Crandler, & Engle (1997); and Hoffman & Novak (1998).

[2]For further discussion of this gap, see *Falling through the Net: Toward Digital Inclusion,* "Executive Summary" (2000).

[3]As noted in the introduction, Carmen Vincent is a pseudonym.

Don't Be Cruel,[4] Dean Woodbeck and his twin brother, Dale, were born on the 24th of February in Vicksburg, Michigan. The two boys grew up in a White, upper middle class family that placed a high value on formal literacy practices. Dean's father finished a master's degree soon after the twins' birth and moved the family to Oxford, Michigan, where he taught math at both the elementary and secondary levels. Dean's mother taught physical education at the high school level and once the twins were older took a job as a third-grade teacher.

As professional educators, both of Dean's parents worked diligently to pass along literacy values to their children and to provide them early instruction that would prepare them for success in school. Both parents were readers and made sure that books and newspapers were readily available in the household. They also read books to their children—Dr. Seuss was a favorite; limited the boys' time in front of the television; and encouraged trips to the library. Although Dean did not remember exactly how he first learned to read, he did remember his father's pride in his early accomplishments:

> I know I learned to read when I was in kindergarten. I have memories of going to my father's third-grade class—at that time, he was teaching third grade—and reading in front of the class. You know, I don't know why he made me do that . . . I just have this memory of . . . sitting on his desk reading out loud to the class. . . .Those kids must have hated me.

As Dean got older, he continued to value reading, discovering, in particular, how newspapers could connect him with events happening outside his community:

> When I was in late elementary school, mid- to late elementary school grades, um, I read a lot of Hardy Boy books. We had, yeah, we owned a whole bunch of those. It's interesting now because my son really likes those. . . . And then, started reading the newspaper regularly probably when I was 11 or 12. And I remember, well, we lived in Detroit, going to get a . . . newspaper in the morning and, so I grew up reading the newspaper and kind of getting interested in current events and that sort of thing.

Certainly, the political events leading up to the twins' school years beginning in 1961 were destined to give Dean dramatic things to read about. Fidel Castro, well ensconced in Cuba by the late 1950s, had captured 37 Americans at the Guantanamo Bay naval base. The Soviet Union had launched both Sputniks in 1957 and during the administration of Nikita

---

[4]See "The 1900s" (1999–2002) for audio archives of these years (http://archer2000.tripod.com/index.html).

Khrushchev in 1958 and had shot down an American U2 spy plane in 1960. John F. Kennedy had been elected to the office of U.S. President in 1961, and by the time the boys enrolled in first grade, in response to the Cuban missile crisis, people had begun building fallout shelters in their backyards and holding atomic bomb drills in public schools.

The Cold War, however, was far from the only threat facing the United States. In 1963, the same year in which Kennedy was assassinated, a bomb killed four children at a Black church in Birmingham, Alabama; and 250,000 people listened to Martin Luther King Jr. deliver his "I Have a Dream" speech in Washington, D.C. Civil unrest followed in Harlem, Philadelphia, Chicago, and Jacksonville. In the summer of 1964, the same year in which King won the Nobel Peace Prize, President Lyndon Johnson signed the Civil Rights Act. By 1966, Malcolm X had been assassinated, and King had led a five-day march in Selma, Alabama ("The 1900s," 1999–2002). In 1967, as Dean attended elementary school and continued his habit of reading newspapers, he must have been following not only the continuing stories of the Cold War and the Civil Rights Movement but also stories about the bombing raids in Vietnam that Lyndon Johnson's administration began in 1965, and about the protest marches that accompanied the President's action ("The 1900s," 1999–2002).

During these years, Dean's twin brother, Dale, was similarly affected by the value the family placed on reading. As Dean noted,

> Yeah, we shared a lot of the same books, and, when we went to the library we would get a lot of the same sorts of books out. He was a more, he had more of a philosophical way of thinking than I did. So he kind of read things that were maybe much deeper than I would. I mean, you know, he would read Marx. . . . Yeah. He got a philosophy degree, so I guess it showed.

At home, Dean's parents maintained an environment that they felt was conducive to both boys' educational success:

> . . . I remember that there were limits in terms of television in our house. You know, we could only watch certain things rather than turn on the tube immediately [when we walked in the house. We couldn't] . . . just turn on the TV to . . . have it on. [There had to be] . . . this certain thing you wanted to watch, and if it was a half an hour, then after the half an hour was up, [you] turned it off. They were, especially my dad, I remember him being strict about that.

Such restrictions must have chafed, especially for teenage boys. It was during the 1950s and 1960s, for instance, that television experienced its period of most dramatic growth. In 1960, Kennedy and Nixon engaged in the first set of televised debates between presidential candidates, and when promoters saw the huge audiences such an event could attract, programs like *Wagon Train, Candid Camera,* and the Beatles' debut on the *Ed Sullivan Show* followed quickly and enjoyed immense popularity. In 1965, ComSat's Early Bird, the first television satellite, was put into orbit, and one of the first broadcasts to use this technology covered a 1966 protest march against the war in Vietnam. The following years saw the broadcast of the first Super Bowl, in 1967; the coverage of Martin Luther King Jr.'s assassination, in 1968; and Neil Armstrong's walk on the moon in 1969. By the early 1970s, shows like *All in the Family* were combining social commentary and entertainment on a regular basis, and television had taken on the coverage of the Watergate affair and the occupation of Wounded Knee by members of the American Indian Movement ("The 1900s," 1999–2002).

The emphasis that Dean's family placed on reading and writing during this time eventually affected the career plans of both twins. When Dean graduated from high school in 1974—the year after North and South Vietnam, the United States, and the Viet Cong signed a peace agreement in Paris ("The 1900s," 1999–2002)—he enrolled at a mid-size midwestern university, majoring, initially, in engineering studies. During his second year in college, however, this child of print and television switched majors to scientific and technical communication and began reporting for the school newspaper. He also joined a fraternity. By his senior year, Dean had become the editor of the university's newspaper. His twin brother, during the same period, enrolled at another midwestern college and pursued an undergraduate degree in philosophy.

When Dean started college in 1974, his initial contact with computer technology involved not microcomputers but their predecessors, mainframe computers. These machines had grown out of alliances between the U.S. military effort and scientists after World War II. The first such computer, dubbed ENIAC, was completed in 1945: It included 17,468 vacuum tubes, weighed 30 tons, took up approximately 1,000 feet of floor space, ran on 130–140 kilowatts of electricity, and ran at a speed of 100kHz (*A Chronology of Digital Computing,* 1994). By 1951, UNIVAC I, the first commercially successful, general-purpose computer, had been purchased by the United States Bureau of Census, and by 1957, only a year after Dean was born, the programming language Fortran had been developed and released. Mainframe computers developed rapidly after that time, and by 1965, the first super computer, the Control Data CD6600, came on the market. By the time Dean entered college, microprocessors had been invented, making possible early "fourth generation" computers that employed integrated circuits with 10,000 or more components on a single chip (White, 1996–2001).

Like many college-age students majoring in engineering during this period, Dean was required to take a mandatory Fortran programming classes in his first year of college. More importantly, however, if the university provided Dean his first technology gateway, it certainly did not motivate him to develop his skills. In fact, almost everything about this particular computing experience—the tasks he had to do, the equipment he used, the environment in which he had to learn—seemed to discourage Dean from valuing the computer literacy skills he learned and from developing them more fully. He tells the story in these words:

> I had to take a computer class and it was, I think it was Fortran, the programming language, so we had punch cards.... Yeah, so we had punch cards, and you would have to do a stack, and they had this, you know, there was this machine that had a keyboard that you typed on and it coded the punch card [with] whatever you were typing in. So if you made one typo, you know ...
>
> You could have 80 cards in your stack [and you] ran the stack through this reader, and then you went away for a while because it didn't generate a printout right away. So you'd maybe go in the morning ... and run your program, [and] go to class, you know, [and] come back a couple hours later. Sometimes you came back the next day to see if the program ran or not and, there it was ... sitting in your mailbox. The program ... may have said "Error," ... and you'd have to do it over again.... So then you would have to go back to your punch cards and say, "OK, did I make a typo here?"
>
> Or, you know, if you dropped them [the cards] and put them back together in the wrong order—everything had to be in a certain order—it [the computer] would just spit [the cards] back at you.... Oh, I hated it ...
>
> Yeah, I mean it was horrible.... They had this big room ... that had the computers and printers and stuff and, of course, you couldn't go back there as a student. It was like Fort Knox. Secured, you know, and you had to have a key to get into the door. They had a little spy thing where they could look out and see who you were.
>
> They would stuff your things into the mailboxes that just opened on the user side, so somebody could come in, take your report by mistake and too bad, you know.

Although Dean doggedly made his way through several programming courses, the specific conditions of his access to computers not only convinced him to switch majors to communication, but also discouraged him from acquiring and developing a robust set of digital literacy skills.

When Dean graduated from college in 1978, he became the Communication Director for a fraternity he had joined as a student, moving from the Midwest to the organization's national headquarters in Richmond, Virginia. After marrying and briefly orienting himself to his new job, Dean enrolled in a journalism and mass communication program at

Virginia Commonwealth University, "just because I was interested in it." At the time of Dean's enrollment at VCU, the field of communication was about to begin a period of transition even more dramatic than that occurring during the television era. In the late 1970s, the invention of integrated microcircuit technologies, such as Intel's 8086 16-bit microprocessor containing 29,000 transistors (Polsson, 1995–2001), fed the rapid and far reaching development of microcomputers. These handy and relatively affordable machines were to prove fundamentally transformative for many aspects of daily life, among them, the field of communication.

By 1981, the IBM PC was launched, and, within a year, IBM was supporting 12 new Microsoft products, and 30 other companies had announced the development of DOS-based software programs. By 1983, the 300 software companies in existence in 1970 had skyrocketed to more than 2,000, and sales in this industry had gone from $750 million in 1977 to $475 billion.[5] In 1984, the Apple Macintosh came on the market, and the Age of Print—and television—had begun to give way to the Digital Age.

With these events on the horizon, Dean was taking communication courses at night, "one class at a time," at Virginia Commonwealth University. This pattern of continuing education was to go on for two years as he enrolled in graduate school. Eventually, his road led back to his original alma mater where he became the Director of Alumni News and Information Services.

> [Taking mass communication courses one at a time] led to getting into the master's program. But . . . there was no way I was going to do it at night. . . . My wife and I . . . started looking for a location where they had a good journalism school that was also in a place where she wouldn't have a problem finding a job, and we ended up in Minneapolis. So I went to grad school for two years at Minnesota.
>
> [T]hen, this guy who was the Director of Alumni Communication [at my old university] was retiring. He wrote to a bunch of people he had known when they were students, including me, and said . . . "This might be something you are interested in 'cause it involves working with volunteers but also involves editing the alumni magazine." So when I got that letter I thought, Well, what the heck. I'll send a resume in. We . . . both knew what we were getting into in terms of location, and actually, [we] were eager to move to a smaller town after living in Richmond for five years and then Minneapolis for two. And that's how I got this job.

Although he had begun a career in a field that was destined to become increasingly dependent on computers, however, it was not until Dean was

---

[5]For an extended description of the history of computing and the influence it had on U.S. literacy instruction from 1979 to 1994, see Hawisher, LeBlanc, Moran, & Selfe (1996).

able to create his own technology gateway at home that he was motivated to use computers as a context for his literacy practices. More importantly, he had to wait until microcomputers had supplanted mainframes before he could shape the specific set of conditions he needed. In 1983, as a graduate student in communication at the University of Minnesota, Dean became fascinated by his brother's description of a new computer "that he called a 'word processor' " and learned about "all this great stuff it could do." Given the lengthy papers Dean had to produce for graduate school, he was motivated to learn more about these new machines. By 1984, he had determined that the fit between the literacy tasks he wanted to complete and the new microcomputers that had only recently been developed was a good one. As he tells the story:

> [I bought] . . . a PC clone. It had, in fact it was one self-contained unit. It had this little amber nine-inch screen built-in. . . . This was called a "portable" at the time, and that sucker weighed about 40 pounds. . . . There were two five-inch floppy drives, and you had to change disks out to run a program because the hard drive was miniscule, you know. You couldn't save anything, basically the hard drive was there to boot this thing up. And then it had this built-in monitor and then the keyboard would flop down. . . .
>
> And that's what I bought it for 'cause I was in grad school, you know, I needed something like that. I had read about computers and I thought this would be great to do a master's thesis on. And, you know, how would people even think about doing a master's thesis without a computer?
>
> So I did my thesis. . . . And I actually started working on the thesis and . . . it was cool. I mean, you know, the program would put in the footnotes and the whole nine yards so it was, it was really neat.

Within the environment of his home, Dean was able to shape the conditions of his technology access—he identified his own exigency for using computers; he recognized the close fit between his personal literacy goals and the computer's capabilities; he created an environment within which he could feel comfortable when working with technology; and he motivated himself to learn more about computers.

Fortunately, Dean could afford to determine the conditions of his access to technology in these ways. The PC clone he purchased in 1984, the same year in which William Gibson published his cyberpunk novel *Neuromancer,* cost approximately $2,000, an expenditure the family could bear because both Dean and his wife were working:

> Actually, I had a pretty good deal because I was working in the women's athletic department doing sports information and that job happened to include both a stipend, but it also, more importantly, included tuition. . . . So my expenses were paid for, and I think in that job I made maybe $8,000 plus per year. You know for grad students that was incredible. . . . [A]nd my wife

worked. She was editing software manuals, and I think she was probably being paid . . . $20,000 a year probably. Something like that.

By the time that Dean assumed his job as Director of Alumni News and Information Services at his alma mater in 1985, he was poised to take advantage of a second gateway for developing digital literacy—the workplace.

In his new job, at a university already quite invested in technology, Dean was able to fashion the conditions of his computer access in ways that supported the further development of his digital literacy practices and values. He convinced his supervisors, for example, to purchase the computers that would allow him to write, edit, and lay out a four-color alumni magazine online. Later, he argued that these computers should be hooked up to a network that would allow him to take alumni communications online and eventually establish a Web site for alumni.

Dean's increasing familiarity with, and reliance on, computers was typical in the larger field of professional communication, which was characterized, at the time, by an emphasis on technology and by rapid growth. The widespread marketing of relatively cheap microcomputers in the early 1980s led rapidly to an increasingly technological workplace for the U.S. corporate sector. In particular, networked environments for workplace communications became increasingly common during the 1980s and 1990s. By 1981, for instance, ARPANET, originally created by the Advance Research Projects Agency to link computer scientists and engineers, had given way to BITNET (Because It's Time Network) in the United States and to the Minitel in France. By 1983, the Internet Activities Board (IAB) had been established and by 1991, the World Wide Web had been released by the Corporation for Research and Education Networking (CERN)[6]

Within this context, professional communicators like Dean found themselves taking on a growing number of computer-based efforts. These professionals became not only layout and design specialists but also communicators working in, and programming for, computer-based communication environments; authors of software and hardware documentation; and the authors of training materials for computer-based environments.[7] By the spring of 2000, Dean did most aspects of his editing job on a computer:

---

[6]See the Internet Society (ISOC) site at http://www.isoc.org/internet/history/ for a variety of resources on the history of the Internet and the World Wide Web.

[7]For examples of professional resources dealing with computer-supported layout and design from this period, see Beach (1986) and White (1982). For examples of resources aimed at professionals working in, and programming for, computer-based communication environments, see Dumas (1988). See also Sides (1984), Horton (1990), and Weiss (1985) for early examples of resources aimed at authors of software and hardware documentation, and Kearsley (1983), Kearsley (1985), and Heines (1984) for resources aimed at authors of training materials for computer-based environments.

I spend my day at this thing [the computer]. And it has made it [editing and publishing the alumni magazine] so much easier because I can draft articles, you know . . . [and], if I quote a faculty member I can e-mail them the quote and say, did I get this right? If I've got a draft, and I [can send it by] other writers in the department to look at to see if they follow my logic. You know how it is, you write something and you edit it and you edit it again and you've seen it so many times, you show it to one of them and say does this really make sense anymore. . . . [T]hen, you know, the designers can import the article that I do in Word Perfect, in Word, into QuarkXpress. You know, the pictures are either digital photos or we scan them so the designer now, he's got all this digital stuff and then he's just putting everything together on his screen and then I can open the program and see what he did. . . .

He was also heavily invested in web development and spent a great deal of time updating the alumni Web site that he had helped create for the university:

This web stuff, now. You know . . . Page Mill was kind of a standard in our department there for a while, and then people started using Adobe GoLive. So I learned that. So particularly when I started with . . . the Web part, Internet part, . . . had to learn how to use PhotoShop. I'm no expert by any means, but at least know how to open a picture, make it brighter, fix the contrast or adjust the color level if it needs to be adjusted so it looks good on the Web. . . . [A]s an editor, too, I had to learn how to use [QuarkXpress], because the designers use Quark. So I had to learn that, at least some of the commands, as an editor. . . .

Right now . . . [I] update the site weekly but sometimes it's daily. You know, during winter carnival, uh . . . I'm launching . . . pictures everyday with the . . . digital camera . . . I never was trained to do or ever thought I would do is be a photographer. [L]ast week when the statutes were really making progress, it's updated at least daily and sometimes two or three times a day. . . .

Dean's increasing involvement with digital literacy practices was reflected in other areas of his life as well. At home, for example, he had established a technology gateway for his own children—a daughter of 10 and a son of 8—purchasing a computer in the late 1990s to serve the family's needs:

I use it, unfortunately, mostly for work. I do some. Sometimes, I do writing at home if I'm working on a magazine article, for example, and there are a lot of phone calls or interruptions here. I'll just pack everything up and go home and work there.

[The children] will use it for school, particularly my daughter who is in a grade now where there is more writing that's expected and more assignments that the computer could be good for. But for my son, he's in third grade and not really to that point yet, so he uses it mostly for games, and he's got an e-mail address too. . . . Games with lots of noise. . . .

[Y]ou know . . . the two of them use the computer differently. . . . There was this thing that came with one of the computers—that is, *Nickelodeon.* It includes these little film clips and sounds, and you can edit your own movie, put together this sort of two-minute movie or however long you want it, I guess. My daughter was really interested in that.

Dean also attended to some of the more specific conditions of access he considered important in the context of the home. He took pains, for instance, to make sure that the environment within which the computer was used was conducive to reflection. As he explained:

And it's much more—we've got this bay window that looks out, and we've got the woods behind our house, so, and the computer is set up right there. That's in our dining room. So it's a much nicer atmosphere to sit and think and write in.

In addition, Dean and his wife established rules to support what they considered to be an appropriate balance between print literacy and digital literacy. As he noted:

Well, actually we are doing this similar to how I grew up. Probably not surprising. I mean we limit how much television they can watch, and we've gotten a little more lax in terms of Saturday morning cartoons lately but, um, yeah. . . . [W]e, for instance, we have a half an hour before bedtime which is reading time. So bedtime is 9:00, you know, at 8:30 you are in bed reading a book or a newspaper, whatever you want to read.

An active member of the local school board, Dean has been heavily involved in making sure that the local schools provide a technology gateway—and the appropriate conditions of access—for local students:

I happen to be on the school board in Hancock. So I've got perspective from that angle too. Everybody seems to value technology and, you know, all of the school systems around here are talking about having computers in their classroom. . . .

You know, we were fortunate in Hancock that there were just alums that gave almost a half a million dollars for computer labs, so we've got a 30-[computer] I-MAC lab in the elementary school, and . . . two applications labs in the high school and one in the middle school.

Because he has developed a sophisticated sense of how complex an issue access really is, Dean has also devoted a great deal of thought to the specific conditions of access in the public schools. He continued to be concerned, for example, that there was adequate support for students and teachers who are using computers, and that the use of computers was integrated in meaningful ways into the academic curriculum.

The unfortunate part I see, kind of putting on my school board hat, is that we don't provide hardly any resources to teachers to learn how to integrate computers into their classrooms . . .

So it's really a challenge. I mean on the one hand it's a tremendous opportunity because all of the hardware was paid for. On the other hand, you know, we don't have many teachers who know how to integrate this stuff into their classrooms. You know, "Superintendent, do you have a plan?" What's going to happen five years down the road when this stuff is all obsolete, and we don't have the half a million dollar sugar daddy out there any more. . . . "What are we going to do with the things? Okay, we've got access to what?"

You know, how this goes, and I kind of run around in a circle about this in my own mind. Because you know I originally thought, "Boy, we get all of this hardware, that's great!" And now I'm thinking, "Well, so what? How is this going to help the high school teachers be better teachers?" Or "How is she going to use this for teaching?" You know, my son happens to have a third grade teacher, and she's tremendous at bringing things from the Web. She's got this TV monitor in the room and she's got her computer hooked up to it so they can be studying the Oregon Trail and they study this out of the book and then she's got this computer game, The Oregon Trail, that the kids can use and then she brings up Web sites about Lewis and Clark and about the Oregon Trail. And so she does a great job, but she's the only one I can think of in the elementary school out of . . . 18 teachers, who does that.

So . . . I think that's the real challenge. From the stuff I read, you know, this is not unique to Hancock. . . . This is really the problem nationwide.

The technology gateway that Dean established in his own home had an influence on other members of his family as well. His mother, for example, recently purchased a computer so that she could correspond with her grandchildren and take advantage of Dean's technological expertise. As he recounted the situation,

You know my mother is . . . going to turn 70 this year. She bought a laptop about two or three years ago, uh, mostly because she wanted to be able to do e-mail with it. Because . . . my father is dead now, so it's just my mother.

. . . She spends half her time in Ohio and half the time in Florida, so she wanted to be able to do this, but she is sort of thinking, "Well if I buy a computer, you know, I've got this monitor thing I've got to lug back and forth" . . . I said, "Well, how about a laptop?" She said, "Well, what's that?" My brother had one, so he brought it out and she said, "Yeah, this is it!" So now she's got a little ink jet printer that's real light, so . . . that and the laptop is what she takes back and forth from Ohio to Florida when she goes down there for the winter.

She originally she said she signed on to this newsletter I . . . [edit], so she gets this thing from me every week, and she responds. Then she sends, e-mail to the kids and to my sister-in-law a lot, and she found, you know, these sites, these Web sites that have animated greeting cards. She's found that and she thinks that's great. So she is sending that stuff to the kids, you know, it seems like almost once a week.

She was afraid of it [technology] at first. She didn't really know if she wanted to do this. But, you know, it's surprising, because more and more . . . of her friends down there were using computers. . . .

Actually I bought it for her because she said, "Well, why don't you just find out what I need and tell me what it's going to cost?" So I did that, and then I became technical support. So, you know, I was getting calls, "Well, I've got my laptop on, and I try to do this, and it won't do that and so what am I doing wrong?"

Thus Dean also became an important sponsor and resource for his mother as she struggled with her own technological literacy abilities.

The Case Study of Carmen Vincent

Carmen Vincent is the daughter of a German-Irish mother and a Native American father—a member of the Ojibwa tribe whose ancestors came from both the Bad River Band in Odanah, Wisconsin, and the Keweenaw Bay Indian Community in Baraga, Michigan. Carmen was born on July 4, 1955, in Highland Park, Michigan. Along with her younger brother, Martin, Carmen grew up in a family that placed a high value on both their Native American heritage and on formal literacy. Looking back, Carmen described her family's economic situations as at "poverty level." She noted, "We always had bills. And we were always getting collection notices."

Carmen's father had been raised on the Keweenaw Bay tribal reservation in Michigan's Upper Peninsula where he, like many other Native Americans, faced both economic and political hardships during the Depression decade of the 1930s. The tone of that decade had been set in advance by the Meriam Report of 1928 which indicated that Native Americans living on reservation lands were among the "poorest, least educated, least healthy, and most depressed populations in the United States" (Champagne, 1994, p. xviii). Although many of the Meriam Report's recommendations were addressed in the Wheeler-Howard Act of 1934, extreme poverty continued to plague Native Americans living on reservation lands. In addition, as the Depression gathered strength in the early 1930s, many Native Americans lost what property they did hold, some to debts incurred during the Depression itself, others to the reallocation efforts of the Office of Indian Affairs (in 1946, renamed the Bureau of Indian Affairs [BIA]). Although the United States had granted citizenship to Native Americans in the General Citizenship Act of 1924, Native lands continued to be allocated by the Office of Indian Affairs until 1934. Between 1887 and 1934, Native Americans in North America lost "over 90 million acres to the allotment process" (Champagne, 1994, p. xivii).

Carmen remembered her own family's stories about this period in the following terms:

> There was eight or nine kids; seven kids, and . . . my dad was born during the Depression, born in 1930. And so his sisters sort of raised him because I guess my grandmother, wasn't really stable. . . .
>   . . . [I]t was hard for him to go to school. . . . They were really poor, but they were mostly more well off than the other families there. . . . My Uncle Jim . . . is in his 70s, and he was telling me that my grandparents took care of the family more or less when there was hard times. . . .
>   And that, my dad told me that my grandfather traded away their land during the Depression in Baraga for a barrel of salt pork. . . .
>   Now, I think there was no work [t]here, and so I remember him telling me that he had to go [downstate to attend school].

Native American activist John Collier became the Commissioner of Indian Affairs from 1933 to 1946. Although he focused his efforts on installing elected tribal governments, forming tribal business corporations, fighting assimilationist legislation, and encouraging cultural artistic expression, "Native Americans continued to suffer from intergenerational poverty and poor health through the decade of the 1940s" (Champagne, 1994, p. xivii).

In 1950, partly in response to such conditions and in an effort to assimilate Native Americans into the cultural, political, and economic mainstream of U.S. life, President Harry Truman appointed Dillon Myer, the former director of Japanese resettlement camps in World War II, as the new Commissioner of Indian Affairs. Under Myer's direction, the newly reorganized Bureau of Indian Affairs inaugurated a systematic program to force Native Americans off reservation lands and into cities where they could be assimilated within the larger culture (Champagne, 1994, p. xiviii). This assimilation effort, which was partially aimed at preparing "Indian children to live in urban areas and to join the urban labor pool" (Champagne, 1994, p. xiviii), was eventually carried out under the Relocation Act of 1956 (Lynch & Charleston, 1990). The BIA also terminated more than 100 Native communities over the next two decades, as part of this larger effort (Champagne, 1994, p. xiviii).

It was against the backdrop of these events in 1950—in the same year the BIA estimated that 19,300 Indian children had no access at all to formal

schooling (Champagne, 1994, p. 321) and director Delmer Davies released
the award-winning film *Broken Arrow*—that Carmen's father left the Keweenaw Bay reservation in the Upper Peninsula and moved to Detroit,
Michigan. There, he enlisted in the Marines and was assigned to a unit in
San Diego, California, for the next four years. When he left the Marines in
1955, Carmen's father moved back to the Detroit area to work in a Ford
plant and finish his GED (Graduate Equivalency Diploma) at Pershing
High School. On October 9 of 1954, the year in which the United States Supreme Court ruled against racial segregation in public schools in *Brown v.*
Board of Education of Topeka, Carmen's father married her mother, whom
he had met at the Ford plant in Detroit where they both worked. Carmen's
father then began an undergraduate course of study in business administration at Wayne State University.

In 1955 Carmen was born, and in 1957 her brother, Martin, joined the
family. In 1958, when Carmen and Martin were still toddlers, Carmen's
mother dropped the children off at an aunt's house on her way to church.
Soon after leaving the children, she was involved in a destructive head-on
collision on the Henry Ford Freeway. Her recovery from the physical and
mental trauma of that accident, which involved more than 52 cars, drove
her feet through the car's floorboard, and pinned her to the wheel for
more than eight hours, took years and involved ongoing hospital stays for
plastic surgery, as well as psychotherapy, institutionalization, and electric
shock treatments. The period following her mother's accident was a difficult one for the family. As Carmen tells her story,

> My father . . . was the first single father I knew. . . . He went to Wayne State
> . . . part time while raising my brother and I.
>
> Well, he always told it like this. He always said, "Well, you know, your
> mom was so different before the accident." He said that she was the most
> meticulous housekeeper, very intelligent. She kept herself so good and, I
> knew that in some ways because she was a good mother when she was on
> task. . . . You know, but when she wasn't on task, it was like forget it, you
> know?
>
> . . . [A]fter the accident it was like, I mean, we had to clean the house all
> the time, my brother and I. And we had to, you know, we had to do every-
> thing. . . . I remember . . . we lived in Kalamazoo, and we would walk to the
> commodity place, and we would take a wagon there . . . I think we walked
> with my dad, and sometimes I think we walked by ourselves, my brother
> and I, to go get the commods.
>
> . . . I know that we were going a long distance. Especially . . . walking,
> you know? And two kids, along with a little wagon—for God's sake.
>
> And then, I know that we, we lived near a Catholic school because we
> went to Catholic school, and my brother and I had skipped one day, and we
> went to the laundromat because they had a playroom there . . . Then [some-
> one] caught us. . . . So we got in big trouble for that . . .

> ... A kid that age dealing with your mom and stuff like that, I mean. . . .
> Think of it . . . we raised ourselves, my brother and I . . . my dad was there,
> too, you know, but . . .

Despite these hardships, however, Carmen remembered the value her
parents placed on education and on literacy practices—even during those
very difficult days:

> Oh, my mother was a reader. [I]f she could have had a library, she would
> have. We had the great books. Great books and classics. My dad read to us.
> My caretakers read to us. . . . Mom read to us once in a while but . . . she had
> her accident and it was hard for her.
>
> My dad was an advocate for Indian education and that's probably why
> I'm here today because of his guidance and role-modeling, you know, when
> I was a teenager. . . .
>
> [Later], Mom would write letters to us from the hospital. We couldn't see
> my mom. . . . We couldn't go in. You could just look out the window, look in
> the window. And, we would write her letters and make her cards and Dad
> would make us do that and then he taught us how to write letters. You
> know, he would say, why don't you write your mom a letter and you have
> to put the date on it and, you know, and then we learned that in school,
> too. . . .
>
> I was always good in spelling and everything. I won a spelling bee in 5th
> grade and 3rd grade. . . . They [her parents], just anytime we wanted a mag-
> azine or a book, they always got it for us. Uh huh. . . . My dad always took us
> to the library in Kalamazoo. . . .
>
> He always read the newspapers, and . . . we would just go lay on the bed
> with him and read the newspaper with him. And he would read articles and
> then he would make a game of it. . . . [H]e always read from the back to
> front, and guess how I read the paper?
>
> And you know I find that easy for me to learn that way, too . . . I'm taking
> a class now because I'm going after my business degree . . . and, in math,
> and I find that if I go from back to front, I learn it better. I don't know what it
> is. I just discovered that within the last term.

In 1969—the year after the American Indian Movement (AIM) was
founded—Carmen's father finished his bachelor's degree in Business Administration at Wayne State University. By this time, American Indian activism had become a strong national movement in the United States. AIM,
a primary inspiration for much of this activity, "sought to reduce police
harassment and to provide alternative, culturally sensitive education for
Native children who were having difficulties in the public school system"
(Champagne, 1994, p. xlix). The organization inspired hundreds of take-
overs and sit-ins from the late 1960s through the mid-1970s, including the
occupation of the island of Alcatraz in 1969.

During this same period—after Carmen's mother had been released from the hospital—the family moved back to Baraga and the Keweenaw Bay Indian Community. The move brought Carmen's father home to familiar surroundings, and he was able to secure a position as the Native American Outreach Coordinator at a local university. Carmen, however, was unfamiliar with life in a small town, and she was faced, in addition, with the difficult task of adjusting to a new high school. It was fortunate that she was resilient:

> . . . [I] went from a class of 500 to a school of 500. Isn't that something? And it was really backwards. . . . It was so backwards . . .
>
> But one thing about being down there [in Detroit], even though I wanted to be involved, I wasn't involved, I was too shy. Here [in Baraga] its just like I blossomed. . . . [I]t was like, "Hey, I know how to do this." We had to respond in class down there.
>
> Up here, the people would ask us something, and then nobody would answer. And . . . I would always be raising my hand, you know, because, you know, we had, in 9th grade English we had already read all these books and up here it was like, what book? You know, "What are you talking about?" It was like so different. . . .
>
> Yeah. I got to be a real class leader and started a lot of things. . . . I got labeled "Most Fun to Be With" and "Class Clown." [Then] somebody else didn't get something so they got to be "Most Fun to Be With," and then I just got stuck with "Class Clown." I was all mad about that but now I laugh about it. I was thinking, "Well I'm glad I was!" you know? I had a lot of pain . . . and that's how I kept it away.

Carmen graduated from high school in 1973, one year after AIM members had organized the "Trail of Broken Treaties" protest in Washington, D.C., and during the year in which AIM members occupied a small trading post at Wounded Knee Village to call attention to "problems on the Pine Ridge Reservation in South Dakota" (*Native American History Timeline*, n.d.). She left the Upper Peninsula of Michigan to attend Kendall School of Design in Grand Rapids, Michigan. That same year, however, Kendall was plagued by a series of unsolved sexual assaults, and Carmen, after narrowly avoiding an assault right outside her apartment, left school after only half a semester. This experience shook Carmen's confidence. As she tells the story:

> . . . I ended up . . . going to California right away visiting my aunt, my dad's sister, and she taught me how to sew and everything because I was sort of lost then. It was like trying to find myself. . . . And, well I felt like a failure after that . . . I mean because I know I had disappointed him [her father] and his dream was for me to finish school, you know. And, it was my dream too but I don't know, I don't know, I wasn't mature enough.

On rocky emotional ground, Carmen came back to the Upper Peninsula; but the next few years were to hold additional challenges:

> Then I came back and then I got married. And I was married for 10 years and I had three children in that marriage and it was going nowhere in my opinion. It was 10 years [later] and we were still . . . you know? [A]nd . . . [I was] raising the kids, and he used to call in sick all the time and drink a lot. And then, I went through that drinking stuff till after we got divorced. . . .

It was at this point, in 1982, while casting about for an alternative to her married life, that a local two-year college provided Carmen with her first significant gateway to digital literacy. Although she remembered seeing her father prepare mainframe punch cards when he was in school and knew that her aunt had used a mainframe, as well, in her work as a bank cashier, Carmen herself had never had the opportunity or the desire to use a mainframe computer. In fact, she had waited until microcomputers were commercially available before taking the technology plunge:

> I took a computer class, and that's when they just had Apples. . . . We learned word processing. And, we made spreadsheets and . . . DOS something.

Carmen liked this course, although, because she lacked access to a computer at home, she could not follow up on her instruction. As she recounted,

> I wanted more, I wanted a career. Being a mother and sewing clothes and cleaning the house and all the things mothers do, baking and all that, wasn't good enough, you know? It wasn't enough, and I wanted to do something and I was wanting to be a nurse. So I went to nursing school. Now that was an experience in itself.

When viewed within the context of U.S. trends, Carmen's efforts to educate and support herself, to develop her own identity and determine her own destiny, were not unusual. By 1980, for instance, women constituted 51.1% of the U.S. labor force, and 39.6% of these women—like Carmen— had children under 18 years of age (*Report on the American Workforce*, 1999, p. 140). Despite their contributions to the workforce, however, women had yet to secure an equitable level of rights, responsibilities, and involvement within the larger cultural context of life in the United States. For instance, it wasn't until 1981 that Sandra Day O'Connor was the first female justice to be appointed to the United States Supreme Court, and that the Court, in *Kirchberg v. Feenstra*, overturned state laws designating husbands as the family's " 'head and master,' having unilateral control of property owned jointly" with their wives (*The Path of the Women's Rights Movement,* 1997–2002). Carmen's struggle mirrored the situation that many women faced, and her successes were both hard won and against great odds.

By 1983, just one year before Louise Erdrich published *Love Medicine* and two years before Wilma Mankiller became the first woman to lead the modern Cherokee Nation, Carmen's divorce became final, and she enrolled in a local two-year college to pursue her associate's degree in nursing. There, however, she faced additional challenges in a profession where women of color represented only a small proportion of licensed practical nurses:

> You know, that was a big thing, too. When I went back they said, "You know, Carmen, we don't think you are going to be able to make it. We may want you to start over from the beginning." And I said, "No, you guys! There is no way I can afford taking another student loan out!" I already had $8,000 in loans, and I said, "No, I can't do it!" I said, "You have to give me a chance . . . I have been in and out of the hospital, and you think I have not been studying everything that's been going on with me. . . ?" And [they said], "Okay, we'll put you on probation and we'll see how you do," and, well, I passed my boards on my first try. And I went right up there and showed them.

Carmen's nursing school, small, rural, and not very well endowed, did not provide her a gateway that she could use to develop additional digital literacy skills, although she remembered her teachers' predicting that she would soon encounter technology on the job:

> We did not have computers in nursing school, but they said we were going to use them someday.

On her graduation from nursing school in 1986, Carmen took on a series of nursing positions that offered her additional access to computer technology. Unfortunately, the conditions of her workplace access to computers—for example, the technical support that she could draw on—were not ideal:

> So, in my job I got introduced to them [computers]. So I knew about them a little more. We had heart monitors . . . we had to enter stuff. . . . [And we] wrote stuff. Even, the ER, or the OB unit has the monitors, you know, the fetal monitors, when you have to enter, information . . .
>
> [And] at the tribal center we had to start using them [computers], for the Indian Health Service for their RMPS system and management information system. . . . All the Indian Health Services are registered in one place, and an Indian can go from this clinic in Keweenaw Bay to the clinic down in

Saginaw Bay, and all they have to do is put in their number and their record
of visits is there.

    The way I was taught at the tribe, you look in the manual and that's how
we were. If you didn't look in a manual, you didn't know how to use it [the
computer]. . . . There is nobody there to support you.

For the next few years, Carmen held several nursing jobs, including one at
the Keweenaw Bay Tribal Center and a stint at a maximum security cor-
rectional institution. She remembered that time in the following words:

> And, I got burned out because I was working at the tribal center and the
> prison. And I would work 12-hour shifts on the weekends, and then I would
> work 40 hours a week at the rez. And . . . it got to be too much.

This situation came to a head in 1993 and 1994, when Carmen's mother
and father both passed away. Shortly thereafter, she accepted the position
of Native American Outreach Coordinator that her father had once held.
And it was the technology gateway that her new university workplace
provided her that seemed to provide the conditions of access—up-to-date
equipment, individualized technical support, tuition-free training courses
congruent with her technology interests—that Carmen needed in order to
develop a robust set of computer-based literacy skills.

> Yeah, when I came here [to her university position] was the most I've
> learned . . . I'm so thankful for this job just because of that. We never had e-
> mail until I came; '96 was my first time with e-mail. . . . Joel Hughes [a tech-
> nical support person], he used to work here, he taught us all . . . he came by
> individually and helped us when we had things [we needed to do]. And so,
> that's . . . [when] I was trained. . . . Right.
>   And then I did take one, course and I believe it was, Word, through work.
> It was a professional development class. And then I did take a course over in
> business, BA 117. And after BA 117, now I understand a lot more . . . man-
> agement information systems, LAN and WAN and all the networks and
> what it means.

Under these conditions, by the time she was interviewed for this project in the spring of 2000, Carmen was using computers at work to write reports and proposals, to complete projects and construct spread sheets. She
was also using computers to recruit students within the Native American
community, store important documents, send e-mail, conduct research on
Native American issues on the World Wide Web, and stay in touch with
her tribal contacts around the United States. She had also purchased a
computer for her home, primarily for use by her children, although this
purchase represented a significant portion of her income.

In establishing a technology gateway for her children at home, Carmen made sure that the conditions of access addressed both their needs and their interests. She set up a special desk and chair in her living room, for instance, so that the whole family could use the computer. In addition, she purchased computer-based games and software to motivate her children's use of computers and a CD burner so that they could create their own music collections. And Carmen was also trying to serve as a role model and a computer-support person for her children, showing them how to learn specific computer applications for the school and personal projects they undertook:

> . . . In high school graduation . . . they show all these slide shows, and it was a terrible slide show because, for one thing, you couldn't see it because they were . . . [projecting] it on a sheet. And I was . . . [saying], "You guys, you don't even need a sheet. . . . And . . . you can just, you can have a CD yearbook. . . ." And they are going, "Mom, I'm sure!" You know? And I'm sitting here, "Yeah, I can do that!" . . . We get our pictures developed on a CD now . . . so you get them on a disk or you get them on a CD.
>
> And . . . then I used them in my son's graduation thank you [notes]. A picture from graduation, I put it on a thank you note, put a saying . . . you know, "Thanks for stopping at my party," and "Thanks for the money," and "I appreciate your coming," and it was a picture of him on that day.

Finally, Carmen, worked to provide conditions that were both structured and safe for her children:

> We just got a new chair at home to sit [for the computer], and the other day I walked in and there is one of them [Carmen's twin daughters] and one of their friends sitting in the [same] chair. I said, "The chair was made for one person." . . . [Y]ou know, they both have skinny butts, and they can fit in there, but, "No, the chair was made for one person and that's all. . . . Get off of it now."
>
> The twins are in 9th grade and they are into the chat thing. And they are on there constantly and then they have their kids over, their friends over 24/ 7, and nothing was getting done. And last week it broke loose, and I said, "You guys are going to have an hour on here [the computer], and you are going to have an hour for chat, and you will have an hour for homework. And then, if you want to use it for research or anything, that's fine. You can have unlimited research time, but this chat . . . stuff, is BS." And, you know, I'm starting to crack down on it.
>
> Uh huh . . . there are some stinky files on there [the WWW] that come up, you know, with the sex stuff. They [the twins] usually delete it . . . now and they go, "This is gross." And . . . I said, "Yeah, it is. You don't need it. You don't even look at it. When it comes on, exit out." And they do.
>
> They had one bad experience where somebody called them at, like, 1:00 in the morning. And we happened to be sitting in the den, and . . . watching

a movie, and I got up and answered the phone. And he said, "Is so and so there?" . . . Well the girls had given a different name, but I knew; . . . it was like their middle name. And I go, "No!" And [he said], "Well I'd like to talk to her." And I said, "Well, I'm sorry, she's not available."

And they [Carmen's twin girls] had picked it [the telephone] up on the other line, so they knew somebody was on there. And so . . . we said, "Okay, this is why you don't do this!" And they got scared from that one call.

Given the access Carmen's children now had to computer technology, and the fact that their mother had shaped the conditions of this access to their technological interests, needs, and safety, Carmen's children, like Dean's children, used computers on a regular basis, for school, for entertainment, and for staying in touch with other family members. As Carmen noted,

They use it for their reports in school, for their, term papers, and science fairs, . . . e-mail . . . , the Web. I know they are using it for the prom. They have to find their prom dresses. . . . They . . . get a good idea of what they want, and then they go, and it tells you what stores it is available at, so then they will go call the store.

My son is in business administration here, and . . . he plans on leaving home. E-mail will be our way of keeping in touch.

Thus computers—and the literate activity that accompanies them—have become essential components of both Carmen's and Dean's families' lives.

Thinking About Access

The cases of Dean Woodbeck and Carmen Vincent and others in this book indicate that schools, homes, community centers, and workplaces represent four important gateways through which people have gained access to computer technology over the last two and one-half decades. Our interviews suggest that the more of these gateways that are open to people, the more likely they are, over their lifetimes, to acquire and develop a robust set of digital literacy practices and to value digital literacy. It is also true, however, that the relative importance of these gateways in the lives of specific individuals varies according to the needs and motivations of the people who use them; the historical contexts in which people exist and are motivated to use computers; their material and economic circumstances; and the social circumstances that both shape, and are shaped by, their actions.

In addition, the cases suggest that the specific conditions of access can affect at what times and in what ways people acquire and develop robust sets of digital literacy skills—or, indeed, if they choose to do so. Among the more significant conditions of access that Dean and Carmen mentioned were the fit, or match, between their needs and the capabilities of available computer hardware and software; the motivation, or personal stake, they had for learning to communicate in online environments; the resources, financial and otherwise, they had available to devote to computers; the immediacy and convenience of computer access; the availability of technical support in a form that fit their particular learning style; and the safety, security, and general ambience of the computing environment they had available for use.

Dean, for instance, had access to mainframe computers at several points in his college career. The conditions of this access, however—the mainframe equipment that had limited applications, the tight security, the awkward interface of punch cards, the delays in feedback—were not congruent with his learning style, his educational values, or his learning goals. It was not until the microcomputers had been invented and marketed that Dean was able to establish his own technology gateway at home. With his first condition of access met—access to equipment appropriate for his interests, needs, and resources—Dean was then motivated to use computers more extensively in support of his academic goals. With a computer at home, he could also establish an environment that matched his own personal working and learning style.

Similarly, Carmen Vincent had access to technology through her work as a nurse for the Keweenaw Bay Indian Community. The lack of technical support for her work on these computers, however, and the relatively narrow range of activities for which she used the computers—entering patient data for a national medical database—did not encourage her to develop additional digital literacy practices. In her university position, however, Carmen had access to a more robust computer system that could support a broader range of her workplace activities and interests: her research efforts, e-mail habits, word processing activities, and recruiting projects. The conditions of her access also included individualized technical support and tuition-free technology courses, both of which suited her learning style and her financial resources, and established a fit with her motivation to finish her degree. At home, Carmen was able to shape her family's conditions of access so that they suited her approach to parenting and her commitment to making sure that her children had a broad range of technological literacies. She provided equipment and systems appropriate for the needs and resources of her family; created a safe and comfortable environment in which her children could use the computer; provided technical support that matched their learning styles and needs; and matched the home computer applications to the needs, interests, and activities of the family. These details also make it clear that

Carmen and Dean took an active role in seeking their own kind of access to computer technology, and in shaping the particular conditions of their access to meet the needs of their families.

Finally, these two case studies indicate that the complexity of access as a social issue becomes clear only when this phenomenon is considered within the context of a larger cultural ecology, and as it is articulated with the other significant formations—poverty and race, for instance—that are part of this ecology. Carmen Vincent's tenacity in pursuing access to computers, for example, acquires additional meaning when it is placed within the context of reports, generally relying on 1990 census data, indicating that one out of every three Native Americans lives in poverty and that over one third of Native Americans live on reservations, trust lands, or in other designated Native communities, areas most frequently located in rural parts of the United States (Benton Foundation, 1999, p. 5). We also understand more about Carmen's efforts to acquire digital literacy if we know that 12% of households on reservations lack electricity, and 53% lack telephone connections, compared with 5% of homes nationally and 9% of homes in rural areas of the United States (*Falling through the Net*, 1999). When we know these facts, it becomes less surprising to learn that only 26.8% of rural Native American households have computers whereas 42% of White rural households have purchased such machines ("Native Americans and the Digital Divide," 1999). It also becomes less surprising to learn that only 19% of Native American homes had access to the Internet, as compared with 29.8% of White households, and an average of 26% of all households nationally ("Native Americans and the Digital Divide," 1999).

Such high rates of poverty when combined with the high cost of telephone connections and services on tribal lands, according to the Benton Foundation, prevent many Native American households from being connected to the Internet, even when such service is available:

> The typical household on a reservation pays $100/month for basic monthly phone service. Because even calls to locations on the same reservation can be considered long distance, inhabitants can incur exorbitant long distance bills averaging an additional $126/month. Many telephone users on reservations have had phone service disconnected at some point in time because of their inability to pay for long distance charges. ("Native Americans and the Digital Divide," 1999)

Such conditions can not only pose a "formidable barrier" to the successful elimination of the technology gap for Native Americans, but they can also exacerbate difficulties involved in accessing government services ("Native Americans and the Digital Divide," 1999).

The case studies of Dean Woodbeck and Carmen Vincent provide a complex picture of access, but one that is nonetheless valuable for educators struggling to create and maintain productive learning environments for digital literacy. Perhaps most important, these case studies demonstrate how racism and poverty, literacy and illiteracy, money and access to technology are linked in the complex cultural ecology that characterizes the United States of America—and how inventive individual people can be in shaping the conditions under which their access to technology can work most effectively.

4

Shaping Cultures:
Prizing the Literacies of Technology

Gail E. Hawisher
Thomas A. Lugo
Melissa Pearson
Cynthia L. Selfe

> [Culture is] the lived experience, the consciousness of a whole society; that
> particular order, pattern, configuration of valued experience, expressed now
> in imaginative art of the highest order, now in the most popular and prover-
> bial forms, in gesture and language, in myth and ideology, in modes of com
> munication and in forms of social relationship and organisation. (The Bir-
> mingham Centre for Contemporary Cultural Studies, as cited in Street,
> 1995, p. 59)

> When I was teaching recently, I was thinking about what do I tell the White
> kids about being in a multicultural society. And I put "Whiteness" into my
> search and I found this really neat site and it's called the Center for White
> Cultural Study. . . . It is a site for White people who need to understand that
> their culture (and our Black culture) is not at the center, but that we are
> among other cultures in America. And I thought, oh my gosh, you know, if I
> could get this site to so many people, you know, how useful that would be.
> (Melissa Pearson, interview, April 6, 2000)

> All the armed services . . . know as well as any institution that culture
> counts. . . . [E]ven in the military, rules are likely to be unenforceable if pre-
> vailing beliefs and attitudes in the institution run counter to what the rules
> require. For this reason, militaries give immense attention to the formation of
> their personnel. (Katzenstein & Reppy, 1999, p. 1)

As we have noted in previous chapters, the degree to which new literacies
assume importance and become accessible to particular groups and indi-

vidual people, or don't, has much to do with the prevailing cultural ecology of the times: that complex intermingling of social, historical, political, and material forces within which human beings live their lives. Within this larger cultural ecology, the concept of culture figures prominently— at the macro-, medial, and micro-levels—in shaping communities' and peoples' attitudes and in encouraging the acquisition of both traditional literacies and the literacies of technology. Cultures, on a micro-level, co- alesce around factors such as race, religion, ethnicity, belief, lifestyle, geography, ideology, and so on. But, in addition, micro-level cultures shape, and are often shaped by, larger cultural groups with which they are affili- ated at the medial and macro-levels, such as society's many institutions, organizations, and even corporate structures. Cultures, in other words, consist of—and are constituted by—the social practices of a people across time and space. Jay Lemke (1995) would say that they are constituted by the texts that people produce and the meanings that they make, through their various semiotic systems: their oral and written discourses, their vi- sual symbols and signs, their behaviors and interpersonal practices. Thus, literacy practices and values are constitutive of culture, and they are fash- ioned by culture at the micro-, medial, and macro-levels.[1]

In this chapter, then, we turn to this wide-ranging concept of culture, recognizing, as explained in the Birmingham Center epigraph at the be- ginning of this chapter, that it is at once "the consciousness of a whole so- ciety" and the province of communities, neighborhoods, and people themselves—all influenced every day by the many overlapping cultures that make up the United States. Before proceeding, however, we need to acknowledge, as Melissa Pearson's comment in the epigraph points out, that in foregrounding cultures—most especially, Latino and African American cultures, as we do in this chapter—we do not wish to imply an absence of cultural influences, race, or ethnicity among those women and men in our study who come from different backgrounds and particularly those who claim White European descent. In other words, regardless of the familiar categories of race and ethnicity into which people are some- times sorted, humans are influenced by, and influence, profoundly and in a multitude of ways the many cultures in which they grow up and move through life and school.

---

[1]In this understanding, we refer to the work of Jay Lemke (1995), who points out that hu- mans constitute social meaning and social systems through a variety of semiotic texts. These texts, Lemke noted, consist not only of language, but also of visual signs, actions, and inter- personal relationships: "It is even useful when speaking of the *text* . . . to add to the verbal record of discourse as much as we can of the visual and actional signs and symbols that con- tribute to . . . social meanings. . . . A theory of meaning cannot limit itself to the semantics of language viewed in isolation from more general forms of human activity . . . [A]n act-in- community, a material and social process . . . helps to constitute the community as a commu- nity" (pp. 8–9).

In addition, we need to note that cultures and ecologies are far from uniform or monodimensional. Although they operate on a micro-, medial, and macro-level, they also vary enormously in their influence and form from person to person, family to family, neighborhood to neighborhood. Moreover, human beings are also shaped by, and shape, many kinds of culture: the cultures of their workplace, the organizations to which they belong, the institutions of which they are a part, and the lifestyles or sports and recreational practices in which they choose to engage, for example. As the final epigraph at the beginning of this chapter points out, the military is one such institutional culture. In telling the stories of the participants in our larger project and in this chapter particularly, we found that expectations in military cultures often had productive influences on families and especially on their literacy efforts—print and digital—that are sometimes overlooked.

This chapter suggests that the dynamic change and upheaval that characterized the 1960s and 1970s affected in dramatic ways a number of different cultures and their attendant value systems. As noted previously, we look at the particular Latino culture and African American culture in which the two co-authors of this chapter participated, and we also examine the ways in which the culture of sports and that of the military shaped their literacy values and activities as they grew up. We ask the following questions, as well: What did it mean to be literate in the United States when these two grew up? What does it mean to them today? How do the different cultures to which each belongs value the literacies of technology? How do these values get taken up and played out in their lives? These are the sorts of questions to consider as we relate the stories of Thomas Lugo, a Mexican-American, born on the West Coast in the United States, and Melissa Pearson, an African American, born in the Southeast.

Today, both Tom and Melissa work as writing instructors at the collegiate level—at a four-year and a two-year institution, respectively—and, when interviewed, were 36 years old and thus born before schools understood the many implications that personal computers might hold for literacy instruction. Both came into the world in 1964, the last year that designates the demographic wave of baby boomers and the first year that marks the large escalation of the Vietnam War.[2] Throughout our presentation of the case studies, we attempt, with Tom and Melissa's help, to highlight key historical and social events that may have left their mark on the local cultures within which the two writing instructors participate.

---

[2]Usually, the Tonkin Gulf Resolution of August 1964 is used as a basis for marking the initial escalation of the war in Vietnam. See http://www.cnn.com/SPECIALS/cold.war/episodes/11/documents/tonkin/ and http://www.historychannel.com/cgi-bin/frameit.cgi?p=http%3A//www.historychannel.com/tdih/vietnam.html

Cultures at Work

As mentioned in previous chapters, the late 1960s, in which Tom and Melissa spent their early childhood, were years of great unrest in the United States. In addition, the geographical areas in which the two grew up were probably as volatile as any in the industrialized world at the time. Both Los Angeles, California, and the southeastern United States were subjected to significant civil turmoil—South Central Los Angeles, where the 1965 Watts Riots took place, and Augusta, Georgia, home to racial turmoil in 1970, are just two examples. Although the Watts civil rights uprisings occurred not far from where Tom was born, their impact was also felt dramatically in the Southeast, as well as in the rest of the United States. Some believe, in part, that the riots themselves grew out of the despair that Blacks and Latinos alike felt over the paucity of available jobs at the time, and of the California legislature's passage of Proposition 14, a move to block the fair housing legislation passed in the Civil Rights Act of 1964.[3] The Civil Rights Act had been designed ostensibly to prevent discrimination "on the basis of gender, creed, race, or ethnic background" in hiring, in wages, and in other conditions of employment, but it also addressed conditions of fair housing ("Events in Hispanic American History," 1997). The rioting itself, however, began after two young Blacks and then their mother were arrested by White police officers who had stopped the young Blacks' car for a traffic violation. The rioting continued for six days leaving more than 30 people dead, hundreds injured, and a whole neighborhood and its buildings in shambles. Watts would be the first in a series of civil uprisings that had at their roots the vexed and violent racial history of the United States.

Unsurprisingly, civil unrest growing out of the unfair treatment of Blacks continued during these years in the Southeast as well. On May 11, 1970, in Augusta, Georgia, not far from Melissa's hometown of Columbia, South Carolina, a peaceful demonstration among Black citizens to protest the fatal beating of a 16-year-old Black county jail prisoner grew violent when one of the protesters tore down the state flag of Georgia. One thousand National Guardsmen were called in to control the ensuing riot in which six of the protesters were killed and many stores and businesses

---

[3]See http://www.eeoc.gov/laws/vii.html. The Civil Rights Act of 1964, which California Proposition 14 sought to limit, reads in part: "To enforce the constitutional right to vote, to confer jurisdiction upon the district courts of the United States to provide injunctive relief against discrimination in public accommodations, to authorize the attorney general to institute suits to protect constitutional rights in public facilities and public education, to extend the Commission on Civil Rights, to prevent discrimination in federally assisted programs, to establish a Commission on Equal Employment Opportunity, and for other purposes."

burned to the ground. The needless deaths of these times—Martin Luther King Jr. among them—continued to distress all people of the United States well into the 1970s and beyond, regardless of their cultural location.

Against this backdrop of righteous rebellion and protest, many African Americans also involved themselves in rediscovering, appreciating, and contributing to their own complex cultural identities. In 1966, for example, the African American holiday of Kwanza, the Swahili term for "first fruits," was created to celebrate family and cultural values (*The Encyclopaedia Britannica Guide to Black History,* 1999). Melissa and her family have come to appreciate Kwanza, in part because they make rather than buy gifts, thus emphasizing generosity "from the heart," as Melissa explains.[4] These years also saw the rise of the Black Aesthetic or Black Arts Movement, which grew out of the "cultural politics" of Black nationalism/separatism and supported authors such as Alex Haley, Eldridge Cleaver, Angela Davis, Toni Morrison, and Alice Walker, to mention only a very few of the well-known writers associated with the movement (*The Encyclopaedia Britannica Guide to Black History,* 1999). Alex Haley would publish in 1965 *The Autobiography of Malcolm X,* and 11 years later *Roots: The Saga of an American Family,* a book that went on to win a Pulitzer Prize in 1977 when Melissa was living as a military dependent in Germany. The book, which traces seven generations of Haley's family, and the subsequent television series based on the book were huge successes and prompted many African Americans, as well as other people in the United States, to trace their own genealogies. These were also the years when African American Studies programs began to slowly make their way onto U.S. college campuses.

Some of the same kinds of political and cultural activity marked the lives of Mexican Americans during this period, as well. Los Angeles, in 1968, for example, experienced what's come to be known as "the Los Angeles Walkout." Earl Shorris (1992) explains that "chicanos showed their power for the first time in Los Angeles in March of 1968 when ten thousand students walked out of barrio high schools" to protest the unequal education that Mexican Americans received and that they believed prepared them for so-

---

[4]From the start, principles guiding this nonreligious but cultural celebration included unity, self-determination, collective responsibility, cooperative economics, purpose, creativity, and faith, with families customarily gathering together on December 26th and each evening thereafter to light a candle and discuss one of these principles and its attendant values. The celebration culminates on December 31st when members of the community come together to share in a feast—the "karamu" as it is known (*The Encyclopaedia Britannica Guide to Black History,* 1999). Melissa explained that these are principles that she today tries "to dedicate her life to, and [she's] joined [her] sons' school's celebrations by dressing in African attire and sharing with them. We have a Kinara [a special seven-branch candleholder]. Justin and Jordan really get into it and have learned to count and give basic greetings in Swahili.

ciety's most menial jobs.[5] During these years, Chicano student organizations were formed, and César Chávez became a hero among Latinos, in part because of his nonviolent efforts to improve the working conditions of migrant laborers through the United Farmworkers Organizing Committee ("Events in Hispanic American History," 1997). Chávez's untiring efforts inspired many Mexican Americans throughout the United States to become political activists and to fight against discrimination.

The Chicano Movement, also known as the Mexican-American Civil Rights Movement,[6] not only attempted to improve educational opportunities for people but also gave rise to a rebirth in the arts among Mexican Americans as they sought to construct new political and cultural identities. Among the many Chicano artists, writers, and musicians that gained attention during the 1970s, to name only a few, are poets such as Ricardo Sanchez and Angela de Hoyos; novelists such as Alejandro Morales and Victor Villasenor; artists Ernesto Palamino, and Judy Baca, who began the City of Los Angeles mural program; film writer José Luis Ruiz, whose film *The Unwanted* portrayed the hardships of Mexican immigrants in the United States ("Events in Hispanic American History," 1997). Thus, in both the African-American and Mexican-American communities, civil rights and protest movements spawned a cultural resurgence that continues to make itself felt across the United States.

As a Mexican American, Tom Lugo helps us capture the spirit of these times in remembering a bit of his childhood growing up in Los Angeles. To understand the nuances entailed in the many labels that accompany being a Mexican American, he defines the several different terms that emerge in this chapter to denote people of Mexican descent, among them "Chicana/ o," "Latina/o," and "Hispanic." We include his comments here:

> Each of those terms means different things, especially that endearing 1970s political designation, Chicano, which warmly reminds me of my sister and her pals, all newly discovering and wearing this identity and its requisite attitude.
>
> To explain, if you called yourself Chicano/a, you'd better be "down" with all that that description/lifestyle entailed: the music (War, El Chicano, Smokey Robinson, Tierra, Richie Valens, et al.), the art, the food, the language (some Spanish, but you didn't have to be fluent), the barrio, and the pride in *La Raza* (the Race) or *Gente de Aztlan* (People of the Aztecs' Land) [loosely translated].
>
> I love all this stuff attached to Chicano and Los Angeles/Southern California because it reminds me of my childhood and my sister, who dropped out of high school at 15 and had some rough going there, for a while.

---

[5]See Earl Shorris' (1992) *Latinos: A Biography of the People,* pp. 103–105.
[6]For further discussion on the impact of Mexican-American activism, see "Chicano: History of the Mexican American Civil Rights Movement" (1996).

As far as using it today to describe myself, that depends: If I want to rile some old, conservative, republican-voting Cubans or Argentines, I might use it just to irk them; the term, remember, is primarily a political one, and many Latinos do not recognize it as a valid (or even serious, to a small extent) affiliation. If you use this term to describe yourself, you'd be wise to be ready to defend it, as it is probably viewed as somewhat antiquated and divisive by some Latinos, especially Cubanos, actually.

Chicano derives from a clipped French mispronunciation of the word "Mexicano." I'm not sure how Mexicanos *verdaderos* [real] perceive the term, but my sense is that they probably chuckle at it. I like Latino, but not Hispanic, because the latter suggests a large group of Spanish-speaking people and there are many Mexican Americans (a description I prefer using), who aren't fluent in Spanish.[7]

Although Mexican Americans continue to succeed in identifying themselves through a variety of cultural contributions, they also, as Tom's words suggest, recognize their larger Latino heritage and the many differences—historical, political, and social—that distinguish them from Cubans, Puerto Ricans, Argentines, Dominicans, and other Latino groups.

Individual Latinos, like individual African Americans, European Americans, Asian Americans, and the multitude of other people who make up the United States, differentiate themselves from one another through varied social practices, cultural sensibilities, and literate activities, even as the multicultural society of the United States places them, more often than not, under the monodimensional term Hispanic or even Latino. Keeping in mind the profound differences among members of the same culture, we now turn to the case studies of Melissa Pearson, born on August 25, 1964, and Tom Lugo, born on August 10, 1964.

Two Case Studies

Growing up, both Melissa and Tom have memories of these early times in their lives and of the unrest that marked the world around them. Melissa's first memory, for example, is of her grandmother crying over the death of

---

[7]In their book *Latinos: Remaking America* Arcelo Suárez-Orozco and Mariela Páez (2002) gave a definition of Latinos that adds to Tom's description of the labels: "We have opted for the broadest, most inclusive, and most generous definition of Latinos: that segment of the U.S. population that traces its descent to the Spanish-speaking, Caribbean, and Latin American worlds. The term *Latino* is a new and ambiguous invention. It is a cultural category that has no precise racial signification. Indeed, Latinos are white, black, indigenous, and every possible combination thereof" (p. 3). For this chapter, we tried primarily to use the terms Mexican American and Latina/o. When Hispanic is used by others for statistical purposes connected with U.S. government reports and the like, we use that category as well. Like Tom, Suárez-Orozco, and Páez, however, we prefer Latina/o over Hispanic as the larger, more encompassing term.

Martin Luther King Jr. in 1968 when Melissa was only four years old. Both Tom and Melissa, however, were somewhat protected from the social disruption that was often portrayed on the televisions in their living rooms. Although Melissa was born into a segregated South Carolina, her father's military career, she notes, gave her and her family more privileges than a typical middle class Black family might have experienced otherwise. And because of the military, her family moved frequently, living in South Carolina, Virginia, Kentucky, Italy, Germany, and Georgia in towns with names that in the United States at least usually began with Fort—Fort Jackson, Fort Knox, Fort Benning.

Tom, who sometimes identifies himself as "a third-generation Angeleno Chicano," stayed mostly rooted in his California neighborhood just east of Los Angeles, his mother moving only once, slightly more to the east, when he was 12 years old to avoid the encroaching gangs of Los Angeles. Although his family was poor at times (he describes, for example, his embarrassment at having to use food stamps for a short period in his life when his mother was out of work), he was actually brought up east of "East Los," as he calls it, in a small apartment he shared with his mother and older sister and brother. Melissa, too, came from a small family in which there were only her mother, father, and a brother, who was seven years younger than she.

As far as parental education is concerned, neither Melissa's nor Tom's fathers finished high school, but whereas Melissa's father went back to school in the military and finished college, thereby making himself eligible for officers' candidate school, Tom's father was never able to finish school. In fact, Tom was amazed to find out when his father died in 1991 that he didn't have a high school education. He always seemed, as Tom put it, "pretty well informed." After leaving the family when Tom was about five, his father worked as a printer and had a low profile in Tom's life, more like that of a distant family member whom Tom regarded as being quite educated. Tom's mother and sister also had to leave high school although his mother went on to earn her GED (Graduate Equivalency Diploma), found work as a secretary, and, since 1983, has worked in an attorney's office as a legal secretary. Of growing up, Tom says:

> You know, I don't remember [my mom] ever reading to me. Never helping me with my homework. She would say, you know, good job when I brought good grades home, but that wasn't her concern. She was a hands-off mom. You know, what I remember clearly is her getting on me for having bad citizenship grades, you know, behavior, 'cause I was kind of obnoxious sometimes. I was always trying to be funny in class. So yeah, she got onto me for that. I remember more of her criticism and yelling at me for that than any lauds I got for good grades, except when I finally got into a four-year university, which no one had in our family before. Then she started paying more

attention to that. My mom had to work two jobs for a long time. I didn't see
her much, and my sister raised me a lot, probably from the time I was 6 to
11—my sister was with me all the time.

Despite his practice of cracking jokes in class, at some level Tom was quite
taken with school. When asked what kind of student he'd describe himself
as, Tom replied, "Good, bored with the rote stuff and always wanting to
be engaged, and the classes were not big, [so I could be]. . . ."

Tom fared well enough in school to attend a junior college, where his
brother had played basketball, and where he too became a walk-on for the
school's basketball team. The culture of sports and its heroes played a major role in Tom's life, and he recalls especially several boxers that hailed
from the Los Angeles area when he was growing up. He lists off the
names of these boxers as

> . . . Bobby Chacon, Danny "Little Red" Lopez, but the biggest/baddest one
> of the seventies was Panama's Roberto Duran, with the *Manos de Piedra:*
> hands of stone. He was a devastating, no-frills brawler, so obviously, L.A.'s
> fight fans (which nearly all my cousins from my mom's side are) loved and
> followed him and his career.

And there were other sports figures who captured Tom's attention:

> I also loved Brazil's Pele, one of the world's best players from 1958 to 1974
> (or so); he's one of the main reasons I started playing soccer at about age
> nine. But most of my other sports interests rested with hoops and Black
> players.

To underscore his love affair with basketball, Tom told us the following
when asked what really made him interested in attending college:

> My first memory of this thing called "college" was via watching UCLA bas-
> ketball games on TV with my brother. I was about six or seven, and the
> games came on late, like 10:00 or 11:00 sometimes, and I got to stay up and
> watch them. My mom usually didn't get home from work till very late.
>
> I remember UCLA playing all kinds of squads, the "University of This"
> and "That University," and I thought that the word "university" sounded
> special somehow. I don't ever recall anyone in my family talking about col-
> lege or university until I was about 12 or so, when my brother first enrolled
> at a local JC. . . .
>
> At that age, my primary connection to universities was through college
> hoops and football, which I got into as a player and fan, the latter occurring
> after my mom got me a subscription to *Sports Illustrated.* I used to love read-
> ing and looking at the College Preview issues for hoops and football (I still
> do!) especially when they included campus photos.

Whether appearing in newspapers or magazines, sports stories assumed prime importance in Tom's literate life, just as team sports themselves came to dominate his athletic life. And, unsurprisingly, during Tom's young years, the UCLA basketball team claimed all sorts of national attention when John Wooden, as UCLA's basketball coach, led his Bruins to 10 national championships, including 7 in a row ("Hall of Famers," 2000–2001). As Tom watched television in the early 1970s, he would have seen the UCLA basketball team, with such superstars as Kareem Abdul-Jabbar, Bill Walton, Marques Johnson, and many others, win again and again, at one time going so far as to garner 88 consecutive victories ("Hall of Famers," 2000–2001).

And if sports initially made higher education exceptionally attractive to Tom, it was the junior college as an institution that served as a significant gateway to additional educational opportunities. Mt. San Antonio College, which he attended for three years before going on to a four-year school, introduced him to the panoply of curricular activities that make up college life and showed him that he could indeed be successful as a student. But, as far as different kinds of colleges are concerned, Tom maintains that he didn't realize what he was missing out on until he visited a friend who was attending a four-year university, the University of California at Berkeley. He says of the experience,

> I had a good time. I stayed with him for like five days. I went with him to his classes, poly sci class and Chinese class, and I loved it.
>   There's like a day and night difference [between a community college and four-year school]. The whole environment, seeing all of these mixed people there, the school is beautiful, the campus is beautiful, and I loved Berkeley. Blondie's pizza and telegraph, I loved. I just loved it.

Tom's experience at Berkeley was enough of an impetus to spur him on to apply for and receive Pell Grants and other federally sponsored loans that enabled him to continue college at four-year California schools.[8] With these monies, he transferred first to California State, Pomona, and then to the University of California at Irvine, where he finished his undergraduate degree and earned a B.A. in English. While there, he also had the op-

---

[8]Many more opportunities for educational funding became available during the years Tom was born and grew up. For an overview of their impact on college admissions, and especially community colleges, see http://www.aacc.nche.edu/Content/NavigationMenu/AboutCommunityColleges/HistoricalInformation/SignificantEvents/SignificantEvents.htm. Included at the site is the following statement: "Beginning with the Higher Education Act of 1965, the 1972 amendments to the act, and subsequent amendments and reauthorizations (including the 1992 higher education amendments), the federal government made it possible for practically every American to attend college. Included in current legislation is the federal Pell Grant program."

portunity to participate in a university exchange program that took him away from California for the first time. This experience outside of California at the University of Tennessee, Knoxville, was very satisfying for Tom. He says:

> When I first left L.A. in September 1987, to attend the University of Tennessee, I was ecstatic to be seeing and living in another part of the nation. We hardly ever went anywhere on vacation when I was little, so I regarded this year abroad as a quasi-vacation. When I got there I loved the tall trees, the mountains, the rivers, the southern people, even the snow. . . .

Tom's love affair with college campuses would continue. He went on to earn his M.A. in English literature at Georgetown University, with the help of a Georgetown Community Scholars Fellowship. Over the years, he discovered that he was a good candidate for minority fellowships without which, he maintains, he would not have had the means to earn an undergraduate or graduate degree. When we first met Tom, who prides himself as being a onetime "at-risk affirmative action beneficiary," he had finished his master's degree at Georgetown and was a very successful writing instructor at Savannah State, a small, historically Black college in Savannah, Georgia.

In turning to Melissa, we see a somewhat different family history of education and childhood progression through schooling. Melissa's mother finished high school and then majored in nursing at Bennett College for Women, a historically Black college in Greensboro, North Carolina, before leaving school to marry Melissa's father, who at that time was an enlisted soldier in the army—in Melissa's words, "a regular old foot soldier"—and to raise a family. Before Melissa's father retired from the military a few years ago, however, he had worked his way up through the ranks and had attained the rank of Lieutenant Colonel. Melissa's mother became a military wife for the most part, but while Melissa was growing up she also worked as a nurse's assistant and then eventually on and off as a deli and bakery worker in supermarkets. The supermarket jobs were easier to find, given the constant relocations that accompanied military life. Like Tom, Melissa was fairly successful in school, influenced to a great extent by the consistently high value her parents placed on education and literacy. During her childhood, she remembers, for example, the literacy activities in which her parents participated:

> Well, my father [was] always reading all the time. You know if I look back over the times in our lives I can always see him stretched out with the paper or some kind of manual or some kind of book or something. I always remember him as a reader.

But my father's punishment for me when I was younger, I had to copy the dictionary. If I got in trouble and was being irresponsible I had to write a paper about responsibility and privilege.

My mother, my mother was like a romance novel reader right before she went to bed. That was her little thing. She would read these little Danielle Steele's or some kind of Harlequin [novel].

As in many middle class families, reading, and writing, were integral to Melissa's upbringing.

Despite her entering school in Columbia, South Carolina, during the height of desegregation, Melissa avoided much of the violence and mayhem that often marked early school desegregation efforts, thanks to her mother. She was enrolled, first, in a special Montessori school, "primarily for African American kids," she explains, and then in an all-Black, Catholic elementary school she attended while her father was in Vietnam. As she elaborates,

This was all during the time that my father was back and forth between Vietnam and, so my mother was trying to put me in places, where, bless her heart, I was being enriched and cultivated, you know. There was so much going on in these schools to put out really good Black children.

Melissa's mother's best efforts, however, could not shield her daughter in the early 1970s from experiencing the outrageous behavior that sometimes accompanied desegregation. When her family moved from Virginia to Louisville, Kentucky, for example, they drove into a huge political protest "complete with burning school busses and picket signs." But it was also during the 1970s, when Melissa was 12 and U.S. Bicentennial celebrations were taking place across the United States, that she had the opportunity to hear one of the premier orators and political activists of our time. Barbara Jordan, then a member of the U.S. Congress, the first Black woman ever to represent Texas in this government body, gave a speech at the Fourth of July celebration on the Washington Mall, and Melissa was there. She says, "I swore at 11/12 years old, that I wanted to be just like her, and I taught myself how to type that year." Barbara Jordan was so articulate and smart that Melissa determined that she herself needed to learn appropriate literacy technologies if she ever was going to be anything like this amazing woman.

Throughout her school years, Melissa primarily attended military-supported schools that were clearly not segregated and which had their own independent administration and bus services. When asked about moving so much, both in the United States and in Europe, she says that she accepted her many moves throughout school "with a grain of salt—and that the transitions weren't so bad." Her main memory has to do with coming back to stateside schools from Germany. Here's how she describes the experience:

> I just don't remember having too much stress [from moving]. The only thing I can remember is when I was in Germany, there was so much enrichment that went on outside the classroom that made you a lot smarter than you realized you were becoming. You know, you just got really savvy about some things and then when I came back to the States and I was confined to the classroom again, because I went to a civilian school for junior and senior year, I found it, I just got really edgy, you know, I got really bored—I really wanted the go-see kind of education again.

Melissa's family returned to the United States in 1980 where her father, now as a Lieutenant Colonel, was stationed in Fort Stewart, Georgia. She graduated from high school in 1983 and attended two southern state universities through her sophomore year, first the University of South Carolina and then Georgia Southern University, moving to Statesboro, Georgia, to be nearer her parents' home. During these years, she remembers attending an all-night college party when Vanessa Williams became the first Black to win the title of Miss America. She says, "As the sun came up and everyone was laying around the living room, the news of a Black Miss America rang in the house like reveille. Everyone was glued to the set." These years of many firsts for Blacks and women gave Melissa confidence to strike out on her own, seeking her own goals regardless of how undefined they might have been at the moment.

As Melissa contemplated her future in the 1980s, technology continued to assume great importance in the U.S. military-industrial complex during what had now become the Reagan presidency. As mentioned in chapter one, the military's need for increasingly sophisticated technological weaponry and high-speed communications had already resulted in ARPANET, a conglomeration of networks that, by 1981, had 213 hosts and was adding a new host every 20 days ("Life on the Internet," 1997). Originally developed to enable U.S. military leaders to communicate with one another in the event of a nuclear attack, it was now becoming a popular communication medium for people outside the military. In 1982, the term Internet was coined ("Life on the Internet," 1997) as the myriad connections of networks that made up the ARPANET came to be viewed as one. And, in that same year, the computer became *Time Magazine*'s "Person of the Year" (Friedrich, 2002). During this time, the personal computer industry grew exponentially, and corporations, along with schools and universities, began to claim microcomputers and the Internet as their own. Although Melissa had benefited a great deal from her education outside the United States, during these years neither the schools for military dependents in Europe nor the high schools and universities she attended in the United

States provided her with access to the new personal computers. In these early years of microcomputer technology, however, many people, including Melissa, had begun to understand that computer expertise and its accompanying literacies were key factors for success in an increasingly technological culture.

In 1986, Melissa left Georgia Southern and joined the army. Like her mother at Bennett College, she first trained as a licensed practical nurse, a profession she too decided to abandon before long. Her next years included marrying a man whom she met in the army, her own discharge from the army, and then her resumption of a military life as she moved from place to place during her husband's ongoing military career. Melissa was always comfortable in the army, but outside the military, she found life, in her words, "a little crazy." She says,

> [Out of the army] I worked as a member services representative in the credit union for a while. That was okay except it really got on my nerves to work with civilians because there was no structure. You basically would do whatever you wanted to do. Whatever you wanted to do; nobody cares about your title or anything. And that drove me nuts a little while. Because I was [so] much a part of the military structure with my husband being in, my father being in, and it was just so engrained [in me] that I found the whole civilian working structure a little crazy. I moved back to the States and worked odd jobs, part-time things, until I became a paraprofessional in a middle school.

Melissa's work in the middle school was sufficiently rewarding that it gave her the motivation to go back to school and finish her degree even though she had also become a mother and had borne two children during this time. Like Tom, she first attended a community college (in the town where her husband's military career finally deposited them) and then went on to a four-year university, receiving her bachelor's and master's degrees in English from the University of Illinois. Funding for her master's degree was provided through a special Scholar's Fellowship from Parkland College that enabled Melissa to return to Parkland as a full-time faculty member in 1998. Since then she has gone on to accept a tenure-line faculty position with Midland Tech, a well-respected two-year college in Columbia, South Carolina.

As we mentioned, Melissa and Tom are just old enough that neither had experiences with computers during high school. Despite being born in the same year, however, their attitudes toward working with the new technologies are dramatically different. Although a friend introduced Tom to computers early in his undergraduate years, he really didn't use word processing until 1988 when he majored in English at the University of California at Irvine. When Tom was asked about how computers fit in with his life and work, he recalled a recent article he had read in the *LA Times* about Latino families resisting computing technology because it failed to provide the necessary personal interaction and connection. At the time of his interview, Tom noted that he preferred not "to write all [this] stuff out," but as long as he was near a university with computers, he also had no desire to buy a computer.

When asked for what purposes he first used computers, he responded, "Almost the same as what I use them for now—only to write papers. That's primarily how I still use them, just for papers and e-mail." He started using e-mail in 1996 for his teaching. Although he has used the Web to find former classmates' e-mail addresses and has recommended a Web site on surfing to his brother, he summed up his attitude toward computer technology with these words:

> I hate—this is one reason why I don't think I'll ever use the Web for a lot of research—I hate just staring at the screen. I want to have something in my hands. So even if I needed [an article], the *Chronicle of Higher Education* is on-line or *College Composition and Communication* is online or something else, I would much rather go somewhere and get it so I can have it in my hands. I just don't like sitting there in those little uncomfortable chairs and facing the screen the whole damn time. I never was a video game person either. I'd much rather be outside doing stuff.

Tom underscores similar reasons for disliking video games in the following excerpt:

> When the boring game of Pong came out, I was about 12 and outside, playing basketball, soccer, football, hide-and-seek. . . . When the boring games of PacMan and Donkey Kong came out, I was about 16 and outside, playing basketball and football, running track, and hanging out with friends who didn't own, or plan to buy, computers. As a street-ball-playing, scraped-knee kid who had to be escorted by an older sibling into the apartment on many a night, I could not grasp why any healthy body would spend time sitting in front of a screen . . . chasing some beeping blip. . . . If you could run, I reasoned, you should be outside with me, Ray-Ray, Javi, and the rest.

Tom much preferred as a boy, and continues to prefer as an adult, the physical contact that outside sports provide to the attraction of video games. In the context of his graduate work and teaching, he frames the problem somewhat differently, but comes up with the same conclusions. He notes that because "graduate studies can be a lonely haul," he copes with that isolation through intramural soccer, basketball, and other sports. Tom extends his world by meeting people from "well over 30 countries" as he plays intramural sports at the universities he attends, not by surfing the Internet.

Even as Tom continues, at some levels, to resist information technologies, there have been times when his not owning a computer has caused him problems. In his travels to other campuses around the United States on fellowships, most recently with a dissertation fellowship at Loyola Marymount University in Los Angeles, for instance, he finds that access for students varies tremendously—that even when there are computer labs, some schools have such old technology that word processing and e-mail take a great many steps and turn into a complicated and difficult process. And sometimes the lab monitors take over the computer tasks so completely that they really don't teach a person how to access their accounts for future use. Difficult access especially bothered Tom in connection with e-mail; he admitted that "one motive that could change [his] outlook toward computers would be [his] desire to be able to use e-mail with students and friends at any time of the day or night." Overall, however, even though he sometimes corresponds with his sister through e-mail, he believes that his family is in "alignment with the article in the *LA Times*—they would much rather talk to me than e-mail me any day."

Although Melissa values deeply her family connections in South Carolina—she accepted her new teaching job in Columbia, in part, so that she and her sons could spend more time with their extended family—she does not view computer technology as interfering with her personal or familial relationships. More than anything, she regards information technologies as contributing to personal success and even sees them as enabling proactive political commitments that she would otherwise neglect. Here's how she understands her community and political activism as far as communication technologies are concerned:

> I'm not out on the street with a sign or anything, but I'm actively [participating], if I cross a site and it's talking about something that I need to be socially conscious about, and there is an area where you can respond to this or something like that, I'll respond . . . if I had to share a face-to-face space with somebody else, I would probably be more introverted about it, you know—I don't always want people to know my political affiliations. But I can share my political affiliations with this tool, you know.

Melissa extends her world through meeting people on the Internet, not through organized sports. Thus, each of these two people enjoys, in his or her own way, the vital exchange that meeting new people provides, but each goes about achieving an expanded sense of community in very different ways.

Wondering whether her early computing experiences had also been favorable, we asked Melissa about her first encounters with information technologies. Her immediate response to questions regarding her early memories of computers included the following memories:

My first memory of a computer? A computer for me was something to be used by skilled people. And it was so far out of my grasp. It probably was not until I was well out of high school—I'm even thinking that it was after the army—yeah, it was when I worked in a bank. All I knew was how to flip it on, put my little password in, and do my own work.

But once Melissa started working with computers, she had no fear of plunging right in. She says:

It wasn't until I wanted this temporary job and it required that I have data processing skills on a certain kind of computer. I lied. I lied. I made my resume sound like I knew every computer program out there and hadn't even learned on it. I was writing stuff like Lotus, you know, and didn't even know what it meant. Excel, didn't even know what it meant. I'm like, yeah, I do it, I do it, you know.

And so when I got the job—I did get the job, because, you know, I've got the gift I guess. I got the job and I remember that on the first orientation day I took the manual home to the computer and I read and I studied that thing all night and the next day I knew how to turn it on, I knew how to get into the program, I knew how to input information just from like familiarizing myself with that manual. And I had those people convinced. I had them convinced that I knew what I was doing on the computer. So that catapulted me into other jobs that required computer skill and I just, that's what I remember doing, getting the book. It all came with the book.

In the same way that Melissa remembered her father learning from the army manuals she watched him read as a child, Melissa took on computers. She read the instruction manuals associated with computing. She says she educated herself through self-application packets and "learned Excel, learned Lotus, learned Word, learned e-mail" and then finally in the 1990s went out and bought herself a Packard Bell. For Melissa, computers denoted privilege; they were for important people, for government professionals, or for bank officials who handled money and important documents. From her father she learned that computers were also intimately connected with systems of war. They required a particular kind of expertise but also gave those who worked with them power over their lives and the lives of others. Melissa's determination and middle class status, reinforced daily by her life in the military, played a significant role in giving her the confidence to gain that power. At the time of her interview, Melissa had taken on the Web for research with her students as her opening epigraph begins to explain. She wanted to encourage them to use the Internet like she did, to focus on social issues that were important to them (and to her). If the online world could help her speak up and out, she contended, then it just might aid her students' literate activities and help them write themselves into global political conversations.

Cultures and Literacy Values

What can we learn from these two case studies? First of all, we can begin to see that culture plays a critical role in shaping values regarding the literacies of technology and that, at the same time, the literacy values and practices of people and groups also shape cultures. Tom uses the *LA Times* article to argue that Latino culture may not be one that generally embraces computing technology. He contends that computer-mediated communication technology deprives the people with whom he identifies from hearing one another's voices. Although Tom viewed his own family as not entirely typical of Latino culture, noting that his mother was divorced, his father deceased, his brother almost divorced, and his sister had moved out of California, he still identifies himself as a Mexican American who has strong family and community ties. Computing technology, although necessary to him for his writing and teaching, has not been, in his eyes, truly a part of what is important to him. As he himself explains, "I have no relationship with computers." Despite placing a very high value on literate activities, Tom views computing skills as ultimately having little to do with literacy. For Tom, the computer, more often than not, is simply a writing tool that replaced the typewriter.

Secondly, we can begin to understand that although local cultures make a difference in the literacy values and practices of individuals, these effects are complexly rendered and often overlap with many other factors at the micro-, medial-, and macro-levels. For instance, although many families with roots in Latino cultures place a high value on certain literacy practices (e.g., Rodriguez, 1982; Villanueva, 1993; Barron, 2003), the cultures of many schools in the United States are determined by other sets of literacy values and practices, often those associated with dominant groups. These practices and values, moreover, may fail to provide contexts conducive to the success of Latino students. One study of Latino workers and their education, for instance, revealed that in 1997 only 55% of Latina/Latinos 25 years and older had graduated from high school, and only 7.4% had graduated from college.[9] According to the 2000 United States Census, these statistics have not, as yet, improved with time. Of the 21.7 million people of Mexican origin in the United States, only 6.9% held a bachelor's degree in 2000.[10] The census also notes that among the 32.8

---

[9]See Carlos Ovando's (2001) review in the *Educational Researcher*, p. 29, in which he discusses these disappointing statistics.

[10]See the U.S. Census Bureau (2001) and the series of tables presented at this U.S. government site for a presentation of demographics related to what the Census Bureau terms those of "Hispanic Origin": http://www.census.gov/population/socdemo/hispanic/p20-535/gifshow/sld001.htm.

million people of Hispanic descent in the United States (for purposes of the census, the category Hispanic includes Puerto Rican, Cuban, South and Central American, Mexican, and another subcategory named other Hispanic), Mexican Americans, who constitute 66% of that figure, made up the lowest proportion of people with a high school diploma or more (U.S. Census Bureau, 2001). In this context, with regard to formal education, Tom stands out as quite extraordinary—statistically an anomaly in his own culture—having earned a bachelor's, master's, and PhD in English studies (although he almost got into a fist fight with his brother about majoring in English because his family doesn't view teaching as a sufficiently lucrative field). We would argue that the value Tom places on conventional alphabetic literacies, his love affair with college campuses (and learning), as well as his love of sports and the communities that sports provided, and continue to provide, motivated him personally and helped him cope with the various cultural contexts he encountered in school.

Melissa's values, too, rooted in her African American culture, her military culture, and the academic culture she inhabited and which she continues to inhabit, seem to have complexly affected her digital literacy practices just as she herself continues to shape the various cultures in which she participates. As an African American, for example, Melissa believes her literacy values and practices, and her digital literacy practices, have been shaped, at least at some level, by her African American heritage. Shirley Brice Heath's (1983) landmark study, *Ways with Words*, for example, maintained that reading among the African Americans she studied was more often than not a communal affair rather than a private affair. Heath noted that "the group activities of reading the newspaper across porches, debating the power of a new car, or discussing the city's plans to bring in earthmoving equipment to clear lots behind the community, produce more speaking than reading, more group than individual effort. . . . On all occasions, [the residents] bring in knowledge related to the text and interpret beyond the text for their own context; in so doing, they achieve a new synthesis of information from the text and the joint experiences of community members."[11]

Melissa, similarly, understands digital environments as a focal point for interacting with people. For her, information technologies can facili-

---

[11]Heath (1983), p. 201. See Shirley Brice Heath's *Ways with Words*, most notably the sections in chapter 6 (pp. 190–235), in which she writes of the literate traditions of Trackton, the Black community in her study. Although written before the advent of people's extensive use of communication technologies, Heath points out that literate practices among the African Americans she studied often occurred in the context of a community activity. See especially the paragraph on p. 200 that begins, "Community Literacy activities are public and social."

tate community building by enabling political activism. Thus, she does not see computers as isolating and alienating. For Melissa, as Heath (1983) noted, "literacy events . . . bring the written word into central focus in interactions and interpretations" (p. 200). In Melissa's case, however, many literacy events occur primarily online. Whereas Tom's use of computers often signals to him that he is apart from people, Melissa participates enthusiastically in online worlds, constructing community and meaningful relations through written, online exchanges.

In the cultural context of Melissa's military background, computers have pointed to success—those who can make computers work also seem to gain power. In this context, just as it was important for Melissa's military father to have acquired and valued traditional literacies, it is important for her and her sons to value the literacies of technology. Her father came of age in an army where it was possible, as an African American man—albeit often extraordinarily difficult—to become an officer and earn the rank of Lieutenant Colonel.[12] In the military, rank, as Mady Wechsler Segal (1999) points out, "is paramount as a determinant of interpersonal interactions" (p. 257). As the daughter of an officer, Melissa was understood in military contexts to be one of the privileged. It is crucial, then, with Melissa, to not only consider the African American culture of which she is a part but also the military culture to which she refers again and again in relating her life story. According to Segal, "characteristics of the military family lifestyle include the risk of injury or death of the service member, frequent moves, periodic separations of the service member from the rest of the family . . . residence in foreign countries, normative constraints on the behavior of family members, and a masculine culture that has implications for families" (p. 252). Segal goes on to argue, however, that "some of [these] characteristic demands . . . also have positive effects" (p. 252). Melissa, too, casts her experiences with the military in a very positive light. She learned early on, for example, that there are certain expectations military culture has for soldiers and their families if they are to succeed—and Melissa was a soldier, as well as a military daughter and wife. She also believes these expectations structured her civilian life in positive ways, in part by making computers and the privileges they afford pivotal to her world.

Similarly, the academic culture that Melissa came to inhabit, and contribute to, also shaped, and continues to shape, her digital literacy prac-

---

[12]Racial desegregation in the United States military took place in the 1940s and 1950s as a result of President Harry Truman's July 1948 executive order, which declared in part, "that there should be equality of treatment and opportunity for all persons in the armed services." (p. 5). See Katzenstein and Reppy (1999, pp. 1–21), for additional discussion of this issue.

tices and values. Without a doubt, she tells us, the academic culture has greatly influenced her valuing of the literacies of technology:

> Thanks to graduate work, I learned the power of cyber(text) and discovered experiential ways of knowing how to learn to write. I hope that makes sense. For instance, I was never aware of what I needed to know or to work on to learn to write better. Using the web board and web portfolio allowed me to examine my own words as if they were legitimate text. I owned them because it was cyber-published (I'm making up a new language :)!)
>
> I continue this strategy in metacognition with my students today [in 2003], especially in the entry or bridge level writing courses. They must discover what they need to know and what they might do. We haven't made it to web portfolios, but we do PowerPoint presentations where the students present and critique their own writing. We try to make it fun and sometimes a little silly so that the emotional aspect and fear of error doesn't override the need for assessment and evaluation.
>
> I just left a class of students, and one woman actually said, "I've come a long way, baby." And she had, I had tears in my eyes. Every day I greet students as 21st century learners. I think I like referring to them as learners more than students. It certainly has a more positive connotation. The reality of the 21st century learner is that the lesson has to be compressed, colorful, catchy, and relevant to their lives. Technology, computers, and alternate multimedia have assisted me in learning and in teaching.

Thus, just as Tom provides his students, through sports, with the model of student-athlete by often participating with them in pick-up basketball games, Melissa uses her own online learning experiences to bolster her students' confidence and learning. In so doing, each instructor borrows from the various cultures that shape him or her while at the same time contributing to the ways in which literacy values within a culture are understood and sometimes transformed.

We do not want to suggest, with this discussion, that the cultures that Melissa or Tom inhabit are simple, discrete, or monodimensional; indeed, we see them as complex, overlapping, and shaded by many factors such as gender, socioeconomic status, and geography. For instance, for several people in our study, military culture, especially in locations where technology abounds, has tended to promote the use of technology even among women.[13] Similarly, for some people, African American culture, especially when nuanced by gender, may also work to do so. Hortense Spillers (1991), a Black feminist at Cornell University, argues that early on,

---

[13]As one example from our study, see chapter 2 and Karen Lunsford's story of her life as part of a military family.

given the experience of their lives, Black women in the United States were excluded from racially dominant notions of femininity. Under the right economic, social, political, and historical conditions, this exclusion may well have provided a cultural landscape in which some African American women, and in this case, Melissa, could pursue computer expertise and digital literacies and be proud of these hard-won accomplishments, even when women from other cultures, operating with another set of influences, might not have done so.

Melissa's activism in and around technological contexts—her commitment to speaking up and out—can also be understood more fully as an interaction of culture and gender. bell hooks (1989), for instance, noted that many Black women in contemporary society have struggled not to emerge from silence into speech but instead to change the nature and direction of that speech, in her words, "to make a speech that compels listeners, one that is heard" (p. 208). For hooks, the act of speech as set forth in writing can be a gesture "that makes new life and new growth possible" (p. 211). Thus, Melissa's active participation on the Web can be interpreted, at least in part, as a function of her gendered position in a culture that may, under some circumstances, value a vital public voice for women.

Will Tom's resistance to acquiring a computer or embracing technology as enthusiastically as Melissa make a difference in his professional life? Maybe. But we need to note that Tom does "do" technology: He uses word processing, e-mail, and occasionally browses the Web. The question then becomes whether his own technological literacy practices will allow him to shape a satisfying life, personally, professionally, and socially, within a larger public sphere that increasingly values communicative exchanges online. In addition, we wonder to what extent the values and actions of specific people and cultural groups that might associate negative values with computer-based literacies will shape the larger public perceptions of these practices and the broad public policies that support them. Or, stated somewhat differently, will resistance to the use and overuse of information technologies create different, but nevertheless productive, opportunities for people participating in overlapping, divergent local cultures?

We conclude this chapter with a quotation from Deborah Brandt's 1995 article, "Accumulating Literacy." Brandt (1995) argues that "[w]hereas at one time literacy might have been best achieved by attending to traditional knowledge and tight locuses of meaning, literacy in an advanced literate period requires an ability to work the borders between tradition and change, an ability to adapt and improvise and amalgamate" (p. 660). Through the cultures in which they participate, Tom and Melissa, in part, have adapted, improvised, and amalgamated the literacies they've acquired during their lifetimes, and there's little doubt that they will continue to do so. Each person has moved both within and without his or her cultural home in coming to literacy in the information age; each has crafted a cultural and personal identity that includes the literacies of technology. But the question as to whether their ongoing learning will achieve the personal and professional goals that they themselves have set and that have, in turn, been shaped and patterned by the cultures in which they engage, remains to be answered.

Those Who Share: Three Generations of Black Women

A. Nichole Brown
Gail E. Hawisher
Cynthia L. Selfe

> *Each family has a particular "ecological niche" created by combinations of nationality, ethnicity, class, education, religion, and occupation and by its individual history. (Celia Jaes Falicov, 2002, p. 274)*

What roles do families play in both changing and sustaining generational patterns of literacy practices and values? In the more than 350 face-to-face and online interviews we conducted for this project, we learned that the answers to this question are as varied as the families with whom we came in contact. One persistent pattern we observed, however, had to do with the ways in which families shared basic literacy values—both within and among generations—if not literacy practices, which were more dependent on cultural values and technological developments that changed with time. In this chapter, we trace three generations of Black women in Nichole Brown's family, all of whom grew up and acquired literacy in South Carolina during the last six decades. Although these stories should, in an ideal world, outline a narrative of promise, of steadily improving conditions for the practice of literacy, in general, and digital literacy, more specifically, they do not.

First, an introduction to those we interviewed. Sheila Martin,[1] born in 1942 in rural South Carolina, attended school in the segregated South of

---

[1] In the interest of keeping the participants' identities anonymous, we have chosen "Sheila Martin" and other names as pseudonyms. The pseudonyms that follow are appropriately footnoted as well. Demographic details, names of schools and towns, and other locations mentioned in the case studies have also been changed.

the 1940s and 1950s. Driven by the twin goals of graduating from high school and becoming a writer, Sheila excelled academically, but she had to leave school after the tenth grade to work in a sewing factory near her home to support herself and her sisters. In 1971, Sheila's sister Jean married and became the mother of Nichole Brown. Nichole grew up in Greenville, South Carolina, during the 1970s and 1980s, and inherited many of the literacy values that her mother and aunt had acquired from their family: a lifetime habit of reading, an insistence on perfectionism in writing, and a general love of learning. Nichole, however, also grew up in a culture that placed a high value on electronic literacy and acquired basic computing skills in high school. She practiced these literacy skills at home on a $300 Sears word processor and became so adept at computer-based communication that she enrolled in a master's level technical communication program at Clemson University.

Yolanda Williams,[2] Nichole's younger cousin born on November 3, 1987, is currently growing up in Spartanburg, South Carolina, where she attends high school. Educated in the technological culture of the 1990s, Yolanda began using computers to play educational games early in her elementary school years, but she has not benefited from a curriculum that fails to consistently integrate technology into learning activities. In the eighth grade, for instance, Yolanda and other students did not have access to the computer that sat on the teacher's desk at school. Yolanda could not use the computers at school to conduct research on the Web, to create multimedia texts, or even to write more conventional school assignments. As a result, she needed to depend on computers at her mother's workplace and in the local library whenever she wanted to read or write online. She was supported in this work by her mother, Beth Williams,[3] who plans on purchasing a home computer soon. Nichole, the most technologically sophisticated member of the family, fears that Yolanda's schooling continues to limit computer-rich instruction to a small set of college-prep students and is depriving her young cousin of a high-tech education.

Our goal for this chapter is to trace the ways in which Sheila, Nichole, and Yolanda acquired and developed literacy, in general, and digital literacy, more specifically, within the context of the historical and social events that characterized their time and milieu. To provide readers with a broader context, we have also located the participants' interview responses in the large-scale historical, political, and social events that occurred during their lifetimes. The selection of these historical frames is a subjective effort, but one that we have tried to corroborate through follow-up interviews and conversations with the participants.

---

[2]"Yolanda Williams" is a pseudonym.
[3]"Beth Williams" is also a pseudonym.

The Case Study of Sheila Martin

On September 9, 1942, against the backdrop of U.S. participation in World War II, Sheila's family, Black South Carolinians who had been sharecropping for two generations prior to her birth, lived in a small town in a rural county of the state that was, by the end of the 20th century, to house a museum honoring the history of the Ku Klux Klan. Sheila's birth, which occurred three years after Marion Anderson was refused the right to perform in a hall owned by the Daughters of the American Revolution and two years after a presidential election in which "only 2.5 percent of southern blacks voted" (Bondi, 1995, p. 302), came at a dramatic historical moment for Black citizens in the United States. During the next two decades, important changes were effected in many of the social, military, and political policies that institutionalized racism in the United States. In part, these changes came as a result of the cumulative exigencies of two world wars and, in part, as a result of a rising tide of political activism on the part of Black citizens across the United States.

As the 1940s began, and President Franklin D. Roosevelt encouraged U.S. citizens to take increasingly firm stands against Nazi racism in Europe, Black activists exploited the opportunity to highlight the racist policies of their own government: among them the existence of segregated military services and school systems, a lack of labor opportunities and equitable salaries for Black citizens, and the abrogation of civil and legal rights in cases involving African Americans. In a targeted effort to address these concerns, A. Phillip Randolph, leader of the Brotherhood of Sleeping Car Porters, threatened a massive march on Washington, D.C., in 1941 to protest labor injustices for Black workers. With this effort, Randolph is said to have initiated the modern civil rights era (Bondi, 1995, pp. 243–244). Roosevelt, faced with the necessity of mobilizing U.S. resources in support of the war in Europe, recognized immediately that the nation's capital could be paralyzed by such a march and bowed reluctantly to the pressures. He issued Executive Order 8802, aimed at eliminating discrimination in government agencies, job-training programs, and defense contracts. The President also established the Fair Employment Practices Committee to investigate violations of his order. Although Roosevelt's order was generally decried by critics and its spirit ignored by employers, the political crisis served to solidify the status of Black labor leaders like Randolph, the "Gandhi of the Negroes"; put the United States military on notice that integration of the armed forces was inevitable; and convince African Americans that mass protest could achieve political ends (Bondi, 1995, pp. 243–244). By 1942, partially as a result of such actions, and the rising tide of Black activism that accompanied them, African American leaders began to assume positions of increasing importance and visibility in the United States: Charity Earley, for instance, had become the first Black commissioned officer in the Woman's Army Auxiliary Corps, and William Dawson had been elected as a congressional representative from Georgia (Harley, 1995).

By 1943, recognizing the continuing need to combat the social institutions supporting racism, the Congress of Racial Equality (CORE) was formed by Black citizens committed to political activism and civil disobedience; and, by 1944, the United States Supreme Court had ruled against all-White political primaries in *Smith v. Allwright*. The work of Black activists during the early 1940s also resulted in *Chambers v. Texas*, which overturned the "conviction of Black defendants in the South on the basis that blacks were legally prevented from serving on juries" (Bondi, 1995, p. 302). Despite the increasing effectiveness of activists, however, a number of barriers to Black voter enfranchisement remained in force "including literacy tests and the poll tax" (Bondi, 1995, pp. 244–245). But although such changes characterized the lives of Black citizens in some spheres, the lives of rural African Americans in the Jim Crow environment of South Carolina remained much the same as they had for a number of generations. In the year Shelia was born, for example, although many Black servicemen had returned from World War II with skills that were marketable in urban areas and many had emigrated with their families to northern cities, at least 44,194 African Americans still earned their living as tenant farmers in South Carolina, 22,061 were employed as croppers, and 73.7% of all farm laborers in South Carolina were Blacks (Smith & Horton, 1995, p. 129). This was true despite the fact that the population of African Americans who lived on farms in South Carolina had decreased 22.2% from 1920 to 1930 (Smith & Horton, 1995, p. 143) and the fact that the population of Black tenant farmers had decreased by 28% in the wake of the Great Depression from 1930 to 1940 (Smith & Horton, 1995, p. 129).

Nor was the employment situation in the South extraordinary during this time. National census figures, for example, showed that, during the year Sheila was born in 1942, 35% of the jobs Whites held were considered to be white-collar positions, 37% were considered blue-collar, and 17% were identified as farming jobs. In contrast, only 6% of the jobs that Black citizens held in this same year were considered white-collar positions, 28% were considered blue-collar, and 32% were considered farming jobs (Smith & Horton, 1995, p. 108).

Sheila, as the daughter and granddaughter of Black tenant farmers in a state known to embrace the spirit, as well as the law, of Jim Crow, grew up in conditions that reflected the combined effects of institutionalized racism and poverty. With her mother, father, and four brothers and sisters, for instance, Sheila lived the first nine years of her life in a three-room house:

It was a little small . . . house, it had about three rooms, and we had like—let's see, I'm trying to remember. How did we heat that old house? I think it was a fireplace in it, and we all slept in that one room, and we had the living room and a kitchen.

And then we moved to a nicer house just before [Mama] died, and it was a, we called it the White House, cause it was a white house, and it had—let's see, one, two—it had two bedrooms, had a living room, it had a kitchen. So it must have been a four-room house, and it had a nice yard with trees in it. And, uh, had a well out in the back, and it was nice. We had a nice house.

But Sheila's parents were determined that their lack of economic resources would not provide an excuse for intellectual impoverishment in the family. Both of Sheila's parents had attended school, and the value on literacy ran high in the family when she was growing up. Her mother, in particular, Sheila remembered,

. . . she wanted us to always go to school, to, get an education, because back then she knew that education was going to be the thing, you know, for people to try to survive in this world. We were going to have to have an education. . . . She stressed that she wanted us to go school, and she asked my grandmother when she was dying to . . . keep us in school. That's one little thing she wanted her to do.

Sheila's mother also took an active role in preparing the five children for school and modeling literacy, even after her husband died in 1951, and the family experienced tighter economic circumstances:

My mother read to us all the time. . . . Before . . . [my dad] died, when they were together . . . she would buy story books like *Snow White* . . . I don't where she got them, but she had all *The Gingerbread Man,* and all that stuff. She did you know, she always read to us. Funny papers . . . Dick Tracy and what's the little man's name? Uh, Dagwood . . . and Little Orphan Annie.

. . . After my Dad died . . . when we were on welfare, people came and gave us books.

When Sheila was 10, her mother died, and the five children moved in with their grandparents, who still had seven children of their own at home.

And then we moved right up the street with my grandmother and we could look from her house to our house. And it was a busy house. It had about—one, two, three—it had about three bedrooms and a living room, dining room, and kitchen. And a big yard with trees all around the house, like an oak grove. . . .

It was crowded, it was crowded, cause we had, the boys had a room, all the boys had a room, and the girls had a room, and my grandmother and grandfather slept in the living room. So it was crowded. We had a long table, great long table and we had benches around the table so everybody could get around the table to eat. . . .

Yeah, [laughing], we had a fireplace in our room, the girls room had a fireplace. And the fireplace was in the living room where my grandparents slept, so we had two fireplaces. And we had water from the well, and my granddaddy had gardens. . . . In the winter time, you know, my grandmother had . . . canned food, put up food . . .

At her grandparent's house, Sheila not only continued reading, she began to write, as well, although the crowded conditions in the house seldom allowed for the kind of privacy for which she hoped.

I've always, I had a very good imagination. So I think I told stories at that time when I was growing up more than writing . . .

I started writing when I was probably about 14. And I remember writing a diary, when I was about 14. It was something personal, and my grandmother she got it and read it . . . it really broke my heart because . . . I think she was looking for something ugly in there and [there] wasn't . . . just my feelings and thoughts about things. . . . So she brought it back to me, you know, 'cause . . . I really didn't want her to read it, 'cause it was just personal stuff. . . . It was how I felt about a lot of things, but she didn't find anything ugly in it so she couldn't say anything about it . . .

I would read . . . those magazines, true stories, and that gave me a lot of ideas about life and what people were going through—you know, other than what we were going through, and how other people lived. . . . Some of those stories I still remember. . . .

I mean . . . stories like when people . . . met and fell in love and got married, and things they went through—challenges, and having families, values, and morals—and all that stuff I learned from books.

The value that Sheila's family placed on literacy reflected the value they assigned to formal education, in general. Sheila, however, enjoyed her elementary and secondary school years not only because they afforded her the opportunity to learn, but because they also provided her the chance to expand her social horizons:

. . . [M]y grandparents were very tight, they were very strict on us. . . . [A]t school I made friends easily . . . and I studied real hard in school. . . . [M]y biggest dream was to graduate from high school, which is what I really wanted to do.

And I wanted to become an actress . . . I used to be in plays, they used to put on plays at school all the time . . . talent shows and all.

Sheila's goal of graduating from high school was not an insignificant effort. At the time Sheila entered first grade in 1948, for instance, Black

schools in the South remained segregated under *Plessy v. Ferguson*, which
was passed in 1896. This Supreme Court decision provided the legal foundation for separate-but-equal educational facilities (Bondi, 1995). In this
environment, per-pupil expenditures for White students in South Carolina were $148.48/year, whereas per-pupil expenditures for Black stu-
dents were only $69.65/year (Smith & Horton, 1995, p. 723). Given such
conditions, it is not surprising that, in 1947, only 8.5% of Black citizens
over 25 years of age had completed four years of high school (Smith &
Horton, 1995, p. 534). Nor was significant improvement of this situation to
occur in the next few years. By 1950, when Sheila was in second grade,
32.5% of U.S. citizens ages 25 and over had finished four years of high
school, but only 12.9% of Black citizens had done so (Smith & Horton,
1995, pp. 534–535).

In fact, systematic attempts to integrate schools in the South would not
begin until 1954, when the Supreme Court ruled on *Brown v. Board of Education of Topeka*—the decision that ruled segregated schools unconstitu-
tional. But the process of integration even after that landmark case was far
from smooth or swift. In 1955, for example, the Georgia Board of Education adopted a resolution to revoke the license of any educator who taught
integrated classes. It wasn't until 1962 that the University of Mississippi
admitted James Meredith as its first Black student (Harley, 1995), or until
January of 1963 that Clemson University, in Sheila's home state of South
Carolina, enrolled Harvey Gantt as its first Black undergraduate.

Sheila herself never had the opportunity to attend an integrated school,
as she told her niece:

> I remember back in 1950—I was really quite young, I must have been about
> nine—I heard someone talk about integration. And my aunt [Annie Lou,
> called Aunt Butch] was working . . . [for] this lady. And . . . [this White lady]
> was talking about people . . . saying they were going to try to integrate
> schools. And she was telling her children that they would never have to
> worry about that because that would never happen.
>
> . . . My aunt came home and told us about it. And at that time this man,
> Martin Luther King Jr., was very young, but he was trying to get that thing
> started . . . about civil rights. And I didn't hear anymore about that until
> probably in the 1960s.[4]

Despite the environment of hatred and inequality in which segregated
schooling was carried out, however—or perhaps, indeed, because of it—
many Black schools, families, and communities placed a high value on ed-

---

[4]Nichole Brown comments, as follows, in her transcript of this interview with her aunt,
"The story goes: the lady's daughter came home and said, 'Momma, they said we're gonna
have to go to school with niggers.' And the mother said not to worry, because that would
never happen."

ucation and saw it as a way of counteracting racism in the United States. Black teachers, despite salaries significantly lower than their White counterparts, were often committed educators who made a difference in the lives of students. From 1948 to 1949, for example, when Sheila was in first grade, White teachers were paid an average of $2,019/year, and Black teachers were paid $1,403/year (Smith & Horton, 1995, p. 718).

Sheila, however, thrived under the care of committed Black educators in her elementary school. She became particularly fond, for example, of her third-grade teacher, Ms. Beasley, who both recognized the sacrifices that Sheila's family made to keep her in school and encouraged her scholastic achievements:

> . . . I had one teacher that particularly took an interest in me. Mrs. Beasley. . . . She did. She was good to me. . . . We went through some hardships . . . She knew that we didn't have any food. . . . We would go to school without any food, and so she found that out, so she would always put me in line to go and eat with the rest of the kids at school. And she was just good to me. So, she was the one, I think, that made me want to do good.
>
> . . . She saw things in me that, you know, that everybody else seem like they overlooked. . . . You know, at one time I was kind of angry, and I would get into a lot of fights. . . . One day, she took me outside, and she told me that I wasn't a bad person, that I was a good person. And it just really, really made me feel like she really cared, and I just cried and cried because she told me, "you're not no bad person."
>
> . . . She knew that I needed somebody to care about me. So I just sucked it up like a little hungry bird, I did. And she was so good to me—I never will forget her. She made me feel like I could do good, made me feel like I was special. . . . Even though I didn't have . . . clothes like other kids had and money . . . she didn't slight me at all; she made me feel like, "You just as good as everybody else."
>
> And that really helped me . . . even though now, you know, I don't feel less than anybody. I might not have as much, but I feel just as good. . . . [S]he did that.
>
> And I think people, they need that, they need somebody to make them feel like they are important . . . not that they are better, but that they are just as good. So she did. And she was the one that really inspired me to do good, to try to do good, do better. So, her name is Marjorie Beasley.
>
> . . . [S]he was my . . . third-grade teacher, but I wasn't close to her when I was in third grade. . . . [W]hen I got in the sixth grade, that's when all this took place.

Outside of school, life in the South under Jim Crow laws wasn't nearly so kind to Sheila or her family. Sheila's father, for example, who had served as a private in the Army during World War II, had returned to a South unchanged, in many ways, from a much earlier time.

When [my daddy] was walking with Mother . . . he saluted one of these . . . officers. Well . . . as a private, you know how you do in the army when you salute one another. And then . . . [the officer] told him, "Don't you see me with my wife?" And Daddy said, "Don't you see me with my wife?"

[The Officer] didn't want to salute . . . [my daddy] because he was with his wife and my daddy was Black. And so they got into it.

And the family suffered even worse situations in the years to come:

I had one uncle that I really adored. And he got killed. . . . Uncle June, my mother's brother. He was the one who took up time with me and acted like I was the most special thing in the world. I loved him more than anybody, you know. . . . He lived in Greenville, but when came home he . . . made me feel like I was just somebody so special to him.

And . . . he wasn't but 25 years old when he got killed. . . . He was coming home and two White guys, soldiers, shot him down and killed him, in Greenville.

The hatred and inequities associated with segregation, however, never completely eclipsed the joy of growing up for Sheila. She was Vice President of the local 4-H club and a member of the Glee Club. And she loved music:

. . . I loved . . . Brook Benton, I loved Nat King Cole, Jackie Wilson, Lavern Baker, and . . . Johnny Mathis. That was back in the late 1950s, early 1960s. . . . But Brook Benton was my favorite . . . "Just a Matter of Time." That was the first one he recorded. And . . . "So Many Ways," "Endlessly" . . .

. . . Back then music was different, it had a meaning to it. You know . . . I love ballads and I like instrumental songs, I don't care for rap music and all that kind of old stuff. But I love good music.

Moreover the segregated schools Sheila attended continued to provide what she considered to be a stimulating intellectual and social environment, especially high school, which Sheila started in 1956, one year after Rosa Parks had been arrested for refusing to move to the back of a bus in Montgomery, Alabama, and just about the time that the University of Alabama enrolled Autherine Lucy as its first Black student (Harley, 1995, p. 272). As Sheila remembers,

The first high school I went to was South High. . . . And that was so exciting. . . . Yeah, the school was segregated, and it was a good school. Like I said, my teachers . . . gave me a lot of opportunities. . . . I would be the one that would fill out the report cards and stuff like that. And . . . I could print really good, so teachers would come and get me out of my class and [I would] print up papers for them. . . . So . . . they gave me a lot of opportunity to excel, to do good. . . .

I didn't hate math but I didn't get to understand it like I should have, you know, 'cause I was out of school so much [helping with the family and children and in the gardens]—especially algebra.

. . . English was a subject that I liked but I had to really, really study on that. Like nouns and pronouns and verbs and adjectives, conjunctions, all that I had to learn all that and what they mean, what to do with them.

School also exposed Sheila to some of the national debates occurring in the press during that time. As she remembers,

When I was a girl, . . . they were talking about . . . the Cuban missile thing . . . and people was kind of worried about a war, a nuclear war. I remember that as a teenager. . . .

I heard a lot about racial issues such as Klans and, stuff like that. And then like in 1960, like when John F. Kennedy was the president, I think I took an interest in that because of the civil rights stuff.

Among the stories Sheila must have heard and read about during that time were the bombing of Martin Luther King Jr.'s home in Montgomery, Alabama, in 1956; President Eisenhower's signing of the Civil Rights Act of 1957, and the integration of Little Rock's Central High School by the Little Rock Nine in 1957.

In 1958, however, during the year that Sheila turned 16 and two years before four Black students from North Carolina A & T College were to sit down at a "whites only" lunch counter at a local Woolworth's store in Greensboro, North Carolina (Harley, 1995, p. 278), Sheila's time in school was cut short by economic necessity:

. . . I had to stop to go to work. . . . My grandmother, moved to Spartanburg and told me that she couldn't carry me. . . . I was 16, so I . . . had to go to work. . . . It wasn't by choice . . . I wanted to be a writer.

I . . . [became] a waitress . . . for maybe about a year, then I was a maid, cleaning up rooms. I was a baker . . . and then I worked at a store, a clothing store. Then I worked at [several factories in the immediate area].

Given the times during which Sheila attended school, and under the conditions in which she was educated, she was not exposed to computers in school. These machines, which grew out of alliances between the U.S. military effort and scientists from major research universities during and after World War II, were not developed until 1945, when the first modern computer, the ENIAC, was invented. By the time Sheila had to leave high school in 1958, the year after the Soviet Union launched the satellite Sputnik, the United States had established the Advance Research Projects

Agency in the Department of Defense to support the development of computer-based research (Zakon, 1993–2003), and Jack Kilby, working at Texas Instruments, had developed a prototype of the first semiconductor integrated circuit (*Timeline of Computing History*, 1996). It was this tiny component that made possible the subsequent miniaturization of U.S. computers and the invention of the personal computer two decades in the future.

However, it wasn't until 1968, when Sheila was 26 years old and had been out of high school for a decade, that she remembers hearing anything at all about computers. In particular she recalls learning that people were "taking a class called keypunching." Computers by this time had grown smaller, faster, and more flexible: Jack Kilby and his colleagues at Texas Instruments had developed a hand-held calculator with four functions (*Timeline of Computing History*, 1996); the first supercomputer—the Control Data CD6600—had been developed; and ARPANET, the original prototype for the Internet, was in the final stages of design (White, 1996–2001). These mainframe computers, of course, were large and expensive. They required a specialized staff to program the routines they performed, input the data they were to manipulate, and troubleshoot the problems that arose in hardware and software. Moreover, early mainframe computers, because they depended on banks of vacuum tubes, generated an incredible amount of heat and were susceptible to malfunctioning when exposed to dusty or dirty environments. Thus, these machines were often kept isolated from users in clean rooms that were maintained under controlled climatic conditions. Although Sheila was not able, herself, to take advantage of the data-entry classes that she heard about, in 1968, she became increasingly aware of the value of computers, especially as technology developed over the next two decades and microcomputers were invented, and word processing became widely available.

Part of her interest in what computers could do stemmed from her continuing commitment to literacy practices. By 1978, the year in which the U.S. Supreme Court ruled that an Affirmative Action policy in place at the University of California, Davis, constituted reverse discrimination (Harley, 1995, p. 330) and approximately two decades after she had been forced to abandon her dream of graduating from high school, Sheila had taken up writing again, focusing her efforts on poetry. As she explained, the intervening years had been too trying and too busy to provide her an environment in which she could devote sufficient time to writing:

> . . . Well, a lot of things were going on in my life as far as trying to survive, raising kids, raising my sister and brother [Jean, (Nichole's mother) and Eddie (called Bo)], and trying to make ends meet. . . . I didn't have time to think about anything other than trying to survive, so that was why.

As her life and circumstances improved, Sheila returned to writing for her own enjoyment and for that of her family. And computers, which she heard more about as her niece Nichole began using these machines in school, seemed to hold potential for her creative work:

> Well, everybody I've talked to about computers, seemed like they are very interesting. . . . For instance, if I want to write my poems or something like that, make copies or stuff, I can use it. . . . That's what I really want to use it for.

By the spring of 2001, with her niece enrolled as a graduate student in a professional communication program at the collegiate level and her grandniece using computers at the local library, Sheila, sounding a great deal like Melissa of chapter 4, was convinced that computers would be of great value in her life, even though she had yet to use one of these machines. As she told her niece,

> . . . I think computers are going to go far. And beyond our imaginations. I really do believe that—I mean, things we, you never thought about. I haven't, you know thought about a lot of things, and . . . [they have] come to pass. So I think in the future it's going to be even greater stuff.

In particular, Sheila mentioned wanting to e-mail members of her family, use computers to design and create greeting cards, shop on the Web, conduct research on antique jewelry and her family's genealogy, and learn more about her arthritis. She had even decided where she would put the computer in her home ("Probably in here in my room . . . I've got a big old space in there") and had done some pricing of machines at Walmart.

Sheila did not find the challenges of learning these applications particularly daunting. As she explained,

> Well, I believe that anybody can do it if they are trained. You know . . . I think a person can do [anything] if they are trained . . . even if they don't know anything about it. . . . If you train them . . . I believe they can do it.

When her niece asked her why she hadn't yet learned to use a computer, Sheila's response was succinct:

> It's a matter of money and someone to teach me.

The Case Study of Nichole Brown

Against the backdrop of a society increasingly enthralled by technology, Nichole Brown, the daughter of Sheila's sister Jean, was born in Greenville, South Carolina, on the 23rd of October, in 1971, into a family she considers working class. The year Nichole was born, Wang, VYDEC, and Lexitron all released dedicated, computer-based word-processing systems. The company became a corporation and began Atari to exploit the marketplace for computer-based video games (*Timeline of Computing History*, 1996). Two years after Nichole was born, the first computer-controlled industrial robot was developed and the rush to develop machines with artificial intelligence and the capacity to learn had heated up considerably (*Timeline of Computing History*, 1996).

Nichole's mother had graduated from high school in 1968 and completed an associate's degree at Greenville Tech in 1980 and a second associate's degree at River College in 1982 while she was an assembly line worker in a local factory. The situation she experienced as a student during this time differed in some important ways from the experiences of her older sister when she went to school. By 1970, for example, 57.4% of White citizens ages 25 and over and 36.1% of Black citizens ages 25 and over had completed at least four years of high school. Further, 8.1% of Whites and 3.5% of Blacks had completed four years of college (National Center for Educational Statistics, 1995, Table 8).

Like her older sister, Sheila, Jean enjoyed school and excelled in those classes she took. As Nichole recalled:

> My mother valued learning. She used to take night classes at Greenville Tech, eventually getting an associate's degree. I don't remember in what though. She took courses in speed reading, shorthand, and other secretarial topics. I don't think she ever concerned herself with finding a job . . . [in which] to use these things, but rather took pleasure in learning them. . . .
>
> In the mid-1990s, when she was in her 40s, she took a series of computer classes and received a certificate of completion. I was very proud of her for this. At that point in her life she was a mother and homemaker, and becoming extremely bored. I like the fact that she was not afraid to learn something new and that she believed in herself enough to do it.

Jean passed along to her daughter her own love of learning and the family's value on literacy activities. As a result, Nichole acquired an early love of books and reading, in part, because this activity allowed her to spend additional time with her mother:

> As a child, I used to beg my family to read my favorite book, *Sam and Jam*. I had so many books as a kid. My cousins taught me to read so that they wouldn't have to anymore. I was reading the classics very early on, books like *Moby Dick* and works by Edgar Allan Poe. I used to read a lot of poetry. I don't remember when I learned to write, though. . . .
>
> My mother and I were always avid readers. As a child, I was encouraged to read and write. It was my primary source of entertainment throughout

my childhood and teen years. My mother and I would take trips to the library every week. When I was older, we would share books because we shared the same taste in reading. It was fun to have someone to talk about the books with. Very few of my friends read.

  After school I would listen to the story hour on the AM station. I read *Red Badge of Courage, Uncle Remus, Lassie,* and some of Mark Twain's works by following along.

Nichole entered first grade in 1978, one year after Steven Jobs and Stephen Wozniak came together to incorporate Apple Computer, and the first computer camp for children was organized in the United States. As she progressed in her schooling, her mother continued to serve as a role model and to encourage her in different ways:

> ... My mother didn't take an active role in my education. Not because she wasn't concerned or involved, but because she was confident that I would do it and do it well. I was a fairly smart student and she knew that I made good grades. Her main concern was that I didn't apply myself more.
>
> I do remember that in elementary school she used to make me do my homework over if my handwriting was too sloppy. She wouldn't let me leave erasure marks or crossed out words.
>
> I don't remember my mother and I talking about the value of education per se, but I do know that it was important to her. I was expected to do well and go on to college. There was never a time in my life that I thought that I would do otherwise.

Nichole's first exposure to computer technology came in 1980, during her elementary school years, when she was in third grade. At that point in history, relatively few public school teachers were familiar with computers, given that the access to the large mainframes was limited to colleges and universities and that the mainframes themselves were so expensive as to be out of reach for most public schools. Nevertheless, the general enthusiasm for computers ran high among educators, if not always among students. As Nichole recalled,

> In third grade, a guest speaker came to our class to tell us about computers. I had no idea what they were. I don't think I had ever heard of them. But I remember the person passing around this card that had little holes all over it and wondering what the big deal was. I was not very impressed and lost interest. I remember being told that the holes were data that the computer read to get information. We learned about binary numbers, too.
>
> It was all so boring and useless to a nine year old. And the pictures showed the computers to be really big. I couldn't understand what it had to do with me.

> What I remember about computers . . . was that they were enormous in size and were mostly for businesses and the government. I know that some people in my school had personal computers that they played games on.

Feeding the enthusiasm of educators in the late 1970s and early 1980s was the invention of the microcomputer. Among the earliest of these machines to enter the market, in 1977, was the Apple II, followed quickly by the Commodore and Tandy personal computers; the Osborne, in 1980; and the IBM PC in 1981 (*Timeline of Computing History*, 1996). One of the major hopes for these small, rugged, and relatively inexpensive computers was that their integration into the educational system could help democratize U.S. classrooms.[5] Unfortunately, however, by the end of the 1980s, computers were increasingly present in many schools, but they were being used in ways that sustained rather than changed existing educational problems aligned along the axes of race and poverty.

By 1984, for example, when Nichole was in seventh grade, 14.3% of students in grades 7 to 12 reported using computers in their homes and 30.7% reported using computers at school. However, students' access to these machines in both homes and schools differed significantly for students in high- and low-income families. For example, whereas 26.1% of high-income students in grades 7 to 12 reported using computers at home in 1984, only 3.6% of low-income students reported doing so. Similarly, whereas 35.8% of high-income students reported using a computer at school, only 21.8% of low-income students were able to do so (*The Condition of Education, 1980*, 1980). This situation was mirrored in schools with high populations of students of color. In 1984, 13.7% of White students reported using computers at home, whereas only 4.9% of Black students reported doing so. Similarly, 30% of White students reported using computers at school, whereas only 16.8% of Black students reported doing so (National Center for Educational Statistics, 1995, Table 415).

Many people, especially those attending schools with high populations of poor students and students of color, continued to have limited access to computers through the decade of the 1980s, even though people were increasingly aware of the power these new machines had to change the nature of learning and to prepare students for an increasingly technological workplace. When Nichole entered the ninth grade in 1986, for example, her high school, which she remembered as enrolling approximately 40% students of color at the time she attended, was not yet integrating computers into a wide range of courses or providing most students a robust program of access to technology.

---

[5]For an extended discussion of how this reasoning was formulated, and how it played out in the decades of the 1980s and 1990s, see Selfe (1999, pp. 64–68).

Given these circumstances, in the summer of 1986 when Nichole was entering the ninth grade, her mother took the practical step of encouraging her daughter to seek access to computers outside of the regular school environment:

> . . . my mother suggested that I enroll in a summer computer course. It was for either six or eight weeks, and I got paid at the end. I think it was for poor, minority students because I had to apply at the employment office, and it was in a rather poor area of town.
> The class taught the basic programming skills of the mid-1980s. I mostly remember using the C:/ prompt and creating queries. I don't think I had access to another computer until my freshman year in college. . . .

To support her daughter's work in computer-based communication environments, Nichole's mother also bought a $300 word processor from Sears, a purchase that, although not as expensive as a fully functional microcomputer, represented a major expenditure of family resources:

> I thought . . . [computers were] something that rich people and spoiled kids had. I knew that I would never have one. Not even a question.
> I was happy when my mother bought a word processor from Sears when I was in the 11th grade. That was 1988.

Nichole and her mother were part of a growing number of people investing in a technological future, acting on their understanding that computers would continue to improve at an increasingly rapid pace for the remainder of the century, if not beyond. By 1987, for instance, it was clear to many that computers were becoming faster and cheaper and more directly applicable to literacy activities than ever before. Moreover, companies like Aldus had responded to frequent consumer requests for more communication software and created desktop publishing packages, such as Pagemaker, that were compatible with both the Macintosh and the IBM microcomputers and perfect for use in personal publishing efforts. All of this was good news for schools. By 1988, teachers were experimenting with networks that allowed students to meet, communicate, and exchange papers online; software that allowed for computer-supported text-analysis and idea-generation; and increasingly sophisticated word processing activities.

Unfortunately, the benefits of integrating computers systematically into curricula were not available to all students—even at this point in history. Nichole's own access to computers through summer programs and at home, for example, did not carry over to her high school experiences. As Nichole remembers the situation, computers may have been present in her high school, but they were not integrated systematically or robustly into the courses she took, even in her senior year:

> I was enrolled in a business class in my 12th grade year of high school, but dropped it to take accounting instead. There were computers in that classroom, but I didn't get to use them. There may have been some days that we got to go in and sit around while someone demonstrated.

Although Nichole's high school offered her only a minimal exposure to the literacies of technology, her own personal experiences with computers, as well as her recognition of the increasingly important role computers were beginning to play in the workplace, had convinced her that these machines were going to shape the future in critical ways. By this time, for instance, Nichole and other high school students in the late 1980s were aware that increasing numbers of U.S. workers were already using computers on the job, employing word processing software, and using computers for work in communication contexts.

With these developments providing a backdrop for her thinking, Nichole enrolled in college in 1990 and signed up immediately for the university's introductory course on computer applications. In that course, she proceeded, along with her fellow students, to learn about a range of computer applications:

> I took a course, CPSC 120. I learned about Excel spreadsheets and Word. At that time, Clemson had both IBMs and Apples. . . .
>
> I don't remember anyone outside of class teaching me to use computers. I mainly learned by trial and error, and asking other students who happened to be in the labs with me. Many of us were just learning to use computers, so it wasn't intimidating to ask questions. The keyboard was easy to use, because I'd used word processors before. Learning the icons was fairly easy. Things like saving and printing were easy to understand also.

By the time Nichole had finished a second university-level course in computer applications in 1991, she had become accustomed to learning computer-based literacies on her own, or with the help of other students in the university computer labs. She had grown accustomed, as well, to the value that the university community placed on computer-based literacies:

> I began to use computers to type papers and to complete the assignments that required computer usage. Mostly Word and Excel stuff. I started using PowerPoint my junior/senior year, around 1994. When I needed help, there were usually students who could answer questions. And I would call the help desk. I had access as long as the lab was open. I generally attended the lab three or four days a week to work on papers and for group meetings.
>
> The labs were standard, with several rows of computers. The times of day

that I was in the labs varied. I spent a lot of late afternoons and evenings there. There was always a gathering of students working individually or with groups. . . . I often had to go to the different labs around campus to find a computer to use. Very few students had computers in the beginning, but a lot more students did when I graduated.

I think Clemson placed a lot of value on computer literacy. Teachers, especially, would assign work that required students to use computers in a number of ways. We had to create charts and tables from data we put into Excel; insert those graphics into a Word document; and submit reports combining everything. We had to do PowerPoint presentations. Of course this is all standard stuff now, but when it was first introduced to Clemson students and faculty, it was exciting. I know that students received higher grades if they gave a presentation using PowerPoint, rather than just doing posters and such.

Clemson, of course, was not alone in the value it placed on electronic literacies. Indeed, the U.S. culture at large perceived the importance of technology as a developing sector of the economy and as a driving force of social change. By 1991, when Nichole was in her sophomore year, for instance, the World Wide Web was fast becoming a reality. At that point in history, 797,000 workers in the United States were employed in the computer services sector (Goodman, 1996, p. 44) and, in 1991 alone, 4,000,000 personal computers were sold to U.S. homes, a number that was to double within three years (Freeman, 1996, p. 48).

In 1995, Nichole graduated from the university with a Bachelor of Science degree in marketing and a minor in speech communication. During the next four years, she was employed as a buying assistant at a shoe conglomerate; as a freelance writer; as a transcriptionist for a video producer; as an assistant to a record producer, and as a reporter for a large publishing firm. In each of these jobs, Nichole used computers on a routine basis. By the time she was 28 years old in 1999, however, motivated by a desire to find a job that went beyond conventional writing and editing and to branch out into computer-assisted design work, Nichole returned to her alma mater to begin a master's level graduate program in Professional Communication. Although she knew graduate school would strain her financial resources, Nichole began her graduate career by purchasing a computer of her own as an investment in her academic success:

I purchased my computer online. When I decided to return for graduate school in August of 1999, I knew that I had to have a computer. I started researching by reading technology and computer magazines like *PC World* and *PC Shopper*. I looked at price and value comparisons, in mags and on the Web.

My computer cost me just under $1,500. I pay $38/month. I was afraid to make the investment because I knew that I would live like a pauper in grad school. But it was imperative that I have one, so I made the sacrifice.

I use the computer in the same capacity as I always have . . . [but] I prefer to work at home rather than a lab because it's more comfortable, and I am not restricted to a lab's operating hours. As far as setting up my computer at home, I call Micron support.

By the time of her interview in the spring of 2001, Nichole had become accustomed to doing quite a bit of her reading, writing, and communicating online. Her on-campus job as the Graduate Assistant Editor at the university's Publication Office, for instance, involved

. . . writing/editing/proofing copy for brochures, posters, catalogs, the alumni magazine, ads, etc. . . . work[ing] with the designers to create the visual images . . . reformatting and redesigning of existing documents . . . using Word, Photoshop, Illustrator, PageMaker.

In addition, Nichole relied on her computer to support many of her academic and leisure-time activities:

I use it to type papers, to read and send e-mail, AOL-IM, to browse the Internet for pleasure and research. I play with document and graphic designs. I listen to the radio with RealPlayer and I download music . . .

I use the Web to research various subjects, and for general news and entertainment. I have a Web-based e-mail account. I look for free graphics and images for presentations and projects. I download free design software.

I think I have an above-average skill level [with computers]. I find that I grasp new technology quickly. I am very comfortable with computers and technology. I am proficient with Microsoft Office programs, except Access. (I'm familiar but not good). I know Adobe PageMaker and Photoshop. I'm comfortable with Macromedia [Director], Dreamweaver. I am still trying to learn Flash. I learn best when I just sit down and play. I've been introduced to MOOing. I want to learn Quark [Express] and Illustrator.

Like many students, although Nichole preferred to work at home on her own computer, she also continued to value the process of working collaboratively with other students, much as she did in her undergraduate years. As a result, she occasionally practiced her design and composition work in the graduate program's specialized computing facility where other graduate students gathered:

Really I use my time in the lab to hone my design skills. It helps that there are other people who may have more knowledge about certain things. I often ask others to give me advice or feedback on my work. We all help each other. We praise and critique each other. It's almost like a social atmosphere, but a productive one.

Mostly I learned to use . . . software by asking and watching. The second-year students were really good about showing me how to use the programs like Dreamweaver and PageMaker and Photoshop. My professors gave introductory sessions, but I had to practice and learn on my own.

Nichole also continued to place a high value on computers in her own life:

I love computers. There is not a day that goes by that I don't use a computer. I am actually trying to find a way to buy a laptop so that I can take it with me when I'm out of town. I feel like I am detached from the rest of the world when I don't have a computer to use. I don't like to be gone long during the holidays because my family doesn't have a computer. I can't imagine my career without a computer . . .

I've become a cyborg. Of course I have no idea in what capacity I'll be able to use computers because technology continues to change. Wherever I live, technology will have to be fairly advanced. I think being at a school like Clemson spoils a person. You can forget that the rest of the world doesn't have this technology at its fingertips. I'll have to plan software upgrades into my budget, just like planning for a vacation or furniture purchase.

Although she fully anticipated the continued presence of sophisticated technology in her own life and profession, as she indicated in her interview questions, Nichole was far less sanguine about the ability of the educational system to provide a high-tech environment for other students in U.S. schools across the country:

The national educational system places a lot of importance on computer use and literacy. I don't think it has the financial means to support instituting those values nationally. By this, I mean that schools and school districts are having to find funds to . . . successfully educate their students. The value becomes even greater because they have to work hard to provide a technological education that the government doesn't fund. A school of 400 in Minot, South Dakota, will not have the same technological materials as a school of 1,200 in northern Chicago, Illinois. The national value system is unbalanced. One school places more value on having the standard books and supplies, while a more modern school places more value on advanced technology and new learning.

Nichole's concerns about technology were exacerbated, at least to some extent, by the experiences of her young cousin, Yolanda, in the eighth grade. As Nichole described the situation:

I am worried about Yolanda's apparent lack of computer instruction because I believe that she needs to be aware of the world that is beyond her immediate surroundings, of the opportunities that are available to her. I think it will open her mind to bigger and better ideas. I think it will instill an inter-

est to challenge and apply herself. I'm concerned that she is being placed in
the group with the non-college-prep students, and therefore, is being shut
out of those important, preparatory courses.

The Case Study of Yolanda Williams

Yolanda Williams, Nichole's second cousin, was born on November 3,
1987, in South Carolina, the year after Nichole attended the computer
camp that provided her first access to digital literacy. Yolanda's mother,
Beth, a real estate property manager, worked part time in the evenings for
the United Parcel Service as a second job. Her father, in and out of prison
over a period of six years, was not a consistent presence in the home. As a
result of her husband's absence, Beth was responsible for passing along
most of the family's literacy values to Yolanda, as well as for providing a
role model for literacy practices in the home and reading to her daughter
as a child. In Yolanda's interview with Nichole, when Yolanda was 13
years old, she described her mother's literacy habits:

> She reads the Bible, she reads the newspaper, she reads *Essence* magazine [a
> Black women's magazine], and she reads—uh, let me see. What else does
> she read? Stuff for her office . . . computer papers, mostly. . . .
>   I don't know that she likes to write, but I do know that she does write. She
> writes . . . oh what does she write? She writes Scripture, most of the time,
> that's the only thing I remember her writing . . . She writes like lease viola-
> tions, and stuff like that.

Given her mother's habits, it is not surprising that Yolanda—who
claimed to have learned to read about the same time she learned how to
walk, "before [the age of] one . . . [or] somewhere around there"—was an
avid reader herself, nor was it surprising that she believed so strongly in
the value of education:

> I read the Bible, I read school work, math, language, literature, Spanish . . .
> Sometimes magazines, novels . . . scary novels.
>   My grandmother thinks reading is very important, my mother does too, I
> think reading is important, too. . . . Oh, education is very important in my
> family.

In the context of these family values, Yolanda developed very specific
reading tastes, especially for those books she read at home. Her favorite
childhood book, for example, was R. L. Stine's *Goosebumps,* but she considered the more popular Harry Potter novels to be both "far fetched" and
"hyped up." The value that Yolanda learned to place on literate activities,
both those conventional literacies associated with formal schooling (e.g.,

reading books, writing reports and writing about her life, writing in journals) and those less conventional literacies associated with her life outside of school (listening to music and singing, reading horror novels, surfing the Web, watching television), was sedimented deeply in her life and permeated her thinking in complex ways.

During the Winter Olympics of 1992, for instance, Yolanda's hero was news reporter Bryant Gumbel, whom she admired because he was both Black and articulate. By time of her interview in 2001, when she was in the eighth grade, her heroes had become "well-educated rich people." And it was not surprising to hear that, at the end of her formal schooling, she hoped to become "a lawyer, a pediatrician, or start my own business like an entrepreneur."

Yolanda entered the first grade at the age of six, in 1993, the year after the term "surfing the Internet" was coined by Jean Amour Polly and the year during which both the United States White House and the United Nations inaugurated their own sites on the Web (Zakon, 1993–2003). Her reading and writing activities in elementary school seemed entirely unremarkable to her. Formal schooling was a part of Yolanda's life, and the typical reading, writing, and language arts activities were a part of that life as well. By the time she was in eighth grade, in 2001, the kind of writing that Yolanda was doing for school focused primarily around her own life experiences. As she described typical assignments for her English composition classes,

> What did you do over the weekend? What was your summer like? What was your spring? What did you do, or how did you like the field trip? What did you learn today? Journals . . .

When she finished these assignments, Yolanda would occasionally be asked to talk about them to the rest of the class, although she held herself to high standards in such matters and did not particularly relish speaking in public about her work:

> If [the teacher] picked you, if you raised your hand and was picked, you would stand up and tell, read out loud what you wrote. . . . Sometimes, if my story was stupid, I would not get up . . .
>   It depends on what I'm talking about. If I'm talking for a long time, I get kind of nervous.

Outside of school, Yolanda lived the life of a fairly typical teenager. Around the house, for example, she felt her life constrained by the routines of school, homework, and chores:

Mostly homework, clean up, that's the only thing I really get to do, clean up,
go to bed, watch TV, sometimes I go outside, that's mostly it . . . I like to ride
bikes, ride my bike, like to draw. I like to . . . read depending on what kind of
book I have . . . I like to watch TV; I like to talk on the phone a lot . . . I love to
shop. . . .

There is a library near our house. It's a pretty nice library. It has computers and stuff . . . mostly we go rent movies from there sometimes. And,
when I have a report to do, I go down there and do it.

These combined activities, Yolanda noted, consumed her interests and
time so completely that she had to give up some of the activities she was
involved in when she was "young"—for instance, the art class she took at
the fine arts center and the journal she kept about her life:

. . . I just write something that I'm thinking down, thinking about what happened to me this weekend . . . I kept one but I lost it. It's somewhere around
here. . . . I have too much homework to worry about—to have time for—
that. I don't have time for it . . .

Like many teenagers who oscillate between the twin disciplining poles
of parents and teachers, Yolanda considered her friends and music to be
her true sources of solace. When Yolanda moved within the sphere of her
friends' influence, however, conventional literacies were accorded little
value. As she noted, she was not even sure her friends spent time reading
or writing:

They don't. If they do, they don't tell me . . . If I see them they are either
watching TV or listening to their music or out with friends or whatever.

Her friends and she were, as Yolanda mentioned, committed music lov-
ers. In particular, Yolanda enjoyed listening to:

. . . rap, R&B, gospel, hip hop mostly . . . Yolonda Adams, . . . Aaliyah,
Usher, Hot Boyz, yeah, Britney Spears. I like, some country I like, a little bit, I
can get into Leann Rhimes, I like that. That's cool. . . . Oh yeah. Maxwell,
yeah. Maxwell, Ginuine, I can feel that.

In fact, Yolanda considered music an outlet for her own personal expression. She sang, mostly hip hop music, both at church and at home.

Like many students in her generation, Yolanda first came in contact
with computers in 1993 and 1994, when she was six and seven, through
her elementary school, a school enrolling primarily Black students and
with a high percentage of students from backgrounds of poverty. In her
first- and second-grade classrooms, Yolanda's teacher let the class play

educational games online—an activity that Yolanda remembered with pleasure. She also learned a bit about keyboarding at that time: "I learned to add and subtract, learned how to try to type. I guess that's it." At that time, however, computers were not integrated systematically or consistently into the language arts curriculum at Yolanda's elementary school given the limited financial resources available to the school. As a result, Yolanda used the machines on an increasingly infrequent basis as she passed into the third, fourth, and fifth grade levels.

Although computer use was generally on the rise in schools across the United States during this period (from the time Yolanda entered first grade in 1993 and graduated from fifth grade in 1998) her experience was not as unusual as educators might like to think. In 1994, few public school educators had adequate preparation for teaching with technology. Nationwide, for example, only 15% of teachers had access to nine hours or more of training in the use of educational technology; in South Carolina where Yolanda attended school, only 11% of teachers had access to this minimal level of preparation (Coley, Crandler, & Engle, 1997, p. 42).

Moreover, because Yolanda went to a school with a high population of students of color and students raised in poverty, she was much less likely to have access to, and sufficient instruction in learning to use, sophisticated computer equipment than were students in schools primarily serving more affluent populations. The distribution of computers along the related axes of race and class remained persistently uneven. Although 19.7% of students from families earning $50,000 to $75,000 in 1993 used computers at home for their school work in grades 1 to 8, only 5.1% of students from families earning $20,000 to $25,000 did so (National Center for Educational Statistics, 1995, Table 415). Nor did these trends bode well for students' employment prospects upon graduation. In the U.S. workplace of 1993, 45.8% of all workers were using computers on the job, and 67.7% of employees in "Executive, Administrative, and Managerial" positions did so (National Center for Educational Statistics, 1995, Table 413). Thus, it seems clear that those students who had access to a high-tech education and high-tech instruction would be best suited for a workplace increasingly dependent on technology.

Yet Yolanda's access to computers, for example, did not improve markedly when she went into middle school in 1999. Both middle schools that Yolanda attended were in neighborhoods with high populations of poor students and students of color. Although these schools, like her elementary school, had computers distributed throughout their buildings, these machines were not integrated effectively into the curricula in ways that reached all students. In the second middle school she attended, Yolanda saw computers as tools primarily for faculty members. Her classroom did have a computer, but this machine sat on her teachers' desk and was used primarily by the teachers: "They use it just about for everything they do—they need it." As Yolanda explained, students could use the computers in the classrooms, but only if they had taken a class in keyboarding skills. So Yolanda and other students who had not been assigned to that particular class had little consistent access to technology under conditions that encouraged them to learn and experiment with online literacies. In Yolanda's English classes, for example, students were not expected to write or revise their schoolwork or homework assignments in online environments, nor were they regularly involved in web-based research projects or multimedia compositions.

This situation, unfortunately, was not particularly rare despite $84 million that South Carolina had pumped into instructional technology between 1996 and 1998. In 1998, although 62% of all eighth graders in South Carolina were enrolled in schools that made at least one computer available in every classroom and 90% of eighth graders were enrolled in schools that made computers available in computer labs, 69% reported that their language arts teachers "never or hardly ever" used computer software for reading instruction, and 39% reported that their language arts teachers "never or hardly ever" used computer software to teach students how to "write drafts or final versions of stories or reports" (Becker, 2000, p. 55). These statistics suggest how difficult it is to gauge students' access to computers based solely on the numbers of computers in a specific school building. As a report by Howard Becker (2000) notes:

> Because schools are so large and composed of so many discrete parts, the amount of technology present in a school building gives only a rough indication of its likely impact on students. The same number of computers may be spread among classrooms or concentrated in a computer lab. A computer with Internet access may be in the library or in the principal's office. A better indicator of students' exposure to technology is the fraction of students with frequent access to current hardware and software in their different classes. According to the TLC-1998 national survey of teachers, the most frequent and creative uses of computers are found in computer classes . . . rather than in English, science, math, and social studies. (pp. 56–57)

One reason that Yolanda's English and language arts teachers have failed to provide her instruction in digital literacy could have to do with their own lack of professional development. In 1998, 32% of the eighth-grade teachers in South Carolina felt less than " 'moderately prepared' to implement software for teaching writing," 31% felt less than " 'moderately prepared' to implement software for teaching reading," and 13% felt less than " 'moderately prepared' in the use of computers" (Technology Counts '99, 1999).

Given the relatively dismal picture of technology use in Yolanda's middle school, it is fortunate that she had some access to computers outside of school. For example, like many students who lack access to computers at home or at school, Yolanda used the computers at the local library to type some of her school assignments; and she used the computer at her mother's office for some of her less conventional literacy activities—as she described it, to

> . . . surf the Net and look for things about stuff that we need—clothes. . . . Oh yeah, music, music videos, the stars, what's going on.

Yolanda did not have a computer at home, however, a situation that Becker (2000) points to as at the heart of the digital divide:

> . . . the digital divide separating children in socioeconomically advantaged homes from children in socioeconomically disadvantaged homes is mammoth. . . .
>
> Because of residential segregation by SES [socioeconomic status], children living in low-SES families without access to home computers also tend to live in low-SES neighborhoods, where they are less likely than children living in wealthier communities to have access through a neighbor or friend. . . .
>
> Even among families with similar incomes and parent education levels, most African-American and Hispanic children had at least 10% less access to home computers and the Internet than white, non-Hispanic or Asian American children. (pp. 56–57)

Given her limited access to technology, Yolanda did not, at the time of her interview in 2001, rate her electronic skills very highly. When asked about her computer skills by her older cousin, this young woman remarked, "I think I'm pretty average."

Family Literacy Values and Practices

In this chapter, we have traced the literacy practices and values of three generations of African American women in one family. At least three important patterns emerged in these stories that are worth noting here. First, although the findings from these cases are not generalizable, in this family and in many others that we studied for our larger project, the importance that a family attached to literacy practices, in general, had an important shaping influence on the ways in which individual family members approached the literacies of technology more specifically. Certainly, Nichole felt that her mother's high regard for literacy practices, in general—her pleasure in reading books, her insistence on attention to detail in writing, her pursuit of higher education—shaped her own willingness to learn new forms of electronic literacy, as well as her ability to do so. Similarly, Yolanda considered her mother's use of computers as part and parcel of her general value on education and her well-established habits of reading and writing. Finally, Sheila's value on writing poetry contributed to her desire to compose poetry and design cards on a computer, and her persistence and personal motivation as a writer may well lead to her success in connection with this goal.

A second important point to note, we believe, is that none of these three women understood computers primarily as machines to be used for computing and calculating. Rather, they understood computers as literacy machines, and they valued these machines because they offered new environments for reading, writing, and communicating. All three women, for instance, mentioned that computers offered spaces within which they could continue to practice reading and writing skills that they already valued (e.g., writing reports for school, composing poetry, reading alphabetic texts) as well as providing environments within which they could expand these skills, appropriately, into new digital forms that allowed for additional communicative reach (e.g., using the World Wide Web to research the provenance of antiques and family history, using software to design documents containing images as well as text, using design programs to create greeting cards featuring original poems, sending e-mail to family members; using the Web to read about music groups and rock stars).

Our third and final point has to do with the notion of progress. At one level, readers might hope and expect the stories of these three Black women to give an account of steadily increasing promise, of improved education, of better and more equitable opportunity, especially because they extend from the time of Jim Crow laws in the segregated South to the 21st century. And in some ways, this promise has been borne out—Nichole's educational opportunities, for example, have proved, in many ways, to be far better than her aunt's. Nichole's chances to develop her literacy skills, in general, and her digital literacy, more specifically, although hard won, have also been greater than those afforded to her aunt. Yolanda's story, however, complicates the family narrative in some important ways. Although she has had an access to education that Sheila would have appreciated and an earlier introduction to digital literacy than her older cousin Nichole, her literacy education has not been unproblematic. More important for this project, her education does not currently include the kind of access to computer-based literacy environments available to many students in schools with high populations of wealthy students who are often, but not always, White. Nor does Yolanda have access to a computer-based literacy environment at home, a situation still far too common among children of color and children from households in poverty (*Falling through the Net*, 2000).

Given the range of factors that people in our larger project have reported as shaping their acquisition and development of the literacies of technology, it is too early to determine exactly how Yolanda's education will proceed in the coming years. We do know, however, that there is an increasingly intimate linkage between literacy and technology in the 21st century, that students now going through educational systems, here and abroad, are not considered fully literate unless they are able to read, write, and communicate in technological contexts. These stories certainly present some evidence, however, to indicate that the technology present in U.S. schools is not being used in ways that benefit all students equally. Further, they indicate that some schools have yet to integrate computers into their English and language arts curricula in ways that provide students like Yolanda the conditions of access they need in order to succeed as readers, authors, and communicators. In this regard— and especially for students in our culture who are poor or of color—this family narrative yields both a complicated and compromised tale of U.S. literacy education.

6

Inspiring Women: Social Movements and the Literacies of Technology

Jane Parenti Blakelock
Jená Maddox Burges
Gail E. Hawisher
Cynthia L. Selfe
Janice R. Walker

> *Movements for social change are not reborn anew each time they resurge, and they do not necessarily die when they decline. Rather, social movements are continuous and move from periods of peak mobilization into decline, abeyance, transition, and back to peak mobilization again. The entry and exit of political generations is central to an explanation of how and when social movements change. (Nancy Whittier, 1995, pp. 257–258)*

In this chapter, we return to the cultural ecology of the last half of the 20th century to relate the stories of three White women who came of age in the late 1960s. What opportunities did these decades offer these three women and how might these opportunities have influenced their acquisition of the literacies of technology? These are the two major questions that organize the case studies in the following pages. As we note in other chapters, the cultural ecology within which literacy values and practices develop, both in general and in the more specific case of digital literacies, is complexly rendered at the micro-, medial, and macro-levels by a constellation of related factors: issues associated with race; overlapping formations of wealth, gender, and education; politics, social movements, and technological inventions, to name only a few. Thus, although some White women in our study who were born in the late 1960s—Paula, Mary, and Karen, as we saw in chapter 2—benefited from increased options for life choices (e.g., admittance to a greater number of colleges; increased job prospects; more educational opportunities at every level), by the time the three presented in this chapter were able to take advantage of these options, they had become almost invisible and were accepted as appropriate rights and privileges. Many of these new opportunities, however, had been brought about by the hard work and efforts of those associated with the Women's Movement. Even as these opportunities became accepted, other choices and challenges had emerged: establishing a productive balance between career participation and parenting, dealing with issues of sexual repro-duction, managing new relationships between and within conventional gender groups. As we have seen, too, some of the difficulties in acquiring literacies experienced by the African American women identified in the last chapter who grew up in the Jim Crow culture of the South changed during, and after, the U.S. protests and riots that marked the Civil Rights Movement (e.g., access to certain educational institutions and some pat-terns of employment), although those difficulties had certainly not disap-peared. Other difficulties and challenges, of course, had also presented themselves (e.g., dealing with less visible, albeit no less invidious, forms of racism; coping with cultural and familial expectations; balancing values of home and school cultures). Clearly, however, the political activism that distinguished the late 1960s and early 1970s made huge differences in some people's lives, at various times shaping, and being shaped by, the literacies that people struggled to attain and their success in acquiring these literacies. That some of the past achievements of social and civil rights activists continue to influence people's lives and literacies today may be less obvious, as Nancy Whittier implies in the epigraph at the head of this chapter, they are nevertheless traceable to particular historical moments. In other words, the effects of these movements—both intended and unanticipated—continue to influence the cultural milieu in which people live, work, and learn.

In this chapter, then, we hope to demonstrate the ongoing importance of social activism, past and present, and to illustrate possible ways in which political movements that were aimed at creating a more just and equitable society—the civil rights and peace efforts, women's rights and second-wave feminism, and other related counterculture projects that emerged with the baby-boomer generation—intersected with literate ac-tivity. We begin with introductions to the three participants in this chap-ter, all situated primarily within a context of women's (and men's) activ-ism and second-wave feminism.

Three Case Studies

As we note in chapter 2, the re-emergence of the Women's Movement, and most especially radical feminism, is often dated as beginning around 1967 (Echols, 1989). During the following year, at a women's anti-war meeting in Washington, D.C., women marched to Arlington National Cemetery and symbolically buried "Traditional Womanhood" (Zinn, 1998, p. 260), while in New York that same year, to protest the Miss America pageant, women "threw bras, girdles, curlers, false eyelashes, and wigs . . . into a Freedom Trash Can" (Zinn, 1998, p. 260). These, of course, were only some of the more publicized activities of the times. Behind the scenes in the years leading up to 1968, women and men had worked with great energy to pass legislation aimed to ensure a more equitable society (e.g., the Equal Pay Act, 1963; the Civil Rights Act, 1964; and the establishment of the Equal Employment Opportunity Commission, 1965).[1] The three women highlighted in the stories that follow came of age on the heels of these difficult but heady years, graduating from high school in 1968, 1969, and 1970.

Jane Parenti Blakelock was born on March 25, 1951, of mixed European-Italian descent, on the outskirts of Dayton, Ohio. She has vivid memories of the many different libraries to which her mother would take her as a child and of the books she would read for herself and subsequently re-read for her younger brothers and sisters. As a middle child among five other siblings, she attended a combination of public and parochial schools, finally finishing up at an all-girls Catholic high school in 1969, before going on to a four-year city college. She dropped out after a year and a half of premed studies at the University of Cincinnati. At the time of her interview, Jane was, and still is, a non-tenure-line lecturer and writing teacher, receiving full-time benefits, and working at Wright State University, a mid-size (15,000-plus) commuter-based school in Dayton, Ohio. Growing up, "we were definitely lower middle class—somewhat on the edge,." she told us. Today, she is the main support for her family of four. The wife of an artist and mother of two teenagers, she lives and works in the same state in which she grew up; has two computers in her office and a makeshift computer lab in her home; and in her spare time introduces neighborhood children to the wonders of computing. In 2001, Wright State University awarded her with the title of Liberal Arts Web Administrator and named her Assistant Director of Writing Programs for Technology. Within her college, her department, and her home, she has become the person everyone goes to when they need any help with technology: she is the consummate humanities computing resource person.

Jená Maddox Burges was born a year and a half after Jane, on September 3, 1952. Jená grew up primarily in the Southwest, despite her family's moving frequently when she was a child. Although her mother attended college briefly, she characterized both her parents as having come from

---

[1]See the Feminist Majority Foundation's *Chronicles* (Part I) for a discussion of some of the efforts leading up to women's rights legislation that distinguished the Kennedy and Johnson administrations. http://www.feminist.org/research/chronicles/part1a.html

"real poverty." Jená told us that she never remembered a time when she didn't read, and she related stories of how, as a child, she would hole up in her mother's closet, immersing herself in old *Good Housekeeping* and *Ladies Home Journal* magazines.

Delaying finishing college until after she was married, Jená earned a B.A. in her late 20s. When she and her husband decided to have children, they had already been married for almost 10 years. To earn extra money when her three children were toddlers, Jená baby-sat. To add value to her services, she would also ensure that her young clients had a couple of sessions a day on a computer, playing games or doing the alphabet, and thus made herself very sought after as a childcare provider. It was during this time that Jená went back to school to become certified as an English teacher. After her graduation, she taught in a small rural school district on a Navaho reservation outside Page, Arizona, where her husband had cobbled together a Pet Commodore computer lab at the local high school and where Jená introduced her students to typing tutorials and word processing. Today she is writing program director at Longwood University in Farmville, Virginia, and since 2002 a tenured associate professor of English.

A third colleague, Janice Walker, born on December 5, 1950, moved from state to state during her first 50 years but always remained within the rural and urban areas of the Southeast. Like many who came of age during the 1960s, Janice's career path zigzagged through the difficult times that marked her childhood, as well as her adult life, as she tried to cope with everyday living and schooling. She attended 11 schools in six years between the 7th and 12th grades, entered several relationships after high school, and went through a divorce, all the while starting and stopping classes in a variety of community colleges and four-year schools. She also participated in the life of a commune, the Athens Family, in the early 1970s and met her first husband there. Janice became pregnant in 1973 and gave birth to a child with severe health problems. Her difficult experiences in trying to find healthcare for her child and to support him financially would have a profound effect on her political activism. During this period, she managed to put together a successful career in marketing and management, only to have the bottom drop out of this sector of the economy in the early 1990s recession, a situation that placed her and her son below the poverty line. Various levels of poverty were not new to Janice, but this was the first time that her complicated and shabby circumstances qualified her and her son for fully financed college educations through Pell Grants[2] and other available means of financial aid. During the next six

---

[2]According to a government report by Christina Chang Wei and Laura Horn, the Pell Grant program continues to be "the largest federal need-based grant program available to postsecondary education students." For a descriptive overview of recipients receiving Pell

years, Janice earned first a B.A. in professional and technical writing, and then a PhD in English with a specialization in technical communication. At age 50, she became a professor of professional writing at Georgia Southern University where she continues to teach today.

The Cultural Ecology of the 1940s, 1950s, and 1960s: Changing Roles for Women?

A closer look at the times in which these three women were born and grew up reveals that even in the years preceding the 1960s, a period in which women were thought to quietly adhere to the roles of traditional wives and mothers, there were rumblings afoot. During World War II, for example, working-class women had entered the labor force in large numbers and taken on jobs in the manufacturing sector (e.g., aircraft industry, weapons industry, machine shops) where they earned a great deal more money than they had working in cafeterias and restaurants, hotels and laundries, and other low-paying jobs before the war (Jezer, 1982). The Depression, and then World War II, had helped to generate media images of women who were strong and self-sufficient,[3] and many women embraced these images as their own.

But this situation changed dramatically after World War II. As service personnel returned from the war and needed jobs now occupied by women, positive attitudes toward strong women in the workforce began to wane, and working women's numbers, often in the manufacturing cities of the Midwest, fell precipitously, especially immediately following the war. In fact, in Detroit alone, the number of women in the automobile industry dropped from 124,000 on May 8, 1945, VE-Day (Victory over Europe Day), to 63,000 in 1946.[4] Postwar attitudes came to value above all women's place in the home. Predictably, women's presence at colleges and universities also dropped significantly during these years. Marty Jezer (1982), for example, notes that "despite the growing demand for professional people and scientists, the number of female college students, in relation to male students, dropped from 47% in 1920 to 35% in 1958, and more than half of their number dropped out before graduation to support

Grants in 1995, see Wei and Horn's (2002) "Persistence and Attainment of Beginning Students with Pell Grants" at http://nces.ed.gov/das/epubs/2002169/.

[3]Marty Jezer (1982) points out that during the Depression and World War II, radio soap operas portrayed women as independent and career-focused. She lists the following titles of some of the radio soap operas of the times: "Dr. Kate," "Her Honor, Nancy James," "Hilda Hope, M.D.," "Portia Faces Life" (about a woman lawyer), "Prudence Dane: Woman of Courage," and "Mary Marlin" (about a woman senator) are just a few that were heard over the radio waves.

[4]See Marty Jezer (1982), pp. 201–218, for a fascinating account of the changing role of working-class women, Blacks, and other minority groups in postwar United States.

husbands or become housewives" (pp. 229–230). If the media of the 1930s and early 1940s sent out signals that supported strong images of women, this was not the case in the later 1940s and 1950s. While paging through the *Ladies Home Journal* and other magazines in her mother's closet, Jená was likely to have come across articles and stories with titles such as "Femininity Begins at Home," "Do Women Have to Talk So Much?" "What Women Can Learn from Mother Eve," "Really a Man's World, Politics," "Cooking to Me is Poetry," and "The Business of Running a Home" (Jezer, 1982, p. 229). Yet despite the prevalence of attitudes designed to keep women in their place, and even as families watched together the popular television situation comedy "Father Knows Best,"[5] the 1950s saw changes in women's opportunities.

As Jane, Jená, and Janice began elementary school in the mid-1950s, those same years in which the United States competed with and lost to the Soviet Union in launching the first space satellite, women had again begun to enter the workforce in large numbers. A quick overview from the late 1950s and early 1960s, for example, reveals that:

Women accounted for 60% of the growth of the labor force in the 1950s, as reported by a Senate Subcommittee on "Employment and Manpower."

More than 53% of female college graduates held jobs.

In more than 10 million homes, both husband and wife worked, an increase of 333% from prewar 1940.

Mothers of children under 18 constituted almost a third of all women workers.

Forty percent of all women over 16 held jobs.

Female employment was increasing at a rate four times faster than that of male employment.

In the sales field, female clerks made 44% of their male counterparts' earnings.

Women's average earnings in 1960 were less than 60% of men's, as compared with 65% in 1950.[6]

---

[5]For an interesting set of images documenting the 1954–1962 popular television show and its portrayal of the role of women, see "Father Knows Best" at http://www.timvp.com/father.html. Note that scenes from the show very seldom venture outside the doors of the family's home.

[6]These facts and statistics are reported in *The Feminist Chronicles, 1953–1993* (Feminist Majority Foundation, 1995). See http://www.feminist.org/research/chronicles/chronicl.html for a further listing of important events during these times, as compiled by Toni Carabillo and the Feminist Majority Foundation.

Notwithstanding the uneven advances in earnings women received for their work and in the kinds of jobs open to them, especially for those women without any college education, the early 1960s recorded significant changes. During this time, there were increased legislation efforts designed to ensure a more equitable society. In 1963, for example, the U.S. Congress passed the Equal Pay Act, amending the Fair Labor Standards Act to provide equal pay for equal work without discrimination on the basis of sex. Twenty years had passed since bills to achieve this goal had been introduced to the U.S. Congress in 1943 (Carabillo, 1993). This same year, the President's Commission on the Status of Women, which had been chaired by Eleanor Roosevelt, published a report titled *American Women* (1963). The report documented instances of sex discrimination and the inadequacy of support systems for women and their changing lives. Its many observations included the tendency for women who attended college to cluster around majors in "education, social sciences, English, and journalism" (p. 69), and it went on to point out that it was often at the graduate level that women's enrollment numbers dropped precipitously:

> The number of women earning B.A.'s was 5,237 in 1900, 76,954 in 1940, and 145,514 in 1961. But since [World War II], the percentage of M.A.'s to B.A.'s has not risen as it did in the previous period; it has remained static at between 16.3 and 18.8 percent, standing at 16.8 percent in 1961. There has been similarly little change in the percentage of Ph.D.'s. In 1961, women earned 24,481 M.A.'s and 1,112 Ph.D.'s; the comparable figures for men afford a sharp contrast—54,459 M.A.'s and 9,463 Ph.D.'s. (p. 69)

The report also underscored the "exceptional need" for women "starting out in life today [1963] . . . to be self-reliant" (p. 70). In calling for women's self-reliance, it noted the tendency for families to be spread all over the United States and the resulting decrease in the number of extended family members able to help out with the care of children and their upbringing. But it also described the reduction of the daily work required of women in the home, stating "woman's work can be finished" (p. 70). Thus, in this report about the lives of U.S. women, the commission members intimated that there would be increased opportunities for young women, like Jane, Jená, and Janice, to do more than "housework." The final paragraph of the report includes the following:

> . . . today's young woman comes to maturity with a special measure of opportunity—to live in a period when American abundance is coupled with a quest for quality, to show forth excellence in her life as an individual, to transmit a desire for it to her children, and to help make it evident in her community. (p. 71)

When the report was published, Jená, Jane, and Janice—at 11, 12, and 13 years of age, respectively—hovered on the brink of adolescence and eventually took advantage of their future opportunities in ways that the report, nonetheless, was not able to fully anticipate.

By the early 1960s, the Civil Rights Movement was well under way. In February of 1960, ostensibly as a result of employees at a Woolworth's lunch counter refusing to serve four African American college students from North Carolina's Agricultural and Technical College, the "sit-in" was born and became a viable nonviolent response to discrimination against Blacks and others. During this same year, a group of southern Black students formed the Student Non-Violent Coordinating Committee (SNCC), whose goal was to marshal support for ending segregation in the South by conducting marches, registration drives, and sit-ins (Carabillo, 1993). Although women from the northern United States who participated in the southern marches for Black civil rights came eventually to realize that they themselves were treated unequally in a movement aimed to end social inequities (Echols, 1989), their determination to bring about positive social change remained undaunted. Students for a Democratic Society (SDS) was also formed this same year and would become later in the decade a powerful voice against the war in Vietnam. In 1961, President John F. Kennedy created the Peace Corps, giving women, as well as men, opportunities to serve and work overseas. Ironically, in 1962, following its creation which was, after all, an initiative designed to send U.S. volunteers around the world to help others through humanitarian efforts and thereby contribute to preserving peace, Kennedy and Russian Premier Nikita Krushchev went down to the wire in negotiations over what has come to be called the Cuban Missile Crisis. What could have been an all-out war was narrowly averted, and armed conflict was avoided.

Arguably at its height during these years, the Cold War also fueled tremendous technological development. The launching of Sputnik in 1957 when Jane, Jená, and Janice had barely entered school, and the United States' subsequent efforts to best the Soviet Union in the race to space resulted in the development of microtechnologies that contributed mightily to the making of the personal computer. Although ENIAC (Electronic Numerical Integrator and Computer) had been developed at the University of Pennsylvania in 1946 and ILLIAC (Illinois Automatic Computers) at the University of Illinois in 1952, these were hardly machines that would make their way into the everyday lives of ordinary people. The ILLIAC I, for example, weighed more than five tons and consisted of 2,800 vacuum tubes,[7]

---

[7]For a more detailed history and photographs of these early machines, see http://www.library.upenn.edu/exhibits/rbm/mauchly/jwmintro.htm for a discussion of the ENIAC and http://cmp-rs.music.uiuc.edu/history/illiac.html for more on the ILLIAC.

not an item that could easily sit on desktops. As Janice notes with irony, "these were machines for countries, not for people." Although microcomputers finally came on the scene in the late 1970s, a number of social and economic forces needed to converge in order to pave the way for these machines to enter English Departments. The post-Sputnik panic that resulted in new funding opportunities for schools and universities promoting curriculum reform, however, was also accompanied by the creation of instructional computing programs that focused on literacy (Hawisher, LeBlanc, Moran, & Selfe, 1996). Eventually, then, when the women of our chapter finally entered university English Departments, they encountered personal computers being used not only as instructional delivery systems but also, more often than not, as writing tools.

Out of this same historical context came what some would argue was the most important social development of the time for women's future independence: the invention of the birth control pill. Although Searle, the pharmaceutical company, had applied as early as 1959 to license a contraceptive drug that came to be called "the pill," it was not until 1960 that the Food and Drug Administration approved its use for birth control. In 1961, the pill appeared on the market at a cost of approximately $10 or $15 per month, and became the first oral contraceptive available to women (Carabillo, 1993). Now women, for the very first time in history, were able to decide with more confidence than ever before whether and when to have children. Twelve years later in 1973, after years of reproductive rights activism throughout the United States, Justice Harry A. Blackmun wrote the Supreme Court decision in *Roe v. Wade* that declared abortion legal. Whether or not individual women took advantage of abortion rights or the birth control pill, the convergence of these two events forever changed decisions many women made regarding childbirth. At the very least, they had decisions to make; childbirth had become less of an inevitable consequence of being a woman.

In many respects, this brief review of the cultural ecology of the Cold War and its momentous events neglects the everyday ordinariness of the three girls' lives as they grew up. The accounts of the three, however, encapsulate the importance of the technological and social transformations that occurred during their lifetimes these last 50 years or so. In their stories we encounter the same difficulties women, and men, face today—enlisting support for college, securing the requisite credentials for jobs, juggling the responsibilities of family and work—but we also encounter challenges and opportunities for women that were less evident in times past. Unlike some of the younger participants in our study, none of these women had extensive support for technological-literacy acquisition, yet each of them managed. And they managed very well indeed. The same resourcefulness they applied to their everyday lived lives they brought to their work with computers. Instead of being the recipients of concerted efforts to provide technological literacy in school-based environments, they led—and lead—the way. Today, the multiple identities that they negotiate in their personal and professional lives are tied intimately to their use of information technologies. But let us back up and relate more of their stories. We want to concentrate on two areas: their literacy and educational background, along with their eventual and perhaps inevitable introduction to computers.

The Case Study of Jane Blakelock

Despite their ultimate technological expertise, none of the three women followed an uninterrupted academic career path as perhaps the *American Women* report might have predicted. Jane, the midwestern writing instructor, who finally completed college at age 29 when the English Department chair told her that she needed only three more courses for a degree, worked off and on in a medical office, trying to fulfill her mother's unrealized dream of becoming a doctor. Always a reader, Jane, after dropping out of college, took night courses in literature just for the intellectual pleasure of it until she learned she was nearing that degree. She married an artist at some point during this time and often found herself the main breadwinner in the family. She took graduate courses sporadically, electing to receive incompletes if something—almost anything, she says—intervened.

During this time, however, the university where she now works called upon her to teach basic writing. The developmental sector was so short of writing instructors that it didn't matter that Jane had only an undergraduate degree. Then, after several years, when she was expecting her second and last child, she describes being tapped on the shoulder by the director of graduate studies. In her words:

> So . . . somebody tapped me on the shoulder and it was a man, who was in charge of graduate studies, and he said "I was looking through your files and I didn't realize you never finished your work." And I said, I know, but the seven years has passed—you have to get the credits within seven years. "But," he said, "they are cutting the red tape right now. There are a number of women that they're doing this for. So get your work done while this is all happening to these other people; the precedent is set."

Jane did indeed then write the 50-page thesis required for a master's degree in literature and received the degree in May of 1988. Three months after writing the thesis on a conventional typewriter, Jane was given her first computer by her mother-in-law. She has now worked at Wright State University since 1980, never dreaming that she would eventually become the Liberal Arts Web Administrator and Assistant Director of Writing Programs for Technology.

The Case Study of Jená Maddox Burges

When we turn from Jane to Jená, who primarily spent her years growing up in the Southwest, we see a similarly uneven pattern of postsecondary education. Marrying a man eight years her senior not long after she finished high school and began and then dropped out of college, Jená assumed various jobs—bartending, woodworking, insurance office employment, and even construction work. She didn't attend school regularly for several years, finally finishing her B.A. in 1978 at the age of 26. In her words, "I got my B.A. in '78—it was off and on." To our minds, Jená was anything but "off" as she persistently made her way through life and school. After her degree, not only did Jená return to college for her teaching certificate, eventually teaching on the Navaho reservation for 10 years, but she also went on to earn a PhD in language studies at Northern Arizona University.

Growing up, both Jane and Jená were precocious readers. Jane was trotted off in kindergarten to read before an eighth-grade class, and Jená read everything she could get her hands on from the age of four. Both spoke very fondly of the Carnegie libraries of their youth where they spent a great deal of time borrowing books and reading. We would argue that each woman's identity as a reader didn't necessarily prepare her to be the proficient computer user she eventually became, but it did enable each of them to succeed in school at the times she wanted to succeed. School was always something at which they could excel, if and when they so chose.

Each woman also came to college teaching rather serendipitously. Jane was called out of the blue by an unknown administrator to whom she had been recommended, and Jená was recruited by a former woman janitor who needed one course to receive her associate degree. As Jená tells it,

> My first college teaching job was bizarre. A woman had been working as a janitor for the school district for many years, taking courses a little bit at a time for her AA degree. She lacked one course, a course in humanities. And I had a B.A. in humanities and so they asked me if I would teach this course. So I had this course as an adjunct, Women in the Arts, that I taught to one woman. She was amazing. It was a wonderful experience.

Because Jená had just received a B.A. in the liberal arts, the two-year college asked her if she'd teach to the janitor a course on Women in the Arts. Here was her dubious entry into the world of college teaching, where both Jená and Jane now make their careers. That the two also became English and writing instructors, we would argue, is also significant and very much a part of their identities as teachers and literate human beings. Much of their motivation to learn computers came, and still comes, from wanting to teach students how to write and communicate more effectively. Whether using typing tutorials, educational games, and word processing to teach to Native Americans in 1984, as Jená did, or engaging in web authoring and maintenance, and developing academic technology support programs, as Jane does today, their motivating goal is to provide students with what they need to operate effectively in an increasingly technological world.

The Case Study of Janice Walker

The brief description we have provided thus far of our third case study, Janice Walker, does little to identify the many accomplishments she achieved in her life, accomplishments intimately connected to her formal education, to her conventional literacy practices and values, and, eventually, to her acquisition of the literacies of technology, as well. Despite her many moves during her school years, or perhaps because of them, Janice was always a "voracious" reader, as she noted, as well as a writer. She prided herself especially on her writing abilities, attributing, for example, her success as a secretary and her work as a corporate executive to her facility with the formal practices of literacy. When she was a beginning secretary, Janice noted, the president of the company sent out a memo to all management personnel instructing them to hold all letters until Janice looked them over. As she summed up her conventional literacy abilities:

> I had a facility with language. So, I had it made—that's why I made good grades in school . . . because . . . you give me an essay exam and I'm going to make an A. I don't care what it is in. I don't need to know anything about it. It just needs to be something that I write. And anyway, so, I had always gone around the workplace calling myself a frustrated writer.

Janice attributed some of her expertise to a very fine early educational system in Miami, Florida, where she was placed in "special resource classes" between the third and sixth grades. A select group of students attended these special classes in which trigonometry, binary codes, and linguistics were taught. Although she did not return to this school system until her senior year in high school, she regarded her experiences within it as the best she received throughout her public education.

In addition to the literacy skills that Janice acquired in formal schooling environments, her family had a history of developing their own technological literacy and expertise. Her grandfather was part of a team that worked on developing the first televisions in the 1940s; her father was similarly involved in electronics in the next generation, earning a GED at age 40 so that he could attend the local vocational school to keep up with changes in technology-color television; and Janice remembers always being able to fix any mechanical device she laid her hands on in much the same way that she was later able to program and work with computers. She joked, "Mechanical devices like me. Computers like me, too. When people are having problems, I don't have to do anything—I just walk near them and the computers start working." But Janice was also very serious about the technological abilities she acquired. The knowledge she came by in the many diverse and sometimes painful workplace settings was often achieved at the expense of time she might have spent with her son or devoted to classes that could boost her standard of living above the poverty line.

During the course of Janice's varied jobs, sporadic courses, and at-home recreation, she managed to accumulate a working knowledge of the many different kinds of electronic machines that populate the workplace. She also acquired the multiple literacy skills needed to operate them. From learning to run a telex machine in her first job at 18 years of age, to mastering databases and entering information in local and national crime centers for a police department, to working with electronic ordering machines that communicate with suppliers' mainframe computers for a supermarket chain, Janice acquired electronic literacy on the job within the workplaces she inhabited. Some of these electronic skills built on skills she learned at school: In high school, for instance, she learned to type 70 words a minute on manual typewriters, and she learned how to program Basic at a community college. Her formal schooling, however, seemed less important than her actual work experience, at least as far as her development of technological literacies was concerned. Her recreation at home was also important. Janice played early computer games such as Pong with her son and built a microcomputer out of spare parts with a friend. In both contexts, at home and at school, Janice was fast becoming a member of a small cadre of computer experts of the 1980s. By the time she received a PhD in technical communication at age 49, Janice had managed to develop an expertise in the literacies of technology that few women her age had acquired.

Despite the three women's fitful passages through the academic world, all, in fact, became proficient in computers in ways that many other 50-something, White working-class women have not. In fact, in many respects, their long educational haul gave them more opportunities for learning digital literacies than a more traditional trajectory would have allowed them. While other women their age, college-educated and not, had already settled into more conventional family roles, Jane, Jená, and Janice were still students, moving from undergraduate to graduate studies in English, just as the first fully assembled microcomputers arrived in the late 1970s on the U.S. landscape. Thus, the educational settings in which they immersed themselves as nontraditional students exposed them to electronic literacies and technologies that other women their age during these times had often only heard about.

Benefactors and Sponsors of the Literacies of Technology

Deborah Brandt (1998) has written of the crucial role that those whom she terms "sponsors of literacy" have assumed in introducing people in the United States to literate activities. In defining sponsors of literacy, she explains that they "are any agents, local or distant, concrete or abstract, who enable, support, teach, model, as well as recruit, regulate, suppress or withhold literacy—and gain advantage by it in some way" (p. 166). The last phrase, "gain advantage by it in some way," is critical to her definition. In making the important connections between "literacy as an individual development" and "literacy as an economic development" (p. 166), Brandt used "sponsor" to denote a relationship where the sponsor has much to gain, often in an economic sense. Here we uncouple sponsor from the purely economic and use it to suggest not so much patronage as once used in supporting artists or sponsorship as used in advertising's commercials but rather in terms of benefactors or supporters who give little thought to the recompense or benefits that they may receive in return.

In examining how Jane, Jená, and Janice came to computers, we will see that as women they did not have access to powerful technological literacy sponsors. But each, nevertheless, had an important benefactor or supporter who made all the difference in the world as far as each woman's experiences with the literacies of technology are concerned.

When Jane was given her first computer in 1988, after she had written her master's thesis, the person who made the gift was her mother-in-law, a woman who continued to have a powerful influence on Jane's computing abilities. She herself a nontraditional student, turned down for a graduate assistantship despite her high grades, nevertheless persisted in her efforts to cobble together a career. She became a contributing editor of a nationally distributed gardening magazine, and, at the same time, provided technical support for their online forum. Today she beta-tests genealogy software for a mostly Russian international team of software developers. The high regard and respect that Jane holds for her mother-in-law is obvious in all her words. When speaking of learning computers, Jane says:

> Whenever I would run into problems I would depend on my mother-in-law, who is very savvy. She would come over and help you troubleshoot something if you had a real problem. I haven't called on her recently but used to more frequently. . . . She's given us more computers [over the years] too and

has even maintained them when something goes wrong . . . she likes to give in an area that she values and she values this and thinks everyone in the family needs good access, so she personally pulled the whole family over the digital divide with a decade of computing gifts and technical assistance.

Largely through the support of this benefactor, and her own determination, Jane was able to develop those technological skills that put her at the forefront of her own college and department. Through her expertise with computers, through her identity as a computing specialist, she attracts additional funding for her work and succeeds in areas that would otherwise be off limits to her.

When we turn to Jená, we see that her technological literacy supporter was, more predictably perhaps, her husband, who established the first computer lab in the rural high school where they both taught and who continued to help Jená learn the intricacies of computing. In writing her dissertation, however, Jená took off on her own and did all the programming and statistical work for her study of second-language writers. Thus, as a recognized professor and writing program administrator today, she has confidence in her computing abilities and is willing to take risks to improve her own learning and provide expertise for her department.

In addition to being born into a family that valued technology from the start, Janice, too, had her sponsors in acquiring the literacies of technology. In her case, although the workplace provided an opportunity to acquire literacies of technology, her knowledge frequently exceeded those of her bosses, who, in Janice's words,

> shouted over my shoulder and told me what to type until I said, no, you are wrong, and because I had just picked it up by doing it because it was language to me. It was, it had grammar, it had syntax, all of the programming languages that I used, you know, had an English language base, you know Basic and PL1, even though you had to learn the specialized grammar and syntax.

But if Janice had the requisite language and computing skills, she did not always have the financial means to acquire and maintain her expertise. Although, when working, Janice had bought a Commodore VIC 20 and then an IBM clone, in the late 1980s she could not afford the $2,000 investment in a computer and turned to a friend who helped her build her own machine out of spare parts. As she tells it:

> I knew a lot about computers, but he did too and probably more than me because he had more money and everything. He was a wonderful guy so I can't say I didn't learn from him because I certainly did. He was a political

activist for AIDS. AIDS activist. He did, he was my best friend and he did die of AIDS a few years later.

Thus, for Janice, her friend's computer expertise in building a 386, "with a tiny hard drive," literally enabled her to own a working computer during this time. Without his help, she would not have been able to afford the requisite technology that eventually supported her efforts in graduate school.

Second-Wave Feminism

Looking again at the large-scale developments and trends on the national and global levels that were taking place at this time, note that the three writing faculty came of age during the early years of second-wave feminism. Nancy Whittier (1995) has written that the "hallmark of the women's movement during the mid-1970s was its success: Activists established organizations, acquired outside funding, won legalized abortion, pushed the ERA through Congress [in] many states, and achieved at least some decrease in the public acceptability of blatant sexism" (p. 64). These were also the years in which women's studies programs proliferated throughout the United States. According to Catharine Stimpson (1986), these programs had as their goals "teaching the subject of women properly" and ending "sex discrimination in education at all levels, from prekindergarten to postdoctorate study" (pp. 12–13). Despite the fact that none of the participants featured in this chapter claimed women's studies as their own field, the reverberations of these changes in academe may well have opened doors for them, if only a crack. As we noted, Jená's first opportunity to teach on the college level was a course in 1983 on Women in the Arts, a course that was rare before the rise of women's studies' programs. In a related way, Jane's master's degree was facilitated by a change in state accreditation policies designed to remove time constraints that barred many women from completing degrees. Finally, Janice's funding for college through Pell Grants, though these awards were not specifically designed to help women, would not have been available before the social activism of the 1970s. As Janice explains:

> I couldn't have gone back to school without the Pell Grant. I'm sure civil rights legislation and open admissions had a lot to do with making that available. And that one year of Pell Grant money made all the difference in the world in my life.

As a single mother with earnings below the poverty line, Janice qualified for financial help and received the necessary support to enable her to graduate with a B.A. from the University of South Florida in August of 1994.

But it is not possible to grasp the momentum of these times without, in part, considering the full context of the radicalism that marked them. In its rejection of mainstream politics, "its embrace of participatory democracy, and its fusion of the personal and political" (p. 13), as Alice Echols (1989) put it, second-wave feminism represented a break with the past. Recognizing early on that their male cohorts in the Civil Rights Movement did not necessarily apply egalitarian principles to women, feminists, during these years, boldly proclaimed women's right to sexual freedom and pleasure. And they were able to do so in times when the possibility of unwanted pregnancy was diminishing.

As a result of the development of the birth control pill and other more effective, if not always safe, methods of birth control in the 1960s and 1970s, some women were able to decide when to bear children. This seems to be the case with Jane and Jená. Jane's two teenage daughters weren't born until she was in her thirties, and Jená made a conscious decision to "have a family," as she put it, when she was almost thirty. Asked what she did after she finished college, she replied:

> Let's see, I'm trying to think what happened then. Hmn, I decided to, once I finished my B.A., instead of going on for an M.A. in religious studies, which is what I had applied to do and had gotten admitted to the program, I decided to take time off and have a family. And I had three kids, you know, within three years and decided, it's so funny, you know, but while there's time. We had already been married seven years.

Although the late 20s and early 30s seem almost young today for having children, these women were not terribly typical of their generation when middle class White females often bore children right after college, right after they married, and sometimes before. Janice, for example, gave birth to her son in 1973 in the heyday of the counterculture when she was only 23 years old. But Jane and Jená were able to resist society's conventional expectations for women in ways that their counterparts of just a few years earlier could not. Although both women ultimately decided to have children, the freedom to decide when to reproduce enabled them to carve out identities and pursue a wide variety of interests that had little to do with traditional women's work. That Janice too was able to carve out such a life while raising a child with ongoing health problems speaks to her tenacity and determination to succeed.

When we consider the retrenchment of the 1980s—what Susan Faludi (1992) terms "backlash," "backlashes," and "backlashings"—the political uprisings and feminist struggles and achievements of the previous decade seem nothing short of remarkable. In 1982, a year after IBM personal computers flooded the market, the U.S. Congress defeated the Equal Rights Amendment. By the end of the decade, the courts had also upheld the limits on abortion rights through the 1989 Webster decision (Whittier, 1995) by allowing states to prohibit public funding for abortion unless a woman's life was endangered. Consider, also, that whereas in Jimmy Carter's administration there had been 13.5% executive appointments for women, under Reagan there were 9%, and 9.6% under the elder Bush (Whittier, 1995). As Faludi (1992) noted, this was the decade when Reagan stated that women now had "so much" that they didn't need to be appointed to public office; when the *New York Times* reported that "Childless women are 'depressed and confused' "; when *Newsweek* said that "unwed women are 'hysterical' and crumbling under a profound crisis of confidence"; and when health manuals announced that " 'high powered career women' are stricken with unprecedented outbreaks of 'stress-induced disorders,' hair loss, bad nerves, alcoholism, and even heart attacks" (pp. ix–x)—all attributed to the successes of the women's liberation movement.

Yet against this backdrop of what some see as feminist retreat and regression, the three women of our chapter got on with their lives and, in many instances, thrived. Although the federal government was cutting back on legislation and educational services that might support women, the states did not—not at this moment in any case. Women assumed more public offices on the state level during the 1980s, introduced more bills dealing with women's issues, and tended to take more feminist stands (Whittier, 1995) than their male counterparts. How these more local activities might have contributed specifically to Jane's, Jená's, and Janice's successes in different parts of the United States is difficult to determine, but this "unobtrusive [feminist] mobilization of the 1980s" (p. 27), to use Mary Katzenstein's (1990) phrase, surely supported their efforts, just as the insights from feminist consciousness-raising of the 1970s continued to spread among women and shape a more complex interpretation of life's experiences and lived identities.

Although for many women orchestrating the intricacies of work and family remains difficult, they do often enjoy the option of pursuing a professional career. Jane, Jená, and Janice came of age when working- and middle class women were typically limited to part-time jobs, employment as sales clerks, nurses, secretaries, and sometimes teachers, all jobs intended to supplement a husband's income rather than to offer lifetime careers in and of themselves. During the 1980s, as the number of college faculty hires was cut back dramatically to meet predictions of decreased enrollments, enrollments that had grown exponentially in the 1960s and 1970s when baby boomers like Jane, Jená, and Janice came of age, adjunct college teaching jobs became readily available. Because the decrease in enrollments failed to match expectations, departments of English, with the responsibility for teaching campuswide first-year writing classes, were especially affected by a shortage in faculty (Schell, 1998). As a result, schools such as Wright State University and the two-year college Jená was associated with in Arizona hired part-time college instructors, among them Jane and Jená, to fill these positions. Although, in the long run, these sorts of positions would lead to exploitation of faculty of both genders, arguably in the short term they offered these two women opportunities. Over time, Jane was able to turn this opportunity into a full-time, satisfying career, and Jená was able to use it as a stepping-stone for further graduate study. Unfortunately, however, many other women (and men), along with the institutions in which they teach, have neither benefited nor profited over the long haul from this use of contingent labor.[8]

By deferring her college degrees until the 1990s, Janice was in a better position to take advantage of a full-time, tenure-line faculty teaching job even though she was almost 50 when she accepted the position; and Jená, although receiving her B.A. in 1978, did not earn her PhD until 1996, which also paved the way for her professorship in 1997 at Longwood University. Although all three women in this chapter took circuitous routes into the teaching profession, new circumstances enabled them to craft teaching not only into a vocation but also into one in which their emerging technological literacies played a significant role in shaping their work and their identities. These circumstances were made possible, in part, by new educational, economic, and social opportunities for women, along with society's inevitable turn to information technologies.

Information Technologies as Gateways

In chapter 3, we introduced the concept of technology gateways, that is, places and situations in which people typically gain access to information technology for the purpose of practicing digital literacy. In this chapter, we suggest that information technologies themselves can serve as gateways to educational and career opportunities, along with advancing a person's digital literacy practices. In other words, the three women of our chapter were able to use their emerging expertise with digital literacies to increase their options for jobs and further their career paths, which, in

---

[8]For further discussion on the rise of the contingent labor force (especially as it relates to women faculty teaching in college settings), see Eileen Schell's (1998) *Gypsy Academics and Mother-Teachers: Gender, Contingent Labor, and Writing Instruction.* See also Eileen Schell and Patti Stock's (2001) *Moving a Mountain: Transforming the Role of Contingent Faculty in Composition Studies and Higher Education* for an excellent set of essays that take on the many issues surrounding the use of contingent faculty in general, both women and men.

turn, led to further technological experiences and learning. Although Janice, for example, was hampered in early attempts at education after high school, her first experience on a computer was a surprising success. Her job in the early 1970s at Southern Bell required that

> you dial in through Fulton National Timeshare and, you know, we had an account number and there were certain things that you had to make sure that were keyed in correctly so you could access it and then you would hit the button and run the tape through the phone lines, and it would give you a signal that it had worked and you were fine. Of course, everyone from all the Southern Bell offices were trying to do this at the same time so we crashed the computer and had to redo it all. And that was my first instance. But I remember this: They had given us instructions, you know, for what you have to key in to log on to the system and all that, and I remember that the instructions didn't work and I said, well, let's try this. Don't ask me why. I said maybe it's this. But whatever I did worked. And I have been doing that ever since, you know. So I guess you could call it hacking in a way, but, very minor, but . . .

Janice would succeed in this job and then go on to work in the mid-1970s first at the Cobb County Police Department where she accessed and entered data into both the local and national crime information centers and then, five years later, she became a buyer at a supermarket chain. There she became the person who was responsible for translating documents exchanged between the programmers and the other personnel. In 1983, when the company bought an IBM personal computer, she took over and trained the others in how to use MultiMate and Multiplan, popular early word processing and spreadsheet programs. A decade later she was similarly able to use her growing competence in computer-based literacies to assume responsibility as a graduate student to direct the English Department's computing facility at the University of South Florida (USF). If her workplaces functioned to provide Janice with facility with the new information technologies, the expertise she acquired through the workplace in electronic literacies advanced her chances for additional opportunities, such as the university assistantships she received at USF.

Jená and Jane had similar positive experiences with the new technologies, and went on to learn the requisite computer technology that supported literacy practices—desktop publishing and page-layout software, photo-manipulation software, web-publishing software—as it came on the market and was integrated into school and workplace settings. Their experiences as early adopters of technology, even when painful, have, furthermore, given them a high level of confidence both about the literacy skills they currently practice in digital environments and about their ability to continue acquiring new literacy skills within these environments. In their current positions as writing program directors and web administrators, they continue, too, to use the university as a gateway through which to enhance their practices in the literacies of technology.

In Sum

The firsthand accounts that we have presented in this chapter can help us trace the ways in which three women acquired electronic literacies with computers during a particularly dynamic period in our nation's history. As Deborah Brandt (1995) argues so persuasively,

> The history of literacy at any moment involves a complex, sometimes cacophonous mix of fading and ascending materials, practices, and ideologies. Literacy is always in flux. Learning to read and write necessitates an engagement with this flux, with the layers of literacy's past, present, and future, often embodied in materials and tools and just as often embodied in the social relationships we have with the people who are teaching us to read and write. (p. 666)

To this thought, we might add "learning to read and write on and off computers," for information technologies today clearly are ingrained in our notions of what being fully literate in the 21st century means.

Although these particular autobiographies, set in the most political of times among passionate social movements, resonate with us, we recognize that interpretations people bring to their reading always vary according to the personal experiences of readers who themselves grew up in particular cultural ecologies. Hence, our observations do not represent the only interpretations readers can or should draw from the cases we have provided. From these particular case studies, however, we note that gender and age, especially when they are articulated with other social, cultural, and material factors, can be key factors in determining whether, how, and when people acquire (or fail to acquire) digital literacies. Janice's autobiography, for instance, indicates how the cultural ecology inhabited by, and constituted by, women, including those who are single parents in economically disadvantaged situations, can affect the acquisition of electronic literacy. Janice's case has also convinced us, however, that economically disadvantaged women whose life experiences are difficult can often still acquire and develop electronic literacies, given that appropriate access, sponsors, timing, motivation, and other conditions are in place.

Finally, we note that Jená, Jane, and Janice were part of the first wave of middle class people living in the United States who came to consider a college education as one of their rights. During these times, more young people began attending college than ever before in the history of the United States (Rudolph, 1972; Schell, 1998), many, like the women of our chapter, belonging to the huge demographic wave of baby boomers (those born between 1946 and 1964) moving through state systems of higher education. Their autobiographies help answer questions about how and why women living during this period acquired technological literacies, and about the social, economic, cultural, educational, and political factors that influenced their acquisition of such literacies.

These three case studies also suggest, however, that people are not simply victims caught in a web of circumstances. Rather, they can—and always do—affect the cultural ecology within which they live although not always in the strategic ways that they might like. Nonetheless, people's actions help to constitute the everyday communities in which either they act out their lives and define what is possible among them, or don't (Lemke, 1995). Thus, personal motivation and interests, individual actions and decisions, we believe, can play a substantial role in the development of electronic literacies. Janice, for example, managed to complete her graduate studies against significant economic and personal odds, in part, because she possessed great personal confidence in her literacy abilities and because she could demonstrate an interest in and experience with technology. Jená and Jane honed their electronic literacy skills, both in college courses and on their own time, because they wanted access to jobs that required such abilities. As these cases suggest, some people, under the right combination of circumstances, may find ways to develop or support their digital literacy activities even when conditions are far from ideal.

These three women are part of that large demographic sweep called the baby boom that came of age in a difficult but thriving ecology; each was part of the counterculture that often resisted mainstream beliefs and values; each benefited in tangible and not so tangible ways from the social movements afoot during her lifetime. In their stories, we begin to glimpse not only the tremendous changes that have occurred in our ways of living during the late 20th and early 21st centuries but also the resourcefulness and persistence of these particular women locally. Today, as Jane, Jená, and Janice go about their everyday work in different parts of the United States, their successes create possibilities for their daughters (and sons), for the young children they taught (and teach), for their own students for whom they continue to shore up their technological expertise, and for all the other women who doubt their own technological literacy abilities.

7

The Future of Literacy

Dànielle DeVoss
Gail E. Hawisher
Charles Jackson
Joseph Johansen
Brittney Moraski
Cynthia L. Selfe

In the next decade, what will the term *literacy* mean, especially within on-line environments? What new kinds of literacy practices will characterize those students now preparing to enter and graduate from our nation's schools? How will these graduates communicate over the globally extended computer networks now distinguishing 21st century workplaces? And how will these networks continue to transform, or not, these graduates' ordinary everyday literacy practices?

Grounded by their education and values in what Jay David Bolter (1991) has called the "late age of print," teachers and schools today face many challenges. They must be prepared not only to work with students and their new literacies in productive ways, but also to modify current curricula to account for students who spend as much time reading the texts of coded simulations or visual arguments as they do the pages of novels. In other words, the U.S. educational system and its teachers must be ready to meet the needs of students who compose meaning not only with words, but also with digitized bits of video, sound, photographs, still images, words, and animations and to support communications across conventional linguistic, cultural, and geopolitical borders.

This chapter offers case studies of four people: two young professionals, a woman and man, both 28 when interviewed in 2001 and who recently completed advanced degrees; and two students, a young woman and man, aged 15 and 16, respectively, who are currently making their way through public high school in two different states. These individuals, along with many others like them, form a vector for literacy in the coming decades. Tracing this vector, considering its direction and pace, can help us glimpse the future and speculate on some answers to pressing questions about the future of 21st century literacies.

As we participate in the early years of this 21st century, parents, educators, and policymakers will find it increasingly important to understand literacy as it has changed, and continues to change, in the digital age, to formulate new insights about what it means to read, compose, and exchange text in electronic environments. The four individuals in this chapter, typical, in some important ways, of students now entering and graduating from U.S. public schools and university classrooms, can help us engage in this task. Their stories, furthermore, challenge us to explore the multiple literacies that now characterize online environments.

The Case Study of Dànielle DeVoss

Dànielle DeVoss, born on August 8, 1973, was the first of two children in her White, middle class, midwestern family. Dànielle's parents pursued their own advanced educations early in their marriage and were committed to the literacy development of their children. As Dànielle noted:

> They encouraged my brother and I to read. I was involved in summer reading programs as young as I can remember. . . . [Around the house, there were] daily newspapers, all sorts of magazines (sports, home improvement, news, politics), books, and novels. My mother preferred historical, cultural, and religious . . . books. My father preferred fiction paperbacks. . . . My mother took us regularly to the library and to used bookstores when we got older.

Dànielle's parents were also responsible, at least indirectly, for the computer-based literacies she began to acquire relatively early in life. As she tells the story:

> I first came in contact with computers when my parents bought a computer . . . when my brother and I were fairly young. I think I was maybe 10. The computer quickly became his domain, but I eventually learned how to use it by looking over his shoulder, and as we got older, we fought for time on the computer. I used the computer as a social space, accessing computer bulletin board systems by phone. . . .
>
> I learned pretty much by looking over my brother's shoulder and then jumping on the computer when he and his friends were gone. He did eventually teach me a few things, but most of my initial learning was on my own. . . . My brother primarily used the computer for the same reason I did—games and bulletin board systems. . . .

Between all the bulletin board systems we called, my brother and I wound up logging about 250 calls a month (I know this thanks to the per-call fees from the local phone company when I was growing up).

As Dànielle progressed through secondary school, her mother made every effort to direct her daughter's interest in computers toward more conventional academic pursuits, but Dànielle continued to enjoy gaming and bulletin board/chat room exchanges. In these gaming environments, she became adept at reading and interpreting imaginary scenarios and composing the exchanges between characters of various types and abilities. She learned, as well, to create elaborate descriptions of her own characters and to respond to the complex situations that other players' characters generated. Her literacy in these electronic environments, Dànielle remembers, had a great deal to do with her increasing confidence as a reader and writer off-line, as well: The exchanges in games and chat rooms, for instance, were especially instructive to her growing sense of rhetorical awareness because they so often resulted in social consequences that she felt keenly:

> Chat rooms and bulletin board systems are complicated spaces where missteps or inappropriate talk can pretty much exclude you from a conversation, or make you the target of venomous textual assaults.

Dànielle also learned other literacy skills and values in the online gaming environments she frequented, those based as much in the visual, kinesthetic, and interactive components of gaming, as in the alphabetic. These practices, moreover, diverged dramatically from the conventional literacy instruction she received in school, where, as she got older, writing instruction was increasingly limited to the alphabetic and to the two-dimensional representational space of the page. Although she certainly did well on such conventional tasks, Dànielle's real attention remained focused on composing the interactive scenarios and exchanges of gaming situations; learning to read and predict the rule based movements of characters in time and space; visualizing, mapping, and navigating her own way through the multidimensional compositional space of games:

> [T]rying to create mental maps of the text-only games I played taught me a lot about mapping out textual spaces and trying to think of them in terms of "real" space. The text-only games required a heck of a lot of imagination, too—often, the games weren't that well written, and it was your interaction with the games that really made the difference. . . .
> [Y]ou had to create complex mental maps. I remember when I first started playing games in these realms and being lost. I'd wander in circles, and wasn't able to return to particular areas within the game. It was frustrating, so I

became much more adept at creating mental maps of where I was and where I wanted to go. I started by paying attention to short distances, mapping how I was moving during one stint of playing. As I did this, I was able to create larger maps and form a stronger sense of the realm in which I was playing in.

Most of these new-media literacy skills and understandings, we should add, Dànielle acquired on her own, without a great deal of systematic help or guidance from others. Few of her teachers, their own understanding of literacy tuned into the relatively narrow bandwidth of the alphabetic, knew enough about computers to take her literacy development in electronic contexts seriously; none were likely to consider the games and chat rooms in which she participated to be an appropriate context for the instruction of literacy.

For the next decade, Dànielle continued her online gaming and, as computers offered increasingly sophisticated environments for both gaming and composing, she developed considerable skill in designing Web sites using HTML code. She also became familiar with Adobe Photoshop; Macromedia Dreamweaver and a variety of other HTML editors; Microsoft Word, PowerPoint, and Excel; Corel WordPerfect and Presentations; QuarkXpress; Aldus PageMaker; and several kinds of bibliographic software. Dànielle enjoyed composing web texts, in part, because these activities resonated with the earlier literacies she practiced in gaming environments. Both kinds of composition allowed her to combine alphabetic and visual elements; to organize texts along temporal and spatial axes; and to explore the structure of large bodies of complicated material. To compose both kinds of texts, Dànielle relied on her ability to predict the movements of readers, to organize and arrange materials according to these predictions, and to navigate space-time creations.

Dànielle's web literacy abilities are especially evident in the main organizational interface of a site she created while working on her PhD at Michigan Technological University (see Figure 7.1). The site opens with a retro-style collage crafted from pictures and texts that Dànielle scanned from popular magazines of the 1930s and 1940s. With these pictures, and borrowing from the layout and design of the historical two-dimensional, print-based texts, Dànielle composed a three-dimensional text in a new-media environment. On top of these images, she superimposed banner headlines—to remind readers of an older style of the magazine cover—and made these alphabetic bits into electronic links that led to other areas of her new-media text. Rather than flipping through pages on which the full text of an article appears, readers click instead on a headline to access additional new-media compositions: hypertextual syllabi, an online photography exhibit, an e-mail connection. In this activity, readers are encouraged to rethink their magazine literacy in terms of the new-media

FIGURE 7.1

literacies structuring the site itself. Through this design, unlike many of her composition instructors, Dànielle sought to connect online literacies with print-based literacies. As she explains:

> Part of what I want readers to feel when they navigate the site is that hypertext isn't a new concept. The ability to read a magazine requires a sophisticated sense of navigation, flipping, moving, and browsing. Creating a collage of images from old magazines and linking them was a move I wanted to make toward disrupting the belief that hypertext is an entirely new technology.

The Case Study of Joseph Johansen

Joseph Johansen, born on July 14, 1973, in Provo, Utah, was the second of 11 children in his White, middle class family. His parents, members of the Church of Jesus Christ of Latter-Day Saints, fostered a strong, intergenerational tradition of literacy. As Joseph described his family's history:

I think a good place to begin would be with my grandfather. I attribute a great deal of my parents' emphasis on education to him. My grandpa grew up on a farm. As a young man all he wanted to be was a sheepherder. He loved to write poetry, read religious and historical books, and to experience nature. Sheepherding gave him ample opportunity to do this. Well, a few years after he got married, I believe he had either four or five children at the time, he was injured to the extent that he couldn't continue working on the farm and tending the sheep. So he decided to go back to school with a family and no job. He worked his way through school and ended up with a doctorate in microbiology. I believe he was the first in his family with any college education. He spent the rest of his career teaching microbiology in various universities. As a result of my grandfather's legacy, each of his seven sons went on to get advanced degrees in engineering, medicine, or computer-related fields.

Although Joseph carried his parents' love of education and reading into formal schooling contexts, his relationship with writing was not always positive:

> Writing . . . [was] a little different. I know that my parents valued communication and understood that writing was important for good communication, but honestly I didn't enjoy writing until my senior year in high school or later. I never did well in English courses as a younger child. I would pull a C, maybe an occasional B, but usually nothing more.

It was through writing, however, that Joseph first encountered computers. He was involved in a course where students were encouraged to learn and then write about a variety of topics including computers. Joseph then began programming with Basic and learned how to create banners and graphics files on computers, getting his first glimpse of the machine's potential as an emerging medium for visual composition. Such a focus fit well with Joseph's longstanding interest in art, a focus encouraged by his parents, if not by his teachers:

> My father is an art teacher. He exposed me to visual literacy at a very young age through art lessons and insights into the way he saw things. He has always encouraged me to develop visual literacies. . . .
>
> For a while I was into comic book art, so I would collect comic books and the character cards that went with them. I would try to recreate the characters I saw and make my own. I became interested in airbrush art in high school. I used to make tee shirts and even painted a mural on my bedroom wall (I am sure my mom hated that but she never said anything).
>
> My teachers . . . convinced me that there was no money in [the love of art]. My dad certainly wasn't making a lot of money and he was a great art-

ist. [And so] I decided to become a computer engineer. That way I could make money and continue doing art work as a hobby.

When Joseph finished high school and completed his missionary work in France, however, he discovered graphic design, a field highly dependent on computer-based communications and networked environments, and one that valued, in addition, his interest in visual arts. Thus, by the time Joseph had finished his bachelor's degree, worked as a graphic designer, and enrolled in a master's-level program in professional communication, much of his composition work took place in new-media environments that involved computer-based graphic design, web design, photo editing, word processing, and multimedia design. In his words, Joseph loved:

> . . . designing visual media . . . Web sites, chat rooms (ironic since I don't really use them), multimedia movies, animations, 3-D imagery and animations, streaming video, flash movies, and CD-ROMs.

In undertaking these new-media projects, Joseph taught himself how to use Office, Photoshop, Illustrator, Image Ready, Freehand, Fireworks, Dreamweaver, Director, Flash, Bryce, Poser, QuarkXpress, and Streamline, with the help of books and CDs he purchased and by engaging in discussions with expert users in chat rooms, discussion boards, and listservs. Although he was enrolled in a graduate-level communications program at a well-regarded university, his teachers, like Dànielle's, had been able to provide Joseph relatively little systematic help in pursuing his visual literacy interests:

> Unfortunately, [neither] of the schools that I have been to are very strong in the visual-computer area. . . . Both schools have great art programs and great computer programs, but neither of them integrated the two very well. I know some schools do but I can't afford them.
> So I have had to tailor what the schools do offer to meet my needs. This has meant a lot of work outside of class researching topics that dealt with the merging of art and computers.

Despite these challenges, Joseph continued to focus on visual literacy, recognizing the culture's increasing dependence on reading, understanding, and composing texts in which meaning is communicated through the visual elements of still photographs, video, animated images, graphics, and charts—a move Gunther Kress (1999) describes as the "turn to the visual" (p. 66). Like Dànielle, Joseph also appreciated the intertextual applications of the new-media literacies:

Working in a variety of media from text to illustration to video has given me a fairly deep arsenal that I can pull from in composing. It allows me to create "textured" works, which I find interesting.

The visual essay *Robojoe* represents an example of Joseph's new-media compositions (see Figure 7.2). Joseph created this Flash movie in a graduate seminar at Clemson University in the spring of 2001, responding to an assignment that asked him to explore the relationship between humans and technology. His goal was to create a totally visual argument that would make a meaningful comment on this topic. *Robojoe* opens on a fore-grounded representation of a triangular cybernetic face glowing blue against a pale gray background of whirling gears and pulsing circuit boards. Superimposed over this representation is a dynamic grid calibrated along x and y axes. The grid follows any mouse movements made by read-ers as they explore this page. With this interface, Joseph argues that technol-ogy—represented by the dynamic grid calibrated along x and y axes, the turning gears, and the pulsing circuit board—has come to both under- and

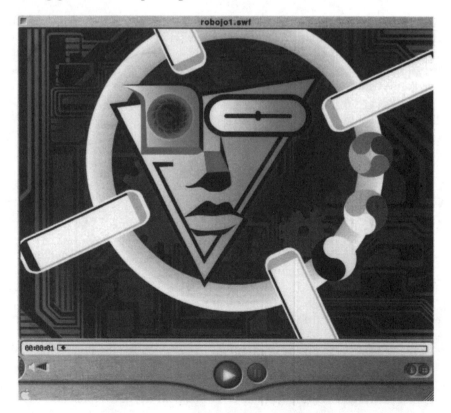

FIGURE 7.2.

over-write the human body, here portrayed as a triangular cybernetic face. This technological revision, Joseph maintains in an accompanying alphabetic commentary on this visual essay, has turned our muscles, the actuators of motion, into moving gears; our heart and nervous system, the body's energy sources, into pulsing circuits; and the human brain into central processing units, represented by the disk input slot in the cybernetic face.

Links from the main screen of this visual essay, three yin-yang symbols of varying complexity, lead to three more perspectives on and stories about technology, each of which was explored in the seminar Joseph took. The first and simplest link takes readers from the splash page to a sequence of moving images that depict the common, reductive, binary perspective that many humans adopt in relation to technology: Technology is either a great good or it is a terrible evil. This story, appropriately, Joseph has composed using shapes that recall only the most primitive of machines: the wedge, the pulley, the lever, and the screw. The second, more complicated, link off the splash page leads to a further complication of the earlier perspective. In this second series of moving images, Joseph indicates that technology's effects may be both good and bad in varying degrees, as represented by the juxtaposition of various images in different combinations: a symbol of atomic energy, an artificial heart, and an airplane come together; a caduceus and a death's head converge; a light bulb, a sailing vessel, and an airship designed by DaVinci move across the screens. In the third and final story, Joseph maintains that computers, represented here by strings of binary code, introduce an increasingly complex instantiation of technology into our culture and suggests the complex ways in which these machines have shaped the human experience: increasing the global reach of communication efforts, as indicated by the transmitting tower; changing our understanding of time, represented by the clock; supporting the spread of multinational capitalism, symbolized by the hand grasping money; and altering our understanding of artificial intelligence, as suggested by the robot. In this argument, Joseph suggests that the imaginary line separating good and bad technologies has disappeared as the boundaries separating the human and the technological have similarly blurred.

The Case Study of Brittney Moraski

Brittney Moraski, born August 28, 1986, into a White, middle class Catholic family living in the rural Upper Peninsula of Michigan, grew up as the youngest of three sisters and three brothers. She attended the elementary school in the same mid-size town where she was born, and went on to attend the local high school. Brittney's mother attended several years of college and her father, a sixth-grade teacher, holds a master's degree in Education.

Both parents place a high value on literacy. Brittney's mother has "always enjoyed reading" and her father "constantly reads magazines on ultralight and powered parachute flying," in addition to daily newspapers. As Brittney notes, her parents

> . . . never stressed the importance of education—it . . . [was] unnecessary. Even in childhood, my brothers, sisters, and I . . . instinctively understood the importance of education.

Brittney, unusually poised for a 15 year old when interviewed, reported that she always had her "nose in a book," and she attributed her love of reading and learning to her family:

> [They were] . . . fantastic about reading to me. I was read to constantly, especially during car rides. Such diligence and attention from my family members has no doubt played a major role in the development of my intellectual facilities. . . .
>
> [Now,] I enjoy history, and I found *Robert Kennedy: His Life* by Evan Thomas to be a fantastic book. I've read many books on the Holocaust, including *Night* by Elie Wiesel and *The Diary of Anne Frank*. I'm beginning to become interested in classical literature (I loathed it before) and recently read *The Pearl* by John Steinbeck. I read the news articles on Yahoo! to stay current in world and national affairs and subscribe to *Time* magazine. I enjoy writing essays and research papers and love creating Web sites.

The first computer that Brittney remembers in the house was her brother's, and it was on this machine that Brittney began her digital literacy practices when she was five:

> My brother Garrett got a computer when I was young, and I remember that I had a dinosaur (my passion at the time) program in which I made a printout that read:
>
> > brittney ligh moraski is 5 years old. her sisters and brothers names are courtney and leslye and brittney garrett brett brandon dad [bob] mom [beth] mitzi is are best friend in the world.

Brittney also used a computer when she visited the home of her best friend, Mitzi. As a result, by the time Brittney got to school she already associated computers with literacy, self-expression, and fun:

> I became comfortable with computers before I started school, so I already had exposure to technology. We had a computerized reading program at

school called Accelerated Reader, where students read books that were assigned a point value. After reading the book, we would take a test on the
computer. Depending on how the student did on the test, points would be
awarded. Being the voracious reader that I was at the time, I acquired over
700 points during my elementary years.

As Brittney progressed in school, she became increasingly adept at using and navigating in computer-supported literacy environments, often
working and learning in Mitzi's company:

> I just dove into computers as a young child, and I used it, especially in word
> processing, often before many of my peers. I used Microsoft Works in fourth
> grade to create my graphs and papers for my science fair project. A huge
> amount of credit goes to the Barras (Mitzi and her father) for my technologi-
> cal progression—they taught me everything.
>
> I would go over to Mitzi's house and together we would try (and try) to
> create the things necessary for my homework. It took us hours to learn how
> to create a graph in Works.
>
> I didn't have a computer of my own until I was a sixth grader, so the only
> time I used the computer was when I was at her house. Needless to say, I
> spent an extraordinary (and worthwhile) amount of time there throughout
> my childhood. Her (and her family's) help and support has been tremen-
> dous.

In her own home, Brittney rapidly became the technology expert. And like
many children coming of age in a technological world, she passed her
growing expertise upstream to her parents, teaching them how to send e-
mail, connect to the Internet, and use Microsoft Money.

Computers became a major part of Brittney's social life as well. As a sophisticated 15 year old, she observed that computer-based literacy had become a means of extending the personal relationships of her friends:

> My friends embrace technology because it allows them to communicate
> with their friends, makes homework assignments easier, and allows them to
> create cards and posters. . . . When my friends have crushes with certain
> guys . . . the computer becomes an important flirting tool. Getting that guy
> on your instant-messenger list can result in conversations that may lead to
> "going out."

By the time Brittney got to high school, she was reading books on web
design, HTML coding, and programs like Photoshop; and enrolling in online distance education classes to supplement her education. As she noted,
a great deal of her day was spent in online literacy activities, although she
believed her outdated computer had cramped her style to some extent:

I have a moderately slow, nondescript PC computer. It has been jazzed up recently; however, one of Mitzi's brothers helped me to install a CD burner, more memory, and an additional hard drive.

. . . I spend a tremendous amount of time using a computer! . . . I have the Internet at home, and I use it for a multitude of functions. I access my Spanish course online, send and receive e-mails, use Yahoo! Messenger to check news headlines and see how my stocks are doing, purchase stocks through ShareBuilder, buy books and CDs at Half.com or Amazon.com, use M-W.com to look up the definitions of words, chat with friends on ICQ, update the school's Web site, look up topics that interest me, download songs, search for scholarships or contests, learn more about the college admissions process and visit the sites of my preferred universities, look for upcoming camps or workshops, research for homework, and more, and more, and more! One recent example of how I use my computer: We were asked at CCD to chose a patron saint and report on it the next week. Well, I used Yahoo! and Google to find sites that list patron saints, and pretty soon I was at catholic-forum.com, trying to find my "personal" saint. I eventually settled on St. Catherine of Alexandria, the patroness of wisdom, philosophers, scholars, and students, but I was tempted to choose St. Vitus, who guards against oversleeping! :)

Given the extent of her online activities, Brittney's computer skills quickly outstripped those of many of her teachers. And, although Brittney was appreciative of those instructors who took the trouble to enter her digital world and was tolerant of their initial efforts, she was also realistic about the time it would take for adults to catch on to the dynamic technologies that were already a part of her life and brutally frank about the instruction she felt her school could offer students like her:

I appreciate [it] when my teachers embrace technology—I understand that it can be a scary thing. However, very few teachers use technology in the classroom. While my algebra teacher has a Web site that he uses to post homework, the art teacher at school gives PowerPoint presentations, and my health teacher had us take a computerized test to see if we were right- or left-brained, there is little use of dynamic technology in school, but I'm certain that this will change as the years progress.

I think my personal initiative in understanding and utilizing computers will serve me better than what my school has taught me. But that's really life in a nutshell. We do best at things we have a genuine interest in, not those that are spoon-fed to us.

Brittney's assessment of the educational system she inhabited was both accurate and incisive. Although Brittney's teachers were supportive of her computer-based learning activities and had even chosen her to attend a summer institute computer-based communication class, many of her online literacy practices remained invisible to the instructors with whom she worked on a daily basis. This was true, at least in part, because many of these online literacy activities fell outside the relatively narrow band-width of the conventional practices her teachers recognized as literate behavior.

None of Brittney's teachers, for instance, realized that her extensive ex-changes in chat rooms helped to define her attitude toward face-to-face conversations and her sophisticated ear for nuance in verbal exchanges. Similarly, Brittney's developing understanding of visual literacy was gen-erally invisible to her high school teachers, as were her digital composing efforts that combined both alphabetic and visual elements. As a result, only Brittney herself knew how much her online activities—for instance, her growing understanding of visual design—had begun to contribute to the success of her conventional alphabetic assignments. As she explained:

> [L]ately ... I've realized that the aesthetic quality and layout of a Web site greatly determines its credibility and effectiveness ... I think cleanliness, readable fonts, and professional-looking graphics are very important. . . . It is important to "read" graphics and understand the relationship between text and how it is displayed (i.e., bold text = main idea, small text = foot-note). . . .
>
> When I write conventional texts, I . . . use visual layouts to contribute to the true message of my writing.

Given her situation, by the time she entered high school, Brittney be-came quite adept at leading a double life in terms of her literacy practices and values. For most of her academic classes, to please her teachers, she composed what she called "conventional" texts like the following essay entitled "Schindler's List." But to challenge herself and to engage in the literacy practices she knew would matter most to her when she gradu-ated, she designed her school's Web site and created visual PowerPoint texts like "Honduras 2001," about a social action project she undertook with members of her church (see Figs. 7.3 and 7.4).

The Case Study of Charles Jackson

Born on October 23, 1985, to a White mother and a Black father, Charles Jackson lived in Salt Lake City, Utah, until his family moved to Geor-gia, and later came to settle in Greenwood, South Carolina. The oldest of five children, Charles lives at home with his four younger sisters and his parents.

Charles' mother and father, both of whom left college to care for their children, have always valued reading and writing within their home. His mother, Charles noted, likes

Brittney Moraski
February 13, 2002
English, Book Report

Schindler's List

Schindler's List, a novel by Thomas Keneally, prevails in its account of the Holocaust and Oskar Schindler's uncanny heroism. The novel fails, however, to convey the very human and personal suffering of European Jewry at the hands of the Nazis. *Schindler's List* presents a cut-and-dry recitation of the tragedies of the Holocaust and does not leave the reader with a strong sense of personal loss at its conclusion. The author's use of complex and, at times, incorrect sentences detracts from the story and makes it difficult to read. The faults of the novel, however, disappear in Steven Spielberg's film adaptation of *Schindler's List*. The movie presents the horrors of the Holocaust visually, and most importantly, poignantly. While Spielberg's film captures an essence of the Holocaust that Keneally's words do not express, it is only when the movie and novel are used in concert that the history of the Holocaust is appropriately depicted.

While *Schindler's List* has considerable faults, it does present an amazing story. Keneally's cantankerous sentences may discredit the flow of the novel, but the lives of Oskar Schindler and the *Schindlerjuden* are so intriguing that the story itself remains captivating. Schindler, a Nazi Party member, used his clout and authority within the Reich to protect over a thousand Jews during the Holocaust. An important industrialist, Schindler contracted Jews, otherwise imprisoned in labor and death camps, to work in his factories under the guise that they were essential workers and that their efforts were necessary to keep up the production of German Army supplies. In his concentration camps, prisoners were cared for and fed. Schindler forbade SS guard beatings and executions of prisoners. While life in Schindler's camps was not easy, the *Schindlerjuden* (Schindler's Jews) considered them a paradise. People on Schindler's list had hope, and better yet, a guarantee of a future beyond the war.

While Keneally does an impressive job telling the *Schindlerjuden's* story, his book lacks the emotional impact that most Holocaust literature possesses. Keneally's style of writing fails in describing the enormous tragedies of the Holocaust. Since a majority of the characters in *Schindler's List* survive the Nazi's Final Solution, their stories lack a certain amount of tragedy and devastation. Readers of the novel are not adequately exposed to the brutality and atrocities present throughout the Holocaust, and, consequently, are not left with a sense of personal grief or loss at the novel's end.

The film version of *Schindler's List*, directed by Steven Spielberg, debuted in 1993. The three-hour video was a winner of seven Academy Awards, including Best Picture and Best Director, and was considered by many to be one of the greatest films of all time. Spielberg's video succeeds in its portrayal of the Holocaust because it uses imagery to make its impact. Spielberg's *Schindler's List* brings the chilling anti-Semitic jeers of village children and the brutality and sheer iniquity of SS guards to the screen. The palpable horror and grief in Jewish families becomes heart-wrenchingly real in the video, and history, however distant, supercedes time and exposes the physical agony of those affected by the Holocaust.

The whole of *Schindler's List* is more than the sum of a moving novel or a cinematic piece of art. Together, the novel and video complement each other, preserving a wide breadth of the Holocaust for future generations to learn and grow from. With the gravity of its subject matter, *Schindler's List*, as a novel and a movie, stands as a testimony, a written and visual witness, to what cannot be forgotten.

FIGURE 7.3. "Schindler's List."

FIGURE 7.4.   "Honduras 2001."

. . . to write stories and stuff like that. . . . My mom reads all the time. In fact my dad gets mad at her sometimes because she reads so much. . . . Whenever I have a book report for school my mom makes me read the book to her. She doesn't trust me to read it by myself so she does that to make sure that I get my readings done.

His father, explained Charles,

. . . likes to read science fiction and stuff . . . [but] my dad does . . . everything on the computer. He reads on the computer. He watches TV on the computer. He looks up stuff on the Internet. He likes to read books and stuff about his games on the computer. . . . His favorite game is "Home World"; you might have heard of it. He likes that game a lot. He buys books and books on that game. He really likes it.

. . . I think he uses computers for his job . . . I think he orders parts or something like that for Lockheed Martin. He uses computers . . . to order parts and look up prices and stuff like that.

Raised in a home environment where his mother and father valued and practiced multiple forms of literacy, and in multiple environments, Charles learned how to read and write online about the same time he learned to read and write in print:

I think I was like four or five years old. I couldn't write well, but I could read. I remember reading *Mercer Meyer*. . . . My parents helped me learn to read, and my teachers helped me learn to write.

. . . the first time I remember using computers [was] when I was four years old. . . . I went to this dude's house. I think he was a friend of my dad. We went down in his basement, and he had computer stuff everywhere, on the walls and everywhere. We took some parts home and set them up. We had this little bitty screen with two colors. You know, green and black. You could type stuff in it. That was about it. Couldn't run games on it.

I took a book from the library and I would try to type it. I tried to learn the shift key and the caps lock key. I remember I wrote like one sentence and it took me an hour. I was about five. My dad told me how to use the shift key. And for a while all my letters were capitalized because I didn't know how not to.

Charles continued to practice literacy in both computer-based and print-based environments as he grew up. In print environments, he developed a taste for comic books—*Ghost Rider, The Incredible Hulk,* and *Captain America*—and a strong preference for historical books and biographies rather than novels. In electronic environments, Charles developed an early love of gaming, spending hours with early games like *PacMan, Aster-*

oids, and *Superman.* Charles also tried out other gaming systems and became especially fond of role-playing environments. As he remembered his initial gaming experiences:

> I had the first *Ultima* game and it was tight. There was a little itty bitty dude wandering around with a little horse and tiny dots on the screen for the village. Later I got into flight simulators like the *Red Baron.* Then as games got more advanced I moved on to new games like *Tomb Raider* and all those games.
>
> Then we went on to the 32 to 64 bit era . . . I played *Crash Bandicoot* and *Final Fantasy.* I have the original *Final Fantasy* . . . it's rated M but I don't care. It's about this dude who has two guns and a sword. The sword is huge; it looks like a buster sword. It is so cool.

Charles' father encouraged his son's interest in online environments and worked with him to build computers out of the spare parts that littered the family's basement. The pair then shared the machines with the rest of the family through a trickle-down system. "Now I have my own computer," Charles noted. "It is actually my dad's old computer. The one in my sisters' room is my old computer. When my dad gets an upgrade, I get his old one and my sisters get mine."

In academic settings, however, particularly in elementary school, Charles had considerably less access to computers. Although his school did acquire a computer lab when he was in the second grade, Charles had only minimal access to these machines and limited help from teachers in learning to use them. When his instructors did integrate computers into their classroom work, they focused on conventional, alphabetic literacy:

> I had about an hour a week [on the computers]. [And], if I was lucky I could [also] use them for 10 minutes before recess. . . .
>
> The teachers helped me learn about computers, but I don't think they really knew what they were doing. They were new to computers like we were. They helped us out by encouraging us to use them and to help us learn to read and write with them. . . . They taught us to use word processors and encyclopedias on computers.

Confronted by such limitations at school, Charles continued to develop an increasingly broad range of online literacies at home. In this effort, he was particularly motivated by his continued interest in computer gaming:

> If you don't know how to read and write then you are going to have trouble using computers, but they can help you read and write better. Say you want

to play games. You are going to have to learn how to read in order to play the games. You have to read on the screen what the menus say.

Charles' gaming activities not only encouraged his reading but his composing skills, as well:

> I do a lot of computer coding. Mostly C++ stuff. I do a lot of writing for my games. I try to come up with ideas. I just sit down and try to come up with ideas. Often I will write down a plot or [try] different methods of coding to get a camera angle to work or a certain character to move, stuff like that.

In the gaming environments he frequented, Charles, like Dànielle, also became adept at reading and interpreting imaginary scenarios, composing the exchanges of characters and gamers within such environments, and responding to the complex situations that games depicted. As he explained:

> [Y]ou need to learn to read between the lines. You need to know the right things to say to people and how to communicate with them. You need to know how to develop friendships. It is important to read between the lines so that you can know what people want you to do and how to go about doing it.

As Charles became increasingly adept at both gaming and game design, he also learned to read the texts of the games themselves—figuring out the grammars, or rule sets, that shaped his interaction with these dynamic environments and acquiring the kinesthetic, intercultural, and problem-solving literacies that the games demanded:

> I think with playing games there is a grammar. Games have different genres just like books do. So when you pick up a game of a certain genre you kind of expect to know how to play that game. Say you pick up an action game you kind of expect, say you expect Mario to move around in certain ways. You expect certain controls to be there and when they are not there then you get confused, because the grammar is not complete in that game or is not what you are expecting. The way controls are used, the menus that are used, the terms, the buttons that are used. You see—like for example the Final Fantasy series—in *Final Fantasy VII*, the button that you use is X. Well in *Final Fantasy VIII* it is O. . . . The Japanese games use the O button and the American games use X for everything.
>   I think that the main skill that I've learned is puzzle solving. Take *Tomb Raider*. Despite the pretty girl, it is a puzzle-solving game. So you have to figure how to move the blocks to fit a certain square, how to swing across the rope a certain way, and how to make all the pieces fit just right. What I even-

tually learned to do, is after about level three I learned how to put the puzzles together and learned what to expect in the game—especially in *Tomb Raider 2.*

In the gaming chat rooms that he frequented online, Charles, like Dànielle, honed his rhetorical skills, not only with people from the United States, but with gamers from other countries as well:

> You have to be courteous. You have to know how to read and write well because people get really annoyed if you are like, "I want to learn how to make a game. How do I do this?" . . . Like some guy from Yugoslavia comes on, and you can hardly tell what he is saying. But I don't feel so bad trying to help them . . . because they can't really help it. English isn't their language. A lot of the people I speak with don't know English that well. You have to be understanding of that. Half the people on there speak German. . . .
>
> I learned to be considerate of people to make sure that I get the respect that I get as well as being respectful to others. You know the old Golden Rule thing. Make sure that you don't put people down. Like if someone thinks they have a great idea and it really isn't you should tell them that it is and then give them constructive criticism on how to make it better. Like some people on there are like, "Oh man that sucks! You shouldn't be out here!" And that just isn't right because everybody is learning how to do new things. Everyone was like that at one point. Calm down a little bit, and let them do it. If you like turn away everybody when they are just learning how to do something, then no one will want to do it again.

If his teachers didn't always recognize that the literacy skills he acquired in the problem-solving environments of online games transferred productively to the more conventional literacy tasks he was assigned in school, Charles certainly appreciated this fact himself:

> Well, playing games has taught me about writing because a lot of games are like problem solving. . . . When you are making a computer game you have to think about everything and what can go wrong, what you are forgetting. And that has helped me in writing because it's the same thing when I am composing a paper for a teacher. I have to think of everything that I am writing, and everything that I can do to make it better and everything that I have done that might make it wrong. Might make it not work or flow correctly. . . .
>
> Games have taught me how to use menus. Lots of games make you apply patches. That forces you to use your computer, set up things and install programs. Video games are good with new technologies anyway, so when I look at a game I can look at how it was made and use the same technologies in my own games.

Charles' online experiences also helped him develop an increasingly keen set of visual literacy skills. As he noted:

> [On my Web site] I have to make sure that the images express what I want them to. I have to make sure that it is accessible, and that it will work on other computers. You have to make sure that you don't just use text. Like if you go to a Web site it is nothing but text then you are like text, text, text, text. If you have an image then you are like, Oh, that's what that means. This is especially true with video. Video tutorials are great to teach you how to like make models or something. They show you like what button to push and how to do things.
>
> . . . I visualize what I am writing. Like in a story. You have to be able to visualize or write things down so that you can make sure you have all your thoughts straight; then you will know that your story won't be messed up. You won't say that he was born in like 1965 and that he is 70 years old. Because I have done that before.

As a result of his own literacy work online, Charles had definite ideas of what coming generations of students, like his younger sisters, should be learning in school. The literacy curriculum he imagined for the future was focused around problem solving in online environments and developing visual as well as alphabetic literacy. As he explained:

> Children watch cable right? They watch Nickelodeon right? Well next thing they see is a commercial for Nick.com and the next thing you know your sisters are all in your room playing games from Nick.com.
>
> The Internet is just like everywhere. Students are going to have to know how to do it. It is going to be required. They will have to do a lot of projects using stuff from the Internet. They will have to get pictures off the Internet and stuff like that. Read maps on the Internet and stuff like that.
>
> I would include like the history of icons. How they went back to the Byzantine Empire, the Roman Catholics when the church split. How to look at icons and know what they mean without words. Like that Nike symbol. I betcha every kid in South Carolina knows what that Nike symbol means because it is on all their shoes and clothes. Which icons are more recognizable? Which icons [do] teens recognize the most? And which [do] they recognize the least? And how [do] advertisers use this to create their slogans and stuff? I'd probably teach them how to create symbols for emotions, new symbols, not the smiley face. And then [we'd] see how easily other students could identify the symbols. That would be interesting.

We've included here a screen shot of the splash page of Charles's Web site, but the image alone doesn't begin to do justice to the expertise he

FIGURE 7.5.

demonstrates in online game-design.[1] At this site, which opens on a splash page dominated by a menacing warrior in black, a character of his own creation, Charles introduces *The Quest of the Golden Fleece,* a game that he began designing after encountering the story of Jason and the Argonauts in his English class at Berea High School. Charles describes his game with some pride in the site's introduction:

> *The Quest of the Golden Fleece* is a real-time, 3-D, action FPG that is set in ancient mythological time. It has been in development for almost a year, and it is looking promising. The game is run on the Genesis3d engine, which rivals that of Half-Life and Quake engines.
>
> *The Quest of the Golden Fleece* is absolutely immersing. You can travel about the known world seeking out treasures or discovering new peoples. You can move through vast ancient cities communicating with townspeople, buying and selling goods, or being a gladiator in the many coliseums.

---

[1]An example of Charles' expertise in online game-design environments can be experienced at http://www.geocities.com/charliensane in which he presents "The Quest of the Golden Fleece: Live the Myth" (Jackson, 2002).

You are Jason who must find the Golden Fleece so he can take the town of Thebes back from his evil Uncle Pelias. The gods play a major part in the journey as they may help or hurt you. The game allows you to choose which path you wish to take while maintaining a . . . flowing story line.

The Web site that Charles has constructed around this complex and intriguing game includes extensive sections entitled "screenshots," "gameplay," "characters," and "tutorials," all composed by Charles. These sections, richly illustrated with colorful computer-based images and animations that Charles has created, are rife with allusions, both to the classical text of the *Odyssey* and to the classical texts of the online gaming world—the *Legacy of Kain* series, for example, with *Soul Reaver 2* among them.[2] With his creation of *The Quest of the Golden Fleece*, Charles has transformed the conventional literacy instruction that he was provided in his high school English class into the kind of digital literacy practices that he values outside of school and that he sees as integral to his success in the future.

The Future of Literacy Studies in a Changing World

The four people in this chapter have all been, and in the cases of Brittney and Charles continue to be, not only insightful students of the new media but also excellent students in general. With a great deal of support from their parents and teachers, they have all developed considerable skill and success in conventional educational settings and literacy environments. They make good grades, they write and read conventional materials with facility, and they have graduated, or will graduate, without difficulty, from the institutions they attended. If these students themselves have been successful, however, the formal literacy instruction they received may have been less so. Their teachers prepared them well for a world of print-based, alphabetic literacy, but these instructors provided very little official instruction or systematic guidance in those literacies that lay outside this very narrow bandwidth. In contrast, it is clear that Dànielle and Joseph, along with Brittney and Charles, consider the reading and composing skills they acquired informally in electronic environments— literacies marked by the kinesthetic, the visual, the navigational, the intercultural; by a robust combination of code, image, sound, animation, and words—to be far more compelling, far more germane to their future

---

[2]These games can be accessed on the Web. See http://www.legacyofkain.com/ for *The Legacy of Kain* and http://www.eidosinteractive.com/gss/legacy/legacyofkain/main.html for *Soul Reaver*.

success than the more traditional literacy instruction they have received in school.

This response should not surprise us. More than 30 years ago, in her book *Culture and Commitment,* Margaret Mead (1970) argued that the kind of educational efforts children found most valuable in preparing them to function successfully as adults depended, to a great extent, on the changes happening in the culture around them.[3] In stable cultures that changed slowly, Mead explained, students valued an education that passed along traditionally based knowledge from an adult-teacher who knew, from experience, how to handle many of the challenges that students would encounter later in life. In less stable cultures, however, cultures characterized by rapid change and disruption, by the "development of new forms of technology in which the old are not expert" (p. 39), young people no longer have the luxury of relying solely on the information provided by their elders to equip them for a changing world. Instead, they depended on the help of their peers and on their own efforts to figure out the skills they needed in the coming years.

---

[3]In her 1970 book, *Culture and Commitment,* Mead describes three different cultural styles, distinguished by the ways in which children are prepared for adulthood. The first, the "postfigurative," characterizes societies in which change is largely imperceptible and the "future repeats the past." In such cultures, adults are able to pass along the necessary knowl edge to children. "The essential characteristic of postfigurative cultures," Mead maintained, "is the assumption, expressed by members of the older generation in their every act, that their way of life (however many changes may, in fact, be embodied in it) is unchanging, eternally the same" (p. 14). Education within such cultures privileges the passing down of traditional values and knowledge through an adult-teacher.

The second of Mead's styles, that characterizing "cofigurative" cultures, arises when some form of disruption is experienced by a society. In this kind of culture, young people look to their contemporaries for guidance in making choices rather than relying on their elders for expertise and role models in a changing world.

A third, and final, cultural style—which Mead terms the "prefigurative"—is symptomatic of a world changing so fast that it exists "without models and without precedent" (p. xx). In prefigurative cultures, change is so rapid that "neither parents nor teachers, lawyers, doctors, skilled workers, inventors, preachers, or prophets" (p. xx) can teach children what they need to know about the world. The prefigurative cultural style, Mead argues, prevails in a world where the "past, the culture that had shaped [young adults'] understanding—their thoughts, their feelings, and their conceptions of the world—was no sure guide to the present. And the elders among them, bound to the past, [can] provide no models for the future" (p. 70).

In the prefigurative culture of the 21st century, then, it is little wonder that most adults have limited success in predicting the changes happening around them, in anticipating and coping with the world as it morphs through successive and confusing new forms. Similarly, it is little wonder that English composition instructors, and most writing programs, have had limited success in predicting and understanding the importance of visual, spatial, and multimodal literacies.

Within this context, it is useful to think about the kind of world, and the pace of change, that confronts Dànielle, Joseph, Brittney, and Charles. When Dànielle and Joseph were born, in 1973, for instance, personal computers had not been invented, nor had any modern computer networks been established. By the time they turned 10, however, Queen Elizabeth had sent her first e-mail message, and France had deployed the Minitel network to millions of its citizens. This rapid pace of change was to continue. By the time Dànielle and Joseph turned 20, and Brittney and Charles had begun attending first grade, both the Internet and the World Wide Web had been invented, and the World Bank and the United Nations had already established their own Web sites. Within another seven years, as Dànielle and Joseph were thinking about their graduate careers, and Brittney and Charles were making their way through secondary school in the year 2000, more than 93 million Internet host systems had been registered and the World Wide Web had reached a size of more than 1 billion indexible pages.[4]

By 2003, as Brittney and Charles were well into their high school careers, and Dànielle and Joseph were embarking on their professional careers, over half a billion people across the world had access to the Internet. A global snapshot at this time would show that among the countries of Europe, Germany, the United Kingdom, and Italy had the largest populations of people who access the Internet at home, and that the United States constitutes 29% of the global Internet, with Europe reporting 23%, Asia-Pacific 13%, and South America 2% ("Global Net Population Increases," 2003). It's also interesting to note that a recent Harris survey (HarrisInteractive, 2002) found that 93% of college students in the United States regularly use the Internet, making them the most connected segment of the U.S. population (92% of them say they own computers).[5]

None of these facts would surprise the four participants we have profiled in this chapter. Nor would they be surprised to learn that the United States Army had already designed and built a multimillion dollar simula-

---

[4]These markers of Internet development and many others can be found in *Hobbes' Internet Timeline,* compiled by Robert H. Zakon (1993–2003). Hobbes' timeline chronicles the growth of the Internet from 1993 to 2003, focusing primarily on the development of hardware, software, and networking systems. This timeline and others can be accessed from the Web site of the Internet Society at http://info.isoc.org/internet/history/.

[5]Here's the information Harris Interactive gives about the study:

The 360 Youth/Harris Interactive College Explorer™ Outlook Study is an online college survey from 360 Youth, Inc. and Harris Interactive. The study covers a variety of topics about the 18–30-year-old college market, from market power and influence, technology adoption and attitudes, to category penetration and spending.

tion facility in which to hold virtual war games or that the Bankers Trust Corporation in New York City had designed and used an online fantasy game, much like *Doom* or *Myst,* to provide corporate training on sexual harassment to its employees in the 1990s (Dillon, 1998). Indeed, it can be argued that Dànielle and Joseph, Brittney and Charles already know a great deal about the world for which they were preparing themselves and a great deal about the specific skills they would need in order to function as literate citizens and productive employees in this changing online world.

These four cases document in very personal terms the dynamic culture of 21st century life in the United States. Dànielle and Joseph, Brittney and Charles live in a very different world from the one inhabited by their parents and teachers. In this environment, the literacy education that teachers and parents provided to students a decade or a century ago will no longer do to equip people for success; too many major changes have altered our world in unexpected ways. Nation states previously isolated by impermeable borders have entered into geopolitical, monetary, trade, and environmental alliances that function regionally and globally. As the influence of nation states gives way, faster transportation, extended computer networks, and almost instantaneous communications systems support the exchange of information and people on a global scale. These transnational patterns, in addition, support the establishment of multiple and overlapping global authorities—The World Trade Organization, the World Bank, the United Nations—that extend people's understanding of political, economic, and social roles beyond the physical borders of their home countries.

These postmodern changes can be disorienting. As Manuel Castells (1997) points out, when power is "diffused in global networks of power, information, and images" (p. 359), disassociated with conventional centralized authorities like geographically determined nation states, social roles, political alliances, and traditional systems of authoritative values, people often feel alienated, fragmented, confronted with a disturbing loss of traditional authorities or conventional certainties.[6] But even as people are confronted by unstable and contradictory postmodern contexts, as Castells (1997) points out, they are also coping strategically with them as

---

[6]In his outstanding series of three volumes, entitled *The Information Age: Economy, Society, and Culture* (1996, 1997, 1998), sociologist Manuel Castells charted the world-order transformations associated with the rise of the information age on a global level. Among the effects of these transformations are the decline of conventional centralized authorities like geographically determined nation states, political alliances, and traditional systems of authoritative values; and the increase of online criminal and terrorist activities. Castells also traced the emergence of identity politics online, especially groups focused on race, gender, history, and language issues.

social and political agents. Increasingly, these groups and individuals assemble and communicate online, within the very computer networks that contributed to the unstable conditions in the first place. In such environments, for example, people like to participate in a new kind of identity politics anchored by the powerful connections of race, gender, history, and common interests, forming interest groups; political action groups; and groups focused on feminist, environmental, religious, or race issues. They also participate in social groups online, groups formed around gaming, dating, chatting about genealogy, films, or music. More important, Castells (1997) noted, as people exchange ideas in such groups—and often take action collectively—they are also involved in contesting, negotiating, and rewriting the new "social codes" under which societies will be "rethought, and re-established" in the coming decades (p. 360).

Literacy practices, it is clear, change dramatically within such online environments; texts must be able to cross national borders, time zones, language groups, and geographic distances; to resist the limitations of a single symbolic system and its attendant conventions.[7] They must communicate on multiple channels, using visual, aural, and kinesthetic elements as well as alphabetic components. To increase their effectiveness, such compositions may also become highly intertextual in terms of their resonance across media boundaries, as Diana George and Diane Shoos (1999) point out. Frequently, for instance, such texts bring communicative elements from television and movies to bear on the related texts of advertisements or games, thus establishing a network of meanings that play off of one another and gain strength from their cumulative allusions, much like what Charles described happening with Nickelodeon or the Nike icon. In such a world, it is of little wonder that Dànielle and Joseph, Brittney and Charles found their formal English composition instruction to be of limited interest. As with most contemporary writing instruction now offered in schools, their work in these classes focused on informative, technical, or creative writing, and it fell almost exclusively within the narrow bandwidth of the alphabetic. The skills they developed in these classes, although useful in some arenas, are not fully capable of preparing young people for a world that will depend on visual literacy, web literacy, gaming/simulation literacy, in short, multimodal literacies.

At the same time, within this dynamic environment, the self-sponsored literacy skills that Dànielle and Joseph, Brittney and Charles have devel-

---

[7]The excellent work of The New London Group makes an eloquent case for multiliteracies in a world characterized by online communications that must cut across traditional geopolitical, linguistic, and cultural borders. We recommend the 1996 *Harvard Educational Review* article entitled "A Pedagogy of Multiliteracies" and the 2000 volume, *Multiliteracies*, edited by Bill Cope and Mary Kalantzis for The New London Group. Additionally, the valuable work of Gunther Kress (1999), " 'English' at the Crossroads," made a closely related case for teachers of English composition.

oped online assume new currency and new importance. In a world dominated by computer networks that extend across language and cultural borders, business and industry, governments and organizations, individuals and groups have already begun to understand and value the visual literacy skills that Joseph has developed. Similarly, the coding and web-design literacy that Dànielle has acquired; the online language studies in which Brittney participates; and the collaborative problem-solving and gaming literacy that Charles has pursued have become increasingly valuable skills within new online environments.

These abilities represent the new literacy practices and values that educators must begin to recognize and integrate into formal classroom instruction if the United States and other countries hope to prepare citizens who can function effectively in the online communication environments that characterize the 21st century. To accomplish this task, educators, certainly those who teach English composition only in its more conventional forms, will need to change their attitudes about literacy in general, and they will need additional technology resources so that they can work more closely with students to learn about the new, self-sponsored media literacies these youngsters are developing and practicing online. Among these resources will be regularly updated computers and software, adequately wired school and university buildings with connections to the Internet, help from knowledgeable technical staff members, and additional professional development aimed at new-media education.

Teachers armed with these resources can then work collaboratively with students to develop meaningful assignments that will bring new literacies into composition classrooms in ways that both engage and challenge contemporary learners. For example, although students like Brittney and Charles have a great deal of situated practice with new-media literacies, they both need more overt instruction to be able to articulate the various rules and conventions adhering to specific kinds of communications within different cultural contexts. These young people also need help in framing their understandings critically so that they can question their own judgment and look at their work from the perspectives of audiences increasingly different from themselves. Finally, these students need a teacher's help in learning how to transform their practices—to transfer their knowledge of new-media literacies into other contexts, cultures, or areas of endeavor.[8]

---

[8]The pedagogical framework we outline here, and the terms we employ, are those of The New London Group. In the groundbreaking book *Multiliteracies*, edited by Bill Cope and Mary Kalantzis (2000), these scholars lay out a multiliteracies pedagogy that relies on four broad approaches to instruction: situated practice, overt instruction, critical framing, and transformed practice (pp. 239–248).

Within such an environment, teachers could pay increased attention to the new-media literacies students bring to the classroom, comparing these literacies to more conventional literacies and seeking to learn from this comparison more about the worlds that students inhabit and believe they will face in the coming years. Students would be able to take advantage of their teachers' perspectives, enhancing their new-media practices in ways that they might not accomplish on their own. With a range of emerging, competing, and conventional literacies in play, and with both teachers and students focused on how to meet the needs of different audiences, how to communicate information in a variety of formats, and how to accomplish their communicative purposes most effectively within a full range of media contexts, classrooms might become more like the places we all wish they would be: vigorous teaching and learning environments, characterized, as educator Paulo Freire (1990) suggested, by a kind of reciprocal learning in which

> ... the teacher-of-the-students and the students-of-the-teacher cease to exist and a new term emerges: teacher-students with students-teachers ... They become jointly responsible for a process in which all grow. (p. 67)

CONCLUSION:
Stories From the United States in the Information Age

Cynthia L. Selfe
Gail E. Hawisher

In this book, we trace the stories of 20 people from the United States of different ages, races, genders, and backgrounds who went about their lives during the period when personal computers were invented or during the time when these machines had found their way—in large quantities—into schools, workplaces, communities, and homes in the United States. These relatively cheap and durable examples of computer technology helped initiate a period of major social and technological change, one in which people's everyday lives, and literacies, were changed in fundamental ways. Today, personal computers have become embedded so deeply into the landscape of our daily lives that they are disappearing, becoming invisible, much like electricity or cars or ballpoint pens, all emergent technologies from previous periods in U.S. history. When this disappearing act is complete, when the memories of what some have referred to as the computer revolution have faded, these first-hand accounts of people's lived experiences will help us remember how computers dramatically altered our lives, and literacy, at one particular point in history.

At the same time, these stories do not purport to be a complete or entirely representative history. Chosen from more than 350 interviews, they still constitute only a small portion of some larger narratives: how individuals and families have adapted their literacy values and practices to computer-supported environments; how individual people's access to computers has varied, in part, along the axes of race, gender, and class; how and why the literacies of technology have thrived within the cultural ecology existing within the United States from 1978 to 2003; how people have struggled to acquire computer-based literacies in an attempt to improve their own prospects or those of their children; how children have shared computer-based literacies with adults and how adults have shared with children.

Thus, we recognize (and hope readers do as well) that no one story we have told here, and certainly not this collection of stories, can be considered indicative or representative of any larger population. There are far too many stories that remain uncollected, unheard, unappreciated for such larger narratives to be considered completely or even accurately rendered. This recognition, however, does not serve to diminish the value of the first-hand accounts told here. On the contrary, to us these literacy histories have proved to be richly sown with insights that have immediate face validity. We believe that other educators, parents, policymakers, literacy workers, and colleagues will react to them in the same way. In the rest of this chapter, we articulate some of the more important themes that emerged about digital literacies and that these stories suggest to us.

We should note, even as we begin, that this particular endeavor—drawing conclusions from a limited set of data—is a dangerous one, so we approach it with some caution. By identifying these themes, we do not mean to imply that they represent the only insights that readers can or should draw from the cases we have provided, nor that these thoughts have been, somehow, scientifically derived from the cases themselves, nor that our articulation of them will remain unchanged as we learn more about the literacies of technology in the United States and abroad.

Rather, we would say that these observations have suggested themselves to us, two women academics and teachers of literacy, because they share similarities with parts of our own stories, as these are situated historically and culturally: our backgrounds and gender; the ways in which we learn and struggle to use technology ourselves; the schools in which we have worked and the institutions that we have visited; the students with whom we have shared a classroom and the colleagues with whom we have shared concerns; the teaching we have done and literacies we have observed; and, finally, our own connections with, and admiration for, the participants whom we interviewed, from whom we learned so much, and with whom we co-authored these chapters. These speculations and themes, in other words, made sense to us, and we hope they do to readers as well.

Emerging Themes

Theme #1: Literacy exists within a complex cultural ecology of social, historical, and economic effects. Within this cultural ecology, literacies have life spans. The cases we have presented in the previous chapters indicate to us that literacies and the processes involved in acquiring and developing literacies are set within a complex ecology of events and effects. This ecology is situated historically, contextualized culturally, and articulated to a real set of material conditions. Composed of many effects and events, this complex ecology serves as the historical, cultural, and economic medium both for the growth and currency of particular literacies as well as for people's processes of acquiring and developing literacy. These cases also indicate to us that new forms of literacy don't simply accumulate. Rather, they have life spans: they emerge; they overlap and compete with pre-existing forms; they accumulate, significantly, perhaps, in periods of transition, but they also eventually fade away.

The cases we present here, especially when viewed in the context of work done by contemporary scholars of literacy,[1] remind us that we can understand literacy as a set of practices and values only when we properly situate these elements in a particular historical period, cultural milieu, or cluster of material conditions. Deborah Brandt (1995) noted that literacies—with the invention of computer-based communication technologies—accumulated toward the end of the 20th century. Proliferating computer-based literacies imparted a "complex flavor even to elementary acts of reading and writing . . . creating new and hybrid forms of literacy where once there might have been fewer and more circumscribed forms" (p. 651). This "rapid proliferation and diversification of literacy," Brandt continued, placed increasing pressure on people, whose ultimate success may be "best measured by a . . . capacity to amalgamate new reading and writing practices in response to rapid social change" (p. 651).

Such work suggests that the definition of literate is far from stable across time; that it changes dramatically and sometimes rapidly; and that specific forms of literacy may have cultural life spans, half-lives, determined by their congruence with, and influence on, current social forces; available communication environments; and political and economic formations that function at the macro-, medial, and micro-levels. In this book, we call this environment the cultural ecology of literacy.

Literacies accumulate most rapidly, these cases indicate, when a culture is undergoing a particularly dramatic or radical transition, much as Deborah Brandt (1995) and Miles Myers (1996) have shown.[2] During such periods of rapid change, humans value and practice both past and present

---

[1]Among the more influential of these scholars, for the purposes of this study, we count Brian Street, James Gee, Harvey Graff, Deborah Brandt, David Barton, Mary Hamilton, Gunther Kress, and The New London Group. We recommend the work of these scholars, which we include in the bibliography, for any readers interested in reading more about literacy.

[2]Both Deborah Brandt and Miles Myers made the point that literacies accumulate (Brandt's specific term from the title of her article, "Accumulating Literacy: Writing and Learning to Write in the Twentieth Century") when cultures undergo dramatic transitions.

forms of literacy simultaneously. In our contemporary culture, for example, which is undergoing a complicated and messy transition from the conditions characterizing modernism to the conditions characterizing postmodernism, change is both dramatic and rapid. Hence, it is no surprise that literacy scholars have noted multiple literacies emerging, accumulating, combining, and competing: print and digital literacies (Deibert, 1997), conventional alphabetic literacies (Brandt, 1995), visual literacies (Kress, 1999, 2003), and intertextual forms of media literacies (George & Shoos, 1999). Eventually, however, this accumulation reaches a limit; humans can cope with only so many literacies at once and the cultural distribution of literacies takes time to unfold, thus, a process of selection occurs.

Sets of literacy practices that fit less well with the changing cultural ecology will fade, whereas other literacy practices that fit better within that context flourish and contend with each other. Examples of emerging, competing, and fading literacies are not difficult to find. The specific literacy practices associated with hand-written letters on paper, for instance, which fit well in a culture that could depend on relatively cheap postal delivery service, a corporate sector based primarily in the United States, and an educational system that provided constant practice in cursive writing and placed a high value on a legible hand, are already fading in the United States. In the same context, e-mail as a literacy practice, which has a robust fit with the growth of electronic networks, global markets, and international financial systems, is flourishing and now competing with the genres of both the personal letter and the business memorandum.

The cases of our last chapter, those of Dànielle, Joseph, Brittney, and Charles, can help highlight the contested nature of the literacy landscape during the late 20th century and early 21st century when technological change has been extremely rapid, and when various forms of digital literacy have been competing with various forms of print literacy for ascendancy. In the early 1990s, for instance, although these young people were working in electronic environments, most of their online literacy practices were still primarily alphabetic. At that time, while desktop publishing, e-mail, and photo manipulation were gaining some currency, the World Wide Web and a graphical browser were just emerging. Only a decade later, however, these young people were all using visual presentation software, downloading web documents, designing sites for the Web, rendering three-dimensional landscapes, animating human figures, manipulating photographs, and inserting both audio and video clips into their online communications. Their online communications, at this point in time, could no longer be considered primarily alphabetic; they had taken a "turn to the visual" (Kress, 1999, p. 66) and to the multimodal.

Clearly, on the macro-, medial-, and micro-levels, there was a close fit between these students' newly acquired digital literacies and the existing cultural ecology. Their new literacies could not have flourished, for instance, without the invention of the World Wide Web, web browsers, and web search engines. Nor could they have existed without new kinds of hardware and software that supported multimedia design and communication. Nor would they have experienced such exponential growth without the accompanying explosion of online communities that used chat rooms, designed and played video games, experimented with digital photography, and designed Web sites—communities made up of people who shared the interests of the young people in the case studies we have mentioned. Similarly, the interests of Dànielle, Joseph, Brittney, and Charles were supported, at one level or another, by parents and friends convinced of the value of digital literacies, the growing enthusiasm of educators who saw the potential of multimedia technology, the technologizing of the U.S. workplace, the establishment of federal and state programs for technological literacy, the increasing global investment in information services, the influence and growth of globalization and transnational finances, to mention only a few influences. All of these factors and many more have contributed to a cultural ecology in which technological literacy practices have been, and continue to be, valued.

It is also important to note, however, that the cultural ecology Dànielle, Joseph, Brittney, and Charles inhabited has not been at all uniform in its predisposition to digital and nonalphabetic literacies. Although the educational institutions these students have attended, for instance, have valued computer-based literacies at some level and in some classes, they also have continued to value—especially in English classes and in most official assessments of communication ability—conventional print literacy. To a large extent, we believe this effect is generational. Print literacy has, after all, been the major shaping force in the educational experiences of faculty members at these schools, and thus, in the ongoing formulation of their official grading and evaluation standards. The context of print literacy had also affected the hiring decisions of these educational institutions, and of the employers who hire their graduates and expect them to be able to meet standards of conventional print literacy. The culture of print literacy also shapes the expectations of parents who enroll children in these educational institutions and the historically defined literacy ideals of the larger society in which the educational institutions exist and are expected to thrive.

This contested situation, in which print-based and alphabetic literacies continue to compete at many levels with computer-based and nonalphabetic literacies, may help explain why the English composition teachers who worked regularly with Dànielle, Joseph, Brittney, and Charles did not address their new-media literacies on a systematic basis. Raised and educated in a print culture, these educators may remain unsure of how to value the new-media literacies or even how to practice these new literacies themselves. Thus, they fail to take advantage of, to build on, and even to recognize, in some cases, the literacy strengths these students bring to the classroom and miss important opportunities to link their own instructional goals to the developing literacy strengths of these talented young people.

   Theme #2: Although a complex set of factors has affected the acquisition of digital literacy from 1978 to 2003, race, ethnicity, and class too often assume key roles. Because they are linked with other social formations at numerous levels, and because their effects are often multiplied and magnified by these linkages, race, ethnicity, and class are often capable of exerting a greater force than other factors.   Many of the interviews that we collected for our project and many of the stories that we have presented in this book indicate that race, ethnicity, and class, because they are articulated with so many other social, cultural, and material factors, have been key in shaping the ecologies within which people acquired (or failed to acquire) digital literacy during these changing years. White, upper middle class status, for example, contributed tremendously in providing opportunities for some of our participants. Dean, Karen, and Mary, among others, were able to capitalize on these opportunities and apply their considerable expertise with alphabetic literacies, itself a result, in part, of society's privileging of their race, ethnicity, and class, to becoming proficient with digital literacies. The stories of Sheila, Nichole, and Yolanda also point to the substantial influence that both race and class exert on people's opportunities to acquire and develop technological literacy, and indeed, literacy in general. Race exerted a major influence on Sheila's educational experiences in the all-Black schools of the segregated South: determining, at least in part, the schools she attended, the teachers she encountered, and the formal literacy practices to which she was exposed. Similarly, class, according to Sheila's own account, played a role in determining the literacy resources she had available in her home, her attitude toward education, and the time that she could devote to her pursuit of formal education.

   Although the relationships were more nuanced and less dramatically evident in integrated schools, race and class continued to affect the education in U.S. schoolrooms through the 1990s and beyond. As numerous reports have documented, schools and universities primarily serving students of color and poor students continued to have less access to computers and other literacy resources than schools primarily serving students who were affluent and often White.[3] It is within this context that

---

   [3]For further discussion of issues related to inequitable access to computers, see Coley, Crandler, and Engle (1997); Healy (1998); Moran (1999); Selfe (1999); Becker (2000); Hawisher (2000); and the *Falling through the Net* series (1995–2000).

we interpret the education that Damon, Carmen, and Tom received and that Yolanda is receiving in the first years of the 21st century. Because race, ethnicity, and class are so closely related in the United States, and because they are aligned with so many other major social formations (e.g., education, employment, social resources, economic opportunity, health and well-being), they have exerted great force within the lives of these people and within the lives of other participants we have interviewed for this project.

Race, ethnicity, and class have also been important factors, we believe, in people's access to computers and digital literacy in home environments. Families of color, for instance, have continued to be less likely than White families to have access to a computer in their homes. Consider, for example, findings from the 1995 U.S. government report, *Falling through the Net: A Survey of the "Have Nots" in Rural and Urban America*:

> Information "have nots" are disproportionately found in [U.S.] rural areas *and* its central cities. While most recognize that *poor* people as a group have difficulties in connecting to the NII [now the Internet], less well known is the fact that the lowest telephone penetration exists in central cities. Concerning personal-computer penetration and the incidence of modems when computers are present in a household, however, no situation compares with the plight of the rural poor. . . .
>
> An examination by *race* reveals that Native Americans (including American Indians, Aleuts, and Eskimos) in rural areas proportionately possess the fewest telephones, followed by rural Hispanics and rural Blacks. . . . Black households in central cities and particularly rural areas have the lowest percentages of PCs, with central city Hispanics also ranked low. . . . For those households with computers, Native Americans and Asians/Pacific Islanders registered the lowest position among those possessing modems. (emphasis in original document)

For Native Americans, then, problems of access in the home are compounded by living in rural areas on tribal lands. In a 1999 report from the Benton Foundation, for example, it was noted that on Native American reservations 12% of households lack electricity and 53% lack telephone connections (Benton Foundation, 1999). It is not surprising, therefore, that only 26.8% of rural Native American households are reported as having computers in 1999 as compared with 42% of rural households across the United States (*Falling through the Net*, 1999).

When considering this state of affairs in light of Damon's technological literacy efforts while attending high school in inner-city Detroit, and Carmen's efforts while living on a reservation in rural Michigan, we find ourselves doubly impressed by the two participants' digital literacy accomplishments. Others in our study also faced similar challenges in their efforts to acquire the literacies of technology and often succeeded against the most difficult odds.

More recently, however, the 2000 U.S. government report *Falling through the Net: Toward Digital Inclusion* (2000), states that conditions have improved, at least as far as Internet access is concerned, or what the report calls "Internet Penetration." In 2000, Black households were more than twice as likely to have home access to the Internet than they were as late as 1998, and Hispanic households made similar gains (*Falling through the Net*, 2000). But overall, even this latest government report maintains that a digital divide in access to computers and the Internet persists especially in Black and Hispanic households where Internet penetration rates remain among the lowest (*Falling through the Net*, 2000).

Finally, we need to note that race, ethnicity, and class have affected people's access to computers, and thus their digital literacy practices, in U.S. workplaces. A great deal of evidence, over time, exists to corroborate this claim:

- In 1993, for example, 48.7% of White workers (18 years and older) used computers at work, whereas only 36.2% of Black workers did, and 29.3% of Hispanic workers did (National Center for Educational Statistics, May 2000, Chapter 7, Table 430).
- In 1997, 53.8% of White workers (18 years and older) used computers at work, whereas only 40.0% of Black workers did, and 30.2% of Hispanic workers did (National Center for Educational Statistics, May 2000, Chapter 7, Table 430).
- In 2000, 14.1% of White workers had access to the Internet at work whereas only 8.6% of Black workers and 5.6% of Hispanics did (*Falling through the Net*, 2000, p. 47).

Of course, these statistics do not reveal the kinds of uses to which computers are put by various people in the workplace. Whether, for example, people sit at a computer all day and enter data that others have created, whether they develop programs and other online materials, or whether they design and manage Web sites makes a huge difference in the kinds of opportunities that their work with computers offers them.

If, however, the participants in our project have convinced us that race, ethnicity, and poverty are key factors that often shape people's digital literacies, they also indicate that these factors alone do not always fully determine the lives and the literacies of people. Influenced by college sports and his acquired love of college campuses, Tom, for example, set in motion an academic career path that began in the community college and continued through graduate school. Sheila, too, was strongly influenced in setting her own educational goals by her mother's beliefs that education could serve as a social counterbalance to poverty and racism; Nichole was keenly aware of her mother's expectations that she attend college and her advice that electronic literacy would prove useful in achieving this goal. Yolanda, moreover, was influenced not only by the value her mother placed on reading and education, but also by the value she placed on computer literacy. Similarly, Damon and Melissa honed their technological literacy skills on their own time because they wanted access to jobs that required such skills. Obviously, however, there are countless others in the United States who have been less able to overcome obstacles that prevent them from acquiring the literacies of technology to their own satisfaction.

Theme #3: Gender can often assume a key role in the acquisition of digital literacy, especially when articulated with other social, cultural, and material factors. These cases also suggest to us that gender, especially when it is articulated with other social, cultural, and material factors, can be a key factor in determining whether, how, and when people acquire (or fail to acquire) digital literacy. White, middle class values associated with femininity, especially, but not exclusively, among those women born before the advent of personal computers, often served as obstacles on the pathways girls and women followed in their attempts to acquire the literacies of technology. For instance, in the cases represented in this book, Mary, whose own professionally educated parents and grandparents placed a high value on alphabetic literacy but not on digital literacy, showed little interest in the new technologies when they first appeared. She was not a computer enthusiast. Coming up through school, she first encountered computers in 1982 when she was a teenager in an honors math class, a class in which mostly boys enrolled. At 13, she was much more interested in achieving good grades, as girls are raised to do, than in becoming a computer aficionado and pal to "techie" guys on the playground. As Roberta Furger (1998) points out, even as late as the 1990s some young girls tended to neglect computers, recognizing "the unwritten yet incredibly powerful rule . . . [that] girls could use them for school . . . but only guys could be *into* computers, only guys could be really good at them" (p. 3, emphasis in the original). In other words, microcomputers, initially at least, often became the province of boys, "boys' toys," or as stated in the title of a 1994 *Wall Street Journal* article, "Computers—The Gender Divide: A Tool for Women, a Toy for Men" (Buckeley, 1994). Although the women in our study ultimately defy the gender stereotypes associated with women and computers, such commonly held assumptions, nonetheless, continue to affect some White, middle class girls' acquisition of the literacies of technology.

It's probably not surprising, then, to learn that despite the growing inroads computers have made into people's lives, the number of women majoring in computer science and technology-related fields continues to be relatively small. Even in the period 2001 to 2002, with women earning the highest proportion of PhDs in computer science since 1985, that figure is only 18% of the total awarded degrees in the United States and also reflects the same percentage of BS degrees that women earned in computer science in 2002 ("CRA Taulbee Trends," 2003). Interestingly, however, although the women in our study showed little interest in computer science as a career per se, many of them have gone on to occupy professional positions that require a high degree of technological literacy. Jane, for example, manages her college's Web site as Liberal Arts Web Administrator; Jená directs the technology efforts of her university writing program; Janice regularly gives technology training workshops and teaches courses on all aspects of digital literacy as an assistant professor of professional writing; Paula oversees computing facilities as director of her college's Cooperative Learning Center; and Mary teaches a web-authoring course for humanities graduate students as part of a 2002 Woodrow Wilson Innovation Award she won as an assistant professor of English. Although these and other women in our study were all born before the advent of personal computers, they have nevertheless successfully acquired the literacies of technology. But we need to note, too, that they have also spent a great deal of time and effort in the process, lacking the early experiences and ubiquitous resources that tend to be more available to the younger participants in our study, regardless of their gender.

These cases convince us, however, that White, middle class women whose access to technology is constrained early in their lives can often still acquire and develop online literacies later, given that appropriate access, sponsors, timing, motivation, and other conditions are in place. Often the educational and societal support these women have been accorded as White and middle class provides them with the necessary confidence to come, finally, to technological literacy after adolescence and, in some cases, even after middle age. But we should also note that second-wave feminism, the Women's Movement, and the rise of the counterculture were also probably instrumental in enabling Jane, Jená, and Janice to strike out on their own and acquire digital literacies. The many social movements encouraged women to define themselves outside the commonplace roles of wife and mother and offered opportunities—educational and otherwise—for them to succeed if they persisted.

There are other factors in particular cultures within the United States, however, that also affect women's acquisition of digital literacies. Lynette Kvasny (2003), for example, argues that technology and gender studies often view women as a collective rather than as a heterogeneous group of women who hold many different attitudes toward information technologies. In an interview study of minorities in Atlanta, Georgia, Kvasny

(2003) found that African American women from low-income communities often understood information technologies as a way to overcome their economic predicament and felt little of the discomfort that, she alleges, some White, middle class women experience toward technology. These observations would hold true of a number of Black women in our study. As we noted in chapter 4, Melissa, as an African American woman, was eager to embrace technological literacies as a means of forwarding her life and career. Although Melissa's material circumstances would classify her across the board as middle class, she nevertheless defined herself outside White, middle class women's notions of femininity and pursued the literacies of technology with enthusiasm. We would also argue that as a teenager Paula, although White, capitalized on her working class roots, ignored values of femininity, and immersed herself in video games and computer programming, even as most of her middle class girlfriends showed little interest.

Other cultural factors that may ameliorate effects of gender come into play as well. The intimate connections that Melissa and also Karen, of chapter 2, experienced with military culture seem to have influenced their relationship with information technologies. As early as 1976, when Karen was only eight years old, Karen's military father introduced her to the first computer games, and soon thereafter to daisy-wheel printers, and then, in the next few years, to the family's Commodore 64. New technological developments were never strangers to women (and men) living on military bases, and Karen took full advantage of the opportunities this exposure provided. Thus, even as a White, middle class girl and woman, Karen valued new media and the literacies of technology as her constant companions very early in life.

Theme #4: Within a cultural ecology, people exert their own powerful agency in, around, and through digital literacy, even though unintended consequences always accompany their actions. All of the cases we have presented in this volume suggest that people exert their own very real and potent agency in, around, and through digital literacies, and that they shape the environment for their own digital literacies through actions that have effects at the micro-, medial, and macro-levels of social operations. This understanding is supported by the work of sociologist Anthony Giddens (1979), who notes that people both shape, and are shaped by, the social systems within which they live in a complex duality of structuration, that "every competent member of every society" (p. 71) not only "knows a great deal about the institutions of that society" (p. 71) but also draws on this understanding of "structure, rules and resources" (p. 71) to make changes in the surrounding environment. Andrew Feenberg (1999), as well, notes that technological systems are productively shaped and influenced by people, in both their design and their use, even as these systems shape and influence the lives of the people associated with them.

Thus, in the stories we have presented in this book, participants both influence, and are influenced by, the social and historical circumstances within which they live. The actions of these people (e.g., their decisions to learn how to work and communicate in computer environments, the ways they shaped their own appropriate conditions of access to these environments, the steps they took to teach both older and younger family members how to use computers as literacy environments), although they occur in micro-level social environments (i.e., in families, peer groups, the life of a person), also extend beyond these environments, and are often magnified by individual talent and cumulative force so that they have effects at higher levels: in medial (e.g., workplaces, schools, organizations) and macro-level (i.e., region, nation, multiple nations) environments, for example.

Consider, too, that people as seemingly diverse as Karen's father, a military officer, who was himself part of a White, military family, and Nichole's mother, a homemaker, who was part of a Black, working-class family, along with other parents of the participants in our study, were influenced by the rapid expansion of the information society in the late 1970s, 1980s, and early 1990s, readily accepting technology as being at the center of progress and advancement in the United States. Educated in a time when scientific discoveries were generally lauded as social advances, these parents understood the computer to be a powerful tool that they should exploit for the benefit of their families, and so they purchased computers as investments in their own and their children's future success. These micro-level family values, themselves shaped by the large-scale ideological formations characterizing U.S. society, fed back into the cycle of consumerism and rapid technology innovation that continues to characterize life in the United States.

At the same time, however, we believe that people often resist, or transcend external expectations and tendencies, depending on their talents, goals, and insights, among many other factors. The cases of Jill, Damon, Tom, Nichole, and Carmen, to name just a few, corroborate this belief. Jill, for instance, made up her mind not to go into web design or multimedia, despite the increasing cachet of these fields, because she saw them as too computer-intensive. Similarly, Damon, Tom, Nichole, and Carmen resisted limiting social expectations linked to race and class to pursue college educations and online literacies. Paula and Janice defied gender expectations in accumulating those literacies of technology most closely associated with techie cultures populated largely by men. The effectiveness of particular people in undertaking such actions, we have learned through these cases, can depend on a range of factors: their innate or learned abilities to pursue both unexpected and predictable goals; their family values and literacy histories; their social, economic, and personal circumstances; their commitment, confidence, and faith in themselves—whatever factors enable them to pursue both unexpected and unpredictable goals.

We do not want to indicate with this discussion, however, that people can always do, or accomplish, anything they so desire within social structures nor that the actions they take are always effective. Clearly, people are constrained in their actions by any number of influential factors: age, class, race, handicap, experience, opportunity, and belief systems are among only a few such factors. Further, we should add that the actions people do undertake, because they occur within a complex cultural ecology, always have what Anthony Giddens (1979) calls "unintended consequences" (p. 56) that escape the bounds of people's intentions. Thus, for instance, although Damon's efforts to acquire certain kinds of technological literacy succeeded in many ways, they also resulted at some level in his failing out of college—an effect he neither foresaw nor desired.

Theme #5: Schools, workplaces, communities, and homes are the four primary gateways through which those living in the United States have gained access to digital literacy in the decades since the invention and successful marketing of the personal computer. Unsurprisingly, the cases in this book remind us that schools, homes, communities, and workplaces represent the four major gateways through which people have gained access to computer technology over the last three decades. In general, our interviews indicate that the more of these gateways people have open to them, the more likely they are, over their lifetimes, to acquire and develop robust sets of digital literacy skills and to value digital literacies. It is also true, however, that the relative importance of these gateways in people's lives varies according to the needs and motivations of those who use them, the historical contexts in which they exist, and the sets of social circumstances that shape them—all factors that shape the cultural ecology in which people come to acquire the literacies of technology.

Many of the interviews we conducted (usually among those who were born sometime in the mid-1950s and later) indicate that public schools and universities have provided the earliest and the most consistently accessible gateways for technological literacy from 1978 onward. In the early years of the personal computer revolution, in fact, when the costs of hardware, software, and technical support precluded easy purchasing of home computers, schools and universities provided countless people in the United States, among them, Sally, Jill, Paula, Mary, Carmen, Dean, and Tom, with their earliest exposure to computers. It's important to note, too, the significant role that two-year colleges have played in opening up opportunities for technological literacy acquisition. Without access to local community colleges, it is unlikely that Paula, Nichole's mother, Carmen, Melissa, Tom, and Janice, to name just a few of the community college alums in our study, would have been able to pursue further education in computer-based literacies if and when they so desired.

Although on every level this access has been, overall, a positive factor, the historical relation between education and digital literacy has proven neither simple nor one-dimensional. For instance, public schools and universities have been criticized for habituating young people to the use of communication technologies, such as computers, without providing them, or their teachers, with a critical perspective on these technologies or on what may be inappropriate uses of computers.[4]

In addition, despite large investments in the new technologies at every educational level, computers remain differentially distributed throughout the United States, with those families who dwell in the upper echelons of society and whose children attend well funded schools often having ready access to digital literacy and its most advanced applications during every step of their schooling. These children are also more likely to have access to teachers who have more extensive training in digital literacies, unlike Damon, who attended some of the poorest of U.S. schools. Yet according to a recent U.S. government report *A Nation Online* (2002), U.S. citizens should be less concerned in 2002 than in earlier times about the existence of a digital divide.

In February of 2002, the U.S. government under George W. Bush's administration published *A Nation Online* (U.S. Department of Commerce, 2002), the most recent publication in the series *Falling through the Net*,[5] designed to report on computer and Internet usage in the United States. The new title was intended to convey the notion that the concerns of the digital divide had been largely addressed and should no longer trouble people in the United States. According to a still more recent report from the Benton Foundation,[6] however, the arguments in *A Nation Online* are contradicted by its own statistics. *The Sustainability Challenge* (Benton Foundation, 2003), for example, maintains that

---

[4]For various takes on this critique, compare Olson (1984); Hawisher and Selfe (1989); Hawisher and Selfe (1991); Birkerts (1994); Selfe (1999).

[5]See the list of references for bibliographical information on the four previous reports published in this U.S. government series.

[6]Throughout this book, we have turned to several reports from the Benton Foundation for timely articles related to information technologies and literacies. According to its web page, "[T]he mission of the Benton Foundation is to articulate a public interest vision for the digital age and to demonstrate the value of communications for solving social problems." Retrieved May 8, 2003, from http://www.benton.org/Library/sustainability/sus_challenge.pdf.

... almost half of American households do not have access to the Internet. Higher-income Americans are more than three times as likely to be online as those with lower incomes. Whites and Asians are six times more likely to use the Internet than Blacks or Hispanics. And 75 percent of lower-income Americans do not have Internet access. (p. 18)

To our minds, the fact that these conditions persist makes it all the more important that schools continue in their role as essential gateways to the literacies of technology, even as access for some people becomes more available in other venues.

The Sustainability Challenge (Benton Foundation, 2003) also reports on successful efforts in U.S. schools to address technology gaps over the past decade, in the following statement:

The percentage of schools connected to the Internet rose from 35 percent in 1994 to 99 percent in 2001. The student to Internet connected computer ratio has improved dramatically in an even shorter time frame, going from 12 students per computer in 1998 to five to one in 2001. Many students who do not have computer and Internet access at home at least have some access at school. However, there are indications that many schools are not using this new infrastructure to maximum advantage. (p. 7)

But, as the report also notes, problems remain. Top on its list of "critical actions" for sustaining and improving schools' technology infrastructure is the need to "accelerate teacher professional development" (Benton Foundation, 2003, p. 7). Thus, although schools are better equipped, more connected, and more capable than ever before in providing greater access to the literacies of technology at every level, they still lack the wherewithal to provide meaningful digital literacy instruction for students like Damon, Brittney, and Charles, who often find themselves in schools where their teachers are less digitally prepared than they would like.[7]

Workplace settings have provided a second major gateway for electronic literacy, as the stories of Nichole's mother, Charles' father, Janice, Carmen, and Melissa suggest, among others. Since the 1980s, businesses and corporations have become increasingly dependent on computer-based communications.[8] Driving this dependence have been the forces of

---

[7]For an interesting discussion of students' responses to digital literacy instruction, particularly among middle and high school students in southern parts of the United States, see the Bell South Foundation (2003) report, *The Growing Technology Gap Between Schools and Students*. According to the report, teachers see themselves as incorporating technological literacy activities into the curriculum a great deal more than students do. The report is also useful in viewing the kinds of online activities in which students take part in and out of school. One interesting finding, for example, is that the average U.S. 15 year old has never "dialed" a phone and purchases movie tickets through the Internet rather than standing in line.

globalization, the rapid growth in computer manufacturing[9] and in the information technology sector, government policies designed to increase the export of U.S. computer goods and services, and the rapid innovation and decreasing costs characterizing the computer industry. As a result of these related trends, workplaces have provided many employees with both access to technology and the pragmatic motivations for taking advantage of this access. This historical tracing does not suggest, however, that access to computer technology in the workplace has been equitable. Computer use in the workplace, as in schools, also continues to be differentially distributed along the axes of race and income as we have already noted.

Communities also serve as critical technological literacy gateways by providing public access facilities, such as community centers, community networks, and libraries for people's online literacy practices. The U.S. government report, *A Nation Online* (U.S. Department of Commerce, 2002), reveals that many in the United States who lack access to computers and the Internet at home turn to libraries for access, and this was certainly true for the participants in our study. Time and again, they mentioned libraries as important gateways for literacy activities. Older participants, like Jane and Jená, spoke of the Carnegie libraries and the weekly trips each made to the library to borrow books; and the younger participants, Damon, or the youngest in our study, Yolanda, not only borrowed books but also talked about writing school papers with word processing and doing research on the Web at local libraries. Significantly, *A Nation Online* reports that "a far higher percentage of Hispanic (39 percent) and Black (45 percent) children rely solely on public access facilities to use computers than White children (15 percent)" (p. 9). Thus these public access facilities also help address the inequitable computing conditions that remain constant problems in the United States.

Finally, families and homes provide the fourth major gateway through which people come to the literacies of technology. Within the environment of their homes, for example, Sally's and Jill's parents provided a rich environment in which their children learned and practiced print and digital literacies; Karen's home was also filled with an impressive array of home crafts, books, magazines, photographic materials and, later, computer games; and Dean and Carmen made sure that their own children had a wide assortment of electronic resources at their fingertips. In fact,

---

[8]For explorations of this claim compare Johnston and Packer (1987); Judy and D'Amico (1997); Meares and Sargent (1999); and U.S. Department of Labor (1999).

[9]Published in 1996, volume 119, number 8 of the *Monthly Labor Review* provides an excellent historical snapshot of how computers were shaping the U.S. economy in 1996. Among the articles in this issue, we recommend those authored by Moris, Warnke, Goodman, and Freeman.

with the exception of Tom, who prefers to use university-access sites for his computing needs, and Sheila, the oldest of the 20 participants, all the adults in this book today compose on computers that they own. When compared to the latest U.S. Census Bureau's (2001) statistics on the percentage of households in the United States owning a computer, the participants are probably more likely to own computers than the average U.S. resident. Fifty-four million households in the United States, or 51% had at least one computer in August of 2000 (U.S. Census Bureau, 2001). The government report goes on to point out that "since 1984, the first year in which the Census Bureau collected data on computer ownership and use, [the U.S.] has experienced more than a five-fold increase in the proportion of households with computers." Along with Internet access and thus ready access to online reading, writing, and communicating at home—computer ownership has been a major factor contributing to the participants' high degree of proficiency with digital literacies. But we need also to note that specific conditions surrounding that access make a huge difference in the ways in which people acquire, or don't, the literacies of technology.

Theme #6: Access to computers is not a monodimensional social formation. It is necessary but not sufficient for the acquisition and development of digital literacy. The specific conditions of access have a substantial effect on the acquisition and development of digital literacy. Interviews in this project suggest that the specific conditions of access are important factors in when and how people acquire and develop flexible sets of technological literacy abilities, or indeed, if they choose to do so. Among the more significant conditions of access mentioned by people are the fit, or match, between their needs and the capabilities of available computer hardware and software; the motivation, or personal stake, they have for learning to communicate in online environments; the resources, financial and otherwise that they have available to devote to computers; the immediacy and convenience of computer access; the availability of technical support in a form that fits their particular learning style; and the safety, security, and general ambience of the computing environment they have available for their use.

The *Falling through the Net* series (1995, 1998, 1999, 2000) illustrates the important role that specific conditions play in shaping people's access to, and activities on, computers. For example, a survey of households that had purchased computers but had never made extensive use of these machines as communication environments by connecting them to the Internet indicated that 1% of families had problems finding a service provider that would support such a connection, 2% of families lacked the knowledge to make the connection a reality, 4% considered their computer or the Internet to be "not user friendly," 5% thought Internet connections to be "not useful," 6.7% evaluated their computers as incapable of Internet access, 9% indicated a lack of time for such activities, and 17.3% thought the cost prohibitive within the context of the family's resources (*Falling through the Net*, 2000, p. 26).

Among the conditions of access that these case studies have encouraged us to consider are the following:

> Home: equitable access to computer equipment and software that supports connectivity; affordable service providers; technical support, preferably, but not necessarily, within the household; role models who use computers, preferably, but not necessarily, within the household; safe, secure, and comfortable environments in which to use computers; computer equipment and software that meet people's needs, interests, and learning styles; financial resources equal to support the costs of computing; personal interest in, and motivation for, using computers to communicate; strong commitment among members of the household to value and practice literacy.

> School: equitable access to up-to-date computer equipment and software that meet the needs and interests of both students and teachers; faculty members who can work knowledgeably and capably in online environments and provide computer-using role models; curricular integration of computers in meaningful ways; building infrastructures that support connectivity; funding policies that provide for technical support and professional development for teachers and staff; comfortable and safe computing environments that are accessible to all students; educational environments that do not discriminate between students on the basis of race, ethnicity, socioeconomic status, gender, sexual orientation, or geographical location.

> Community: equitable access to up-to-date computer equipment and software that meet the needs and interests of a broad range of people; support personnel who can work knowledgeably and capably in online environments like public libraries and literacy centers and provide computer-using role models; the integration of computers in civic life in ways that are meaningful; building infrastructures in libraries and community centers that support connectivity; funding policies that provide for technical support and professional development for staff; comfortable and safe computing environments that are accessible to community members; educational environments that do not discriminate between people on the basis of race, ethnicity, socioeconomic status, gender, sexual orientation, or geographical location.

> Workplace: equitable access to up-to-date computer equipment and software that meet the needs and interests of employers, employees,

and organizations; technical support that provides help for employees with different learning styles and different levels of computer expertise; tuition free, on-site training classes that employees can attend; computer equipment and software that support connectivity within the organization and within professional circles; safe, secure, and comfortable environments in which to use computers.

To add to this picture, we can consider the situation of households like Carmen's and Janice's that have been headed by a single female parent. In the United States in 2000, two-parent households were much more likely to have home Internet access than single-parent, female-headed households (52.7% for dual-parent, versus 30.6% for single, female-headed; U.S. Census Bureau, 2001). Within this context of overlapping social conditions, Carmen and Janice's own stories—of seeking access to computers and arranging the specific conditions they needed in order to make that access meaningful, of acquiring digital literacy and sharing this literacy with their children—assume new meaning.

Theme #7: Some families share a relatively coherent set of literacy values and practices—and digital literacy values and practices—and spread these values among their members. Information about, and support of, electronic literacy can flow both upstream, from younger to older, and downstream, from older to younger members of a family. The stories that people tell about literacy, both print and electronic, in this book indicate that some families share, among their members, a relatively coherent set of values associated with education generally, and literacy more specifically. Further, these stories suggest, such values can transcend the boundaries between print and electronic literacies. To explore this claim, we refer to the specific cases of Sheila, Nichole, and Yolanda, in chapter 5, although this observation holds true, as well, for many of the other families in this study.

All three generations of Sheila's, Nichole's, and Yolanda's family, for example, believed that education, in general, represented an important key to their future success, and that literacy, more specifically, was an essential component of a good education. Sheila, for instance, pursued her high school degree with a single-minded dedication, even though she had little evidence that such a degree would change the world she encountered in the segregated South. She also dreamed of being a writer and authored her own poetry whenever the circumstances in her life allowed. Nichole, similarly, saw both her undergraduate and graduate education as an investment in her own future, and her ability to read, write, and design communications as the focus of her career. Yolanda, who was convinced that she devoted the majority of her young life to completing homework assignments, recognized her own investment in reading as a natural reflection of her mother's and grandmother's valuing of that same activity.

These literacy values, as indicated by Sheila, Nichole, and Yolanda, were passed along within the family in many different ways, not only through the more elaborated stories that the family shared (e.g., Sheila's story about how Aunt Butch's White employer reacted to the possibility of integrated schools), but also through the nature, frequency, and context of family members' literacy practices (e.g., Nichole's mother reading to her daughter and teaching herself to use the dedicated word processor that she purchased at Sears; Yolanda's mother teaching her daughter to use the computer at her workplace), in their informal passing conversations (e.g., Nichole mentioning various computer applications to Sheila; Yolanda mentioning her lack of computer access to Nichole), in family members' observations of each other's actions (e.g., Sheila's writing poetry, Nichole's working for the University Communications Office, Jean's attending night school, Yolanda's online shopping excursions, her mother's Bible reading), and in the literacy materials kept and used around the house (e.g., books, newspapers, the Bible, magazines, computers). Also passed along within a family are less positive literacy experiences. Sheila, for instance, was able to recall the humiliation she felt when her grandmother read her private diary looking for evidence of inappropriate behavior and thoughts. In a child with less of a commitment to writing as a way of making sense of the world, this experience could have discouraged personal writing. From all these sources, it is clear to us that literacy values and practices are sedimented deeply and at many different levels in a family's lived experiences.

These cases also indicate that the importance a family attaches to literacy practices, in general, may shape the ways in which they approach the literacies of technology, more specifically. Certainly, Nichole felt that her mother's high regard for literacy practices, her pleasure in reading books, her insistence on attention to detail in writing, her pursuit of higher education, shaped her own willingness to learn new forms of electronic literacy, as well as her ability to do so. Similarly, Yolanda considered her mother's use of computers as part and parcel of her general value on education and her well established habits of reading and writing. Sheila's value on writing poetry contributed to her desire to compose poetry and design cards on a computer, and her persistence as a writer may well lead to her success in connection with this goal.

Within this context, none of these three women understood computers primarily as machines to be used for computing and calculating. Rather, they understood computers as literacy machines, and they valued these machines because they offered new environments for reading, writing, and communicating. All three women, for instance, mentioned that computers offered spaces within which they could continue to practice reading and writing skills that they already valued (e.g., writing reports for school, composing poetry, reading alphabetic texts) as well as environments within which they could expand these abilities, appropriately, into new digital forms that allowed for additional communicative reach (e.g., using the World Wide Web to research the provenance of antiques and family history, using software to design documents containing images as well as text, using design programs to create greeting cards featuring original poems, sending e-mail to family members; using the Web to read about music groups and rock stars).

These three case studies also provide a complex mapping of the routes by which literacy values and practices are passed along within a family. Under the right conditions, literacy practices and values can flow upstream as well as downstream in a family, as indicated by an NPR/Kaiser/Kennedy School poll conducted in 1999, which found that 33% of adults reported asking their children for help with computer problems, and 55% of children reported asking their parents for such help ("Survey Shows Widespread Enthusiasm for Technology," 1999). Thus, it is not surprising to find that Sheila has influenced her niece Nichole's value on literacy practices in general, and that Nichole has also influenced her aunt's specific understanding of computers, as well as her desire to purchase a computer that would support her writing. Similarly, Yolanda has recognized in her older cousin Nichole a literacy role model and inherited from her a sense of what literacy practices are both possible and desirable. At the same time, however, Nichole's own literacy practices, and at least part of her approach to graduate studies, have been shaped by her understanding of the inadequate digital literacy instruction that Yolanda is receiving and how that instruction is affecting her younger cousin's life.

This particular finding is corroborated in other case studies within the larger project. Jill's uncle and aunt, for instance, passed computer equipment downstream to their niece and nephew; Jane's mother-in-law gave her family computers and even provided technological support for their literacy efforts. These same relatives served both as teachers and role models. Similarly, the fathers of Paula, Carmen, and Charles provided their children not only with computer equipment, but also with software that encouraged their children to use the computer for activities that mirrored—and went beyond—the more formal literacy instruction they received in schools. In examples that illustrate the upstream flow of digital literacy, Dean and his brother advised their mother on her purchase of a laptop computer and served as her technical advisors while she learned to

use this machine to send e-mail to her grandchildren; Mary and her siblings selected the computer their parents bought and color-coded the key-
board so that her parents could more easily understand its workings (they
needed to know, for example, that *del* really meant *delete*). Similarly,
Paula, Janice, Melissa, Brittney, Jill, and Nichole all serve as their family's
technology experts, and pass their expertise upstream to parents and relatives. Many of the interviews also indicate that access to computers at
home may be increasing as generations of old technology are used and re-
cycled among families, with computers being passed from children to
parents, from aunts to nieces, and from grandchildren to grandparents.

*Theme #8: Faculty members, school administrators, educational policymakers,
and parents need to recognize the importance of the digital literacies that young
people are developing, as well as the increasingly complex global contexts within
which these self-sponsored literacies function. We need to expand our national
understanding of literacy beyond the narrow bounds of print and beyond the alphabetic.* The cases in this book suggest to us the new responsibilities that
U.S. literacy educators—and parents, educational policymakers, and people in general—have toward emerging, competing, and fading literacies
at a time when the cultural ecology of literacy is changing so rapidly. Literacy scholars Brian Street, Harvey Graff, Gunther Kress, and Elspeth
Stuckey, among many others, remind us of the dangers we face when we
cling too tightly to one single official version of literacy, like Standard
English or alphabetic literacy, or even, we would suggest, digital
literacies. Thinking only in terms of one official way of composing, one
way of reading, Street (1995) notes, not only fails to acknowledge and respect the complexities of literacy as situated historically, culturally, economically, and politically but also supports "patronizing assumptions
about what it means to have difficulties with reading and writing in contemporary society" (p. 17).

Further, because students from different cultures, races, and backgrounds bring different literacies and different experiences with literacy
to the classroom, focusing so single-mindedly on only one privileged form
of literacy encourages a continuation of the literate/illiterate divide that
perpetuates violence and functions in a conservative, reproductive fashion to favor existing class-based systems.[10] Thus, when educators adhere
to a narrow understanding of alphabetic literacy, when they recognize the
activities we call composing or reading only when they occur in conventional contexts, they contribute to a situation in which people consider

---

[10]For an explanation of the violence evoked in the name of literacy, see the outstanding
work of Stuckey (1991), Street (1995), Graff (1987), and Wysocki and Johnson-Eilola (1999).

themselves (and, worse, others) more or less literate or illiterate depending on their facility within that small range of abilities. Within this context,
we can better understand why schools, in general, and composition and
literacy programs, more specifically, need to understand, value, and work
actively with the multiple literacies that students bring with them to classrooms, literacies in which students have—like Damon, Dànielle, Joseph,
Brittney, or Charles—considerable and deeply sedimented personal and
cultural investments.

In addition to considering a U.S. context for digital literacy, we also
need to recognize another, more globally situated context. As Manuel
Castells (1996, 1997, 1998) explained in his three-volume series on the information age, the rapid growth of transnational mass media and computer networks requires new kinds of texts that can effectively cross national borders, time zones, language groups, and geographic distances;
texts that use emerging discourses expressed in a rich mix of video, audio,
graphics, animation, and alphabetic elements and that resist the limitations of a single symbolic system and its attendant conventions. The new-
media texts that grow out of these contexts differ so radically from those
print texts with which we are familiar, Gunther Kress (1999) noted, that a
conventional "emphasis on language alone simply will no longer do" (p.
67) to adequately or accurately represent how meaning is generated:

> The focus on language alone has meant a neglect, an overlooking, even sup-
> pression of the potentials of representational and communicational modes
> in particular cultures; an often repressive and always systematic neglect of
> human potentials in many of these areas; and a neglect equally, as a conse-
> quence, of the development of theoretical understandings of such
> modes. . . . [T]o put it provocatively: the single, exclusive and intensive fo-
> cus on written language has dampened the full development of all kinds of
> human potentials, through all the sensorial possibilities of human bodies, in
> all kinds of respects, cognitively and affectively, in two and three dimen-
> sional representation. (Kress, 1999, p. 85)

Kress's claim is supported, we believe, by the stories of Damon, Dànielle,
Joseph, Brittney, and Charles, among others. These cases indicate, moreover, that if literacy educators continue to define literacy in terms of
alphabetic practices only, in ways that ignore, exclude, or devalue new-
media texts, they not only abdicate a professional responsibility to describe the ways in which humans are now communicating and making
meaning, but they also run the risk of their curriculum no longer holding
relevance for students who are communicating in increasingly expansive
networked environments.

Some Final Observations

The digital divide will never be fully addressed until access to computers, and to the acquisition and development of digital literacies, are understood as multidimensional parts of a larger cultural ecology. The preceding discussion of case studies from this project illustrates only some of the complexity associated with access to computers, and thus, to digital literacies, as well as the specific conditions characterizing this access. Given both the complexity and the overdetermined nature of this ecology, it seems most reasonable to conclude that no one action or set of solutions is going to address the entire range of access and literacy issues associated with the digital divide in the United States. The case studies on which we have focused in this book indicate that closing such gaps will depend not so much on providing people with access to computers through one technology gateway, but rather on providing them with access through several such gateways.

In addition, the case studies indicate that equitable access, by itself, is only a starting point, especially for the poor or for people of color, and sometimes for women and people living in rural geographic locations. The specific conditions of access must also be addressed in order to assure people productive environments within which access can make a real difference. One necessary, but not sufficient, element of these conditions must be a broad understanding and valuing of multiple literacies— emerging, competing, and fading—in home, school, community, and workplace environments. None of these considerations, of course, can be addressed in isolation from the cultural ecology within which access to computers, and the acquisition and development of the literacies of technology, make a difference for people.

In concluding, we wish to thank the people who participated in this investigation of digital literacies for their intellectual and personal generosity, those who are represented in this book and those who are not, those who decided to join us as co-authors and those who decided to remain anonymous. Each participant in this study, named or unnamed, helped to author its contents by teaching us about literacy both online and in print. The participants' words have become part of the text that we wrote in these pages and the texts that we will continue to compose throughout our lives. We have found each story, each literacy autobiography, each life history interview to be a compelling narrative about extraordinary human beings—even when they seem to be living the most ordinary of literate lives in the information age.

APPENDIX
Interview Protocol

We're doing research to find out primarily how people came to computers and what their experiences using computers have been. We're interested in what experiences different generations of people living in the United States have had with computers.

Demographic Information

Name:

Current Occupation:

Previous Occupations:

Nationality:

Race:

Orientation (only if volunteered by subject):

Let me get down a few facts about your family as you were growing up.

Immediate family members and ages:

How would you describe your family circumstances?

Income Level:

    Growing up:
    Now:

Parents' Literacy Histories (e.g., literacy values, education, reading/writing/computing activities):

Did your parents value literacy? How? Any literacy stories?

Parents' Education and Professions:

Can you tell us a bit about yourself? Where were you born? Where did you grow up? What is your family like? What are you like?

Place and date of birth:

Where did you live?

    Growing up:
    Now:

Schooling History:

    Elementary   College
    Secondary   Other

Early Exposure to Literacy/Computers

Can you tell us how/when/why you learned to read and write?

Can you tell us the story about when, where, how you first came in contact with computers?

Can you tell us the story about when, where, how you *first learned* to use computers?

Do you remember what the prevailing images/representations of computers were when you were growing up (e.g., movies, television, magazines, books)?

At home

If your family had a computer at home when you were growing up, can you tell us the story of buying the computer? Who bought it? When? Why?

Can you tell us how much the computer cost? Can you talk about how significant/serious that investment was in terms of your family's regular budget?

For what purposes did you use the computer when you first started? As you continued to learn?

Can you tell how a typical session might have gone in your home computing environment?

How often did you use the computer? What contributed to your use of it or not? Are there any stories/incidents that you can remember about this?

Can you remember any books/texts about computers that you had at home? Any that you read? Any computer games?

Can you identify any images that you remember about computer use?

What did you and your siblings and parents use the computer for at this time? As you continued to use it?

At school

Tell the story of how you first learned to use the computer at school: What was your motivation? Age? Who helped? How did they help? What kind of support did you have? In what classes did you learn to use the computer? How much access did you have to a computer per day/week/month?

Describe your use of this computer: Who was there? What times of day? What were the surroundings like?

For what purposes did you use this computer?

For what purposes did other kids use the computer at school when you were all first learning to use technology? As you continued to learn?

Can you tell how a typical session might have gone in this environment?

What determined how frequently you used the computer? Are there any stories/incidents that you can remember about this?

Can you remember any books/texts about computers that you had access to at school? Any that you read? Any computer games?

Can you identify any images that you remember about computer use that you encountered at school? Educational images?

What did your family think about computers? Your learning computers? Your parents? Sisters and brothers? Uncles and Aunts? Cousins? Grandparents? What values did they place on this activity? On your participation? On their role? Do you have any stories you can tell us that would illustrate the value your family placed on computers or computer literacy?

What did your friends think about computers? What values did they place on this activity? On your participation? On their role? Do you have any stories you can tell us that would illustrate the value your friends placed on computers or computer literacy?

What did your teachers/the school you went to think about computers? What values did they place on this activity? On your participation? On their role? Do you have any stories you can tell us that would illustrate the value the educational system placed on computers or computer literacy?

Did you used to read about computers? If so, where? When?

Can you remember any pictures of computers or computer use that struck you as memorable? Where did you see these?

Current Exposure

Do you (or your family) own a computer *now*? If so, please describe it.

If "yes"

Can you tell us the story of buying the computer? Who bought it? When? Why?

Can you tell us how much the computer cost? Can you talk about how significant/serious that investment was in terms of (your, your parents, your family's) regular budget?

Describe for us where you keep the computer in your house/apartment/dorm room: What are the things you have around the computer? What items of furniture do you associate with the computer?

For what purposes do you use this computer (e.g., what kinds of work, what applications)?

For what purposes do your siblings/parents/children use the computer? Who taught them? Who provides support (e-mail)?

Do you access the Web? What do you use it for?

Tell the story of how you learned to use the computer in this environment: What was your motivation? Who helped? What kind of support did you have? Do you continue to have?

What are the rules associated with using a computer in your home/apartment/dorm? Who made up these rules? How do they affect you?

Can you identify books/texts about computers that you have access to at your home/apartment/dorm? Any that you read?

Also

Do you currently have access to a computer someplace other than at home? Where (workplace, school)? When? For how long? How do you get there? How much does it cost to use this computer? How do you get that money to pay for access?

Describe the surroundings in which you use this computer: Who is there? What times of day? What are the surroundings like?

For what purposes do you use this computer?

For what purposes do other students/co-workers use the computer?

Can you tell how a typical session might go in this environment?

Tell the story of how you learned to use the computer in this environment: What was your motivation? Who helped? What kind of support did you have? Do you continue to have?

What are the rules associated with using a computer in this environment? Who made up these rules? How do they affect you?

Can you identify books/texts about computers that you have access to at your school/workplace/other? Any that you read?

Can you describe your current level of skill with computers? Novice, competent, expert? Any stories about your expertise?

What do you think about computers now? Why?

What do your family think about computers now? Your parents? Sisters and brothers? Uncles and aunts? Cousins? Grandparents? Your friends? What values do they place on computer use? On your participation? On their role? Do you have any stories you can tell us that would illustrate the value your family and friends now place on computers or computer literacy?

What values does the educational system currently place on computer use? Do you have any stories you can tell us that would illustrate the value your schools now place on computers or computer literacy?

How/when/where/why do you see yourself using computers in the future?

Do you read about computers? If so, where? When? What do you read **on** computers?

Can you identify any images of computer use that have struck you recently? Where have you seen these images?

Do you use a particular brand of computer? If so, why? Which one? Names of programs?

Anything more you'd like to say about your relationship with computers?

References

American women: Report of the president's commission on the status of women. (1963). U.S. Government Printing Office: Publications of the President's Commission on the Status of Women.

Annals of America, volume 21, 1977–1986. Opportunities and problems at home and abroad. (1987). Chicago, IL: Encyclopedia Britannica, Inc.

Barron, Nancy. (2003). Dear Saints, Dear Stella: Letters examining the messy lines of expectations, stereotypes, and identity in higher education. *College Composition and Communication, 55*(1), 11–37.

Barton, David, & Hamilton, Mary. (1998). *Local literacies: Reading and writing in one community.* London: Routledge.

Beach, Mark. (1986). *Getting it printed.* Cincinnati, OH: North Light Books.

Becker, Henry. (2000). Who's wired and who's not: Children's access to and use of computer technology. *The Future of Children: Children and Computer Technology, 10*(2), 44–75. A Publication of The David and Lucile Packard Foundation.

Bell South Foundation. (2003). *The growing technology gap between schools and students.* Retrieved May 10, 2003, from http://www.bellsouthfoundation.org/pdfs/pltreport03.pdf

Benton Foundation. (1999). *Native networking: Telecommunications and information technology in Indian country.* Retrieved April 17, 2003, from http://www.benton.org/Library/Native/

Benton Foundation. (2003). *The sustainability challenge: Taking EdTech to the next level.* Retrieved May 6, 2003, from http://www.benton.org/Library/sustainability/sus_challenge.pdf

Bertaux, Daniel. (1981). *Biography and society: The life history approach.* Beverly Hills, CA: Sage.

Bertaux, Daniel, & Thompson, Paul. (1993). *Between generations: The life history approach.* Beverly Hills, CA: Sage.

Bertaux, Daniel, & Thompson, Paul. (1997). *Pathways to social class: A qualitative approach to social mobility.* Oxford, UK: Clarendon Press.

Birkerts, Sven. (1994). *Gutenberg elegies: The fate of reading in an electronic age.* New York: Fawcett Columbine.

Bolter, Jay David. (1991). *Writing space: The computer, hypertext and the history of writing.* Hillsdale, NJ: Lawrence Erlbaum Associates.

Bondi, Victor. (Ed.). (1995). *American decades: 1940–1949.* Detroit: Gale Research, Inc.

Brandt, Deborah. (1995). Accumulating literacy: Writing and learning to write in the twentieth century. *College English, 57,* 649–668.

Brandt, Deborah. (1998). Sponsors of literacy. *College Composition and Communication, 49,* 165–185.

Brandt, Deborah. (1999). Literacy learning and economic change. *Harvard Educational Review, 69,* 373–394.

Brandt, Deborah. (2001). *Literacy in American lives.* Cambridge, UK: Cambridge University Press.

Brettell, Caroline B. (Ed.). (1996). *When they read what we write: The politics of ethnography.* Westport, CT: Bergin & Garvey.

Britzman, Deborah P. (2000). "The question of belief": Writing poststructural ethnography. In Elizabeth St. Pierre & Wanda Pillow (Eds.), *Working the ruins: Feminist poststructural theory and methods in education* (pp. 27–40). New York: Routledge.

Bruce, Bertram C. (Ed.). (2003). *Literacy in the information age: Inquiries into meaning making with new technologies.* Newark, DE: International Reading Association.

Bruce, Bertram, & Hogan, Maureen P. (1998). The disappearance of technology: Toward an ecological model of literacy. In David Reinking et al. (Eds.), *Handbook of literacy and technology: Transformations in a post-typographic world* (pp. 269–281). Mahwah, NJ: Lawrence Erlbaum Associates.

Buckeley, William M. (1994, March 16). Computers—the gender divide: A tool for women, a toy for men. *The Wall Street Journal,* p. B1.

Carabillo, Toni. (1993). A passion for the possible. In Feminist Majority Foundation's *The feminist chronicles, 1953–1993.* Retrieved February 25, 2003, from http://www.feminist.org/research/chronicles/chronicl.html

Cassell, Justine, & Jenkins, Henry. (Eds.). (1998). *From Barbie to Mortal Combat.* Cambridge, MA: MIT Press.

Castells, Manuel. (1996). *The rise of the network society* (Vol. 1 in *The information age: Economy, society, and culture*). Malden, MA: Blackwell.

Castells, Manuel. (1997). *The power of identity* (Vol. 2 in *The information age: Economy, society, and culture*). Malden, MA: Blackwell.

Castells, Manuel. (1998). *End of the millennium* (Vol. 3 in *The information age: Economy, society, and culture*). Malden, MA: Blackwell.

Center for Reproductive Rights. (2000). Nations worldwide support a woman's right to choose abortion. Retrieved May 16, 2003, from http://www.crlp.org/pub_fac_atkwwsup.html

Champagne, Duane. (Ed.). (1994). *Chronology of Native North American history: From pre-Columbian times to the present.* Detroit, MI: Gale Research, Inc.

Chicano: History of the Mexican American civil rights movement. (1996). National Communications Latino Center. Retrieved April 24, 2003, from http://chicano.nlcc.com/

Chiseri-Strater, Elizabeth. (1996). Turning in upon ourselves: Positionality, subjectivity, and reflexivity in case study and ethnographic research. In Peter Mortensen & Gesa E. Kirsch (Eds.), *Ethics & representation in qualitative studies of literacy* (pp. 115–133). Urbana, IL: NCTE.

Chronology of Digital Computing Machines (to 1952). (1994). Retrieved November 23, 2003, at http://uk.geocities.com/magoos_universe/chronology-of-dcm.htm

Coley, R. J., Crandler, J., & Engle, P. (1997). *Computers and classrooms: The status of technology in U.S. schools.* Princeton, NJ: Educational Testing Service.

Cooper, Marilyn M. (1986). The ecology of writing. *College English, 48,* 364–375.

Cope, Bill, & Kalantzis, Mary. (Eds.). (2000). *Multiliteracies: Literacy learning and the design of social futures.* London: Routledge.

Council of Economic Advisors. (1985, February). *Economic report of the president.* Washington, DC: Government Printing Office.

Council of Economic Advisors. (1990, February). *Economic report of the president.* Washington, DC: Government Printing Office.

Council of Economic Advisors. (1997, February). *Economic report of the president.* Washington, DC: Government Printing Office.

CRA Taulbee trends. (2003). Washington, DC: Computing Research Association. Retrieved May 6, 2003, from http://www.cra.org/info/taulbee/women.html

DeCerteau, Michael. (1984). *The practice of everyday life* (S. Randall, Trans.). Berkeley: University of California Press.

Deibert, Ronald J. (1997). *Parchment, printing, and hypermedia: Communication in world order transformation.* New York: Columbia University Press.

Dillon, Nancy. (1998, September 25). *Games make training child's play.* Computer World site. Retrieved May 2, 2003, from http://www.computerworld.com/news/1998/story/0,11280,26370,00.html

Dumas, Joseph S. (1988). *Designing user interfaces for software.* Englewood Cliffs, NJ: Prentice Hall.

Echols, Alice. (1989). *Daring to be bad: Radical feminism in America.* Minneapolis: University of Minnesota Press.

Encyclopedia Britannica guide to Black history, The: Timeline. (1999). Retrieved April 23, 2003, from http://blackhistory.eb.com/

Events in Hispanic American history. (1997). The Hispanic-American Almanac. The Gale Group. Retrieved April 24, 2003, from http://www.galegroup.com/free_resources/chh/timeline/index.htm

Falicov, Celia Jaes. (2002). Ambiguous loss. In Marcelo M. Suárez-Orozco & Mariela M. Páez (Eds.), *Latinos: Remaking America* (pp. 274–288). Berkeley: University of California Press.

Falling through the net: A survey of the "have nots" in rural and urban America. (1995, July). United States Department of Commerce, Economic and Statistics Administration, and National Telecommunication and Information Administration, Washington, DC. Retrieved April 16, 2003, from http://www.ntia.doc.gov/ntiahome/digitaldivide/

Falling through the net II: New data on the digital divide. (1998, July). United States Department of Commerce, Economic and Statistics Administration, and National Telecommunication and Information Administration, Washington, DC. Retrieved April 16, 2003, from http://www.ntia.doc.gov/ntiahome/net2/

Falling through the net: Defining the digital divide. (1999, July). United States Department of Commerce, Economic and Statistics Administration, and National Telecommunication and Information Administration, Washington, DC. Retrieved April 16, 2003, from http://www.ntia.doc.gov/ntiahome/digitaldivide/

Falling through the net: Toward digital inclusion: A report on Americans' access to technology tools. (2000, October). United States Department of Commerce, Economic and Statistics Administration, and National Telecommunication and Information Administration, Washington, DC. Retrieved April 16, 2003, from http://www.ntia.doc.gov/ntiahome/digitaldivide/

Fallon, M. A. C. (1993). Apple Computer Corporation. In A. Ralston & E. D. Reilly (Eds.), *Encyclopedia of computer science* (3rd ed., pp. 70–73). New York: Van Nostrand Reinhold.

Faludi, Susan. (1992). *Backlash: The undeclared war against American women.* New York: Anchor Books.

Father knows best. (2002). Tim's TV Showcase. Retrieved April 12, 2003, from http://www.timvp.com/father.html

Feenberg, Andrew. (1999). *Questioning technology.* New York: Routledge.

Feminist Majority Foundation. (1995). *The feminist chronicles, 1953–1993.* Retrieved April 12, 2003, from http://www.feminist.org/research/chronicles/chronicl.html

Freeman, Laura. (1996). Job creation and the emerging home computer market. *Monthly Labor Review, 119*(8), 46–56.

Freire, Paulo. (1990). *Pedagogy of the oppressed* (Myra Bergman Ramos, Trans.). New York: The Continuum Publishing Company.

Friedman, Susan. (1998). *Mappings: Feminism and the cultural geographies of encounter.* Princeton, NJ: Princeton University Press.

Friedrich, Otto. (2002). The computer. Time, Inc. Retrieved April 27, 2003, from http://www.time.com/time/personoftheyear/archive/stories/1982.html

Furger, Roberta. (1998). *Does Jane compute? Preserving our daughters' place in the cyber revolution.* New York: Warner Books.

Gee, James Paul. (1996). *Social linguistics and literacies: Ideology in discourses* (2nd ed.). London: Taylor and Francis.

Gee, James Paul. (2003). *What video games have to teach us about learning and literacy.* New York: Palgrave Macmillan.

George, Diana, & Shoos, Diane. (1999). Dropping bread crumbs in the intertextual forest: Critical literacy in a postmodern age. In Gail E. Hawisher & Cynthia L. Selfe (Eds.), *Passions, pedagogies, and 21st century technologies* (pp. 115–126). Logan: Utah State University Press.

Getting America's students ready for the 21st century: Meeting the technology literacy challenge, a report to the nation on technology and education. (1996). A report from the U.S. Department of Education, Washington, DC.

Giddens, Anthony. (1979). *Central problems in social theory: Action, structure and contradiction in social analysis.* Berkeley and Los Angeles: University of California Press.

Global Net population increases. (2003, February 25). Retrieved May 2, 2003, from http://www.nua.ie/surveys/?f=VS&art_id=905358729&rel=true

Goodman, William. (1996). The role of computers in reshaping the work force. *Monthly Labor Review, 119*(8), 37–45.

Graff, Harvey J. (1987). *The legacies of literacy: Continuities and contradictions in Western culture and society.* Bloomington: Indiana University Press.

Hall of Famers. (2000–2001). Naismith Memorial Basketball Hall of Famers, Inc. Retrieved April 25, 2003, from http://www.hoophall.com/halloffamers/Wooden.htm

Harley, Sharon. (1995). *The timetables of African-American history: A chronology of the most important people and events in African-American history.* New York: Simon & Schuster.

HarrisInteractive. (2002, July 29). College students spend $200 billion per year. Retrieved May 1, 2003, from http://www.harrisinteractive.com/news/allnewsbydate.asp?NewsID=480

Hawisher, Gail E. (2000). Accessing the virtual worlds of cyberspace. *Journal of Electronic Publishing.* 6.1. Retrieved November 1, 2003, from http://www.press.umich.edu/jep/06-01/hawisher.html

Hawisher, Gail E., & Selfe, Cynthia L. (Eds.). (1989). *Critical perspectives on computers and composition instruction.* New York: Teachers College Press.

Hawisher, Gail E., & Selfe, Cynthia L. (1991). The rhetoric of technology and the electronic writing class. *College Composition and Communication, 42,* 55–65.

Hawisher, Gail E., & Selfe, Cynthia L. (1993). Tradition and change in computer-supported writing environments: A call to action. In Phyllis Kahaney, Linda Perry, & Joseph Janangelo (Eds.), *Theoretical and critical perspectives on teacher change* (pp. 155–186). New York: Teachers College Press.

Hawisher, Gail E., LeBlanc, Paul, Moran, Charles, & Selfe, Cynthia L. (1996). *Computers and the teaching of writing in American higher education, 1979–1984: A history.* Norwood, NJ: Ablex.

Healy, Jane M. (1998). *Failure to connect: How computers affect our children's minds for better and worse.* New York: Simon & Schuster.

Heath, Shirley Brice. (1983). *Ways with words: Language, life, and work in communities and class-rooms.* New York: Cambridge University Press.

Heines, Jesse M. (1984). *Screen design strategies for computer-assisted instruction.* Bedford, MA: Digital Press.

Hiltz, Star Roxanne, & Turoff, Murray. (1978). *The network nation.* New York: Addison Wesley.

Hobbs, Catherine. (1995). *Nineteenth-century women learn to write.* Charlottesville: University Press of Virginia.

Hoffman, Donna L., & Novak, Thomas P. (1998). Bridging the racial divide on the Internet. *Science, 280,* 390–391.

hooks, bell. (1989). *Talking back: Thinking feminist, thinking black.* Boston: South End Press.

Horton, William K. (1990). *Designing & writing online documentation: Help files to hypertext.* New York: John Wiley & Sons.

Internet Society (ISOC). (2002). Retrieved April 16, 2003, from http://www.isoc.org/internet/history/

Jackson, Charles. (2002). The quest of the Golden Fleece: Live the myth. Retrieved May 1, 2003, from http://www.geocities.com/charliensane

Jaffe, Alexandra. (1996). Involvement, detachment, and representation on Corsica. In Caroline B. Brettell (Ed.), *When they read what we write: The politics of ethnography* (pp. 51–66). Westport: Bergin & Garvey.

Jezer, Marty. (1982). *The dark ages: Life in the United States 1945–1960.* Boston: South End Press.

Johnston, William B., & Packer, Arnold H. (1987). *Workforce 2000: Work and workers for the 21st century.* Indianapolis, IN: Hudson Institute.

Jones, Delmos J. (1979). Toward a native anthropology. *Human Organization, 29*(Winter), 251–259.

Judy, Richard W., & D'Amico, Carol. (1997). *Workforce 2020: Work and workers in the 21st century.* Indianapolis, IN: Hudson Institute.

Katzenstein, Mary F. (1990). Feminism within American institutions: Unobtrusive mobilization in the 1980s. *SIGNS, 16,* 27–54.

Katzenstein, Mary Fainsod, & Reppy, Judy. (Eds.). (1999). *Beyond zero tolerance: Discrimination in military culture.* New York: Rowman & Littlefield.

Kearsley, Greg. (1985). *Training for tomorrow: Distributed learning through computer and communications technology.* Reading, MA: Addison-Wesley Publishing, Co.

Kirsch, Gesa. (1993). *Women writing the academy: Audience, authority, and transformation.* Carbondale: Southern Illinois University Press.

Kress, Gunther. (1999). 'English' at the crossroads: Rethinking curricula of communication in the context of the turn to the visual. In Gail E. Hawisher & Cynthia L. Selfe (Eds.), *Passions, pedagogies, and 21st century technologies* (pp. 66–88). Logan: Utah State University Press.

Kress, Gunther. (2003). *Literacy in the new media age.* London: Routledge.

Kurzweil, Raymond. (1990). *The age of intelligent machines.* Cambridge, MA: MIT Press.

Kvasny, Lynette. (2003, April). *Triple jeopardy: Race, gender and class politics of women and technology.* Paper presented at the Association for Computing Machinery's Conference on "Freedom in Philadelphia: Leveraging Differences and Diversity in the IT Workforce," Philadelphia, PA.

Laclau, Ernesto, & Mouffe, Chantal. (1985). *Hegemony and socialist strategy. Towards a radical democratic politics.* London: Verso.

Lather, Patti. (2000). Drawing the line at angels: Working the ruins of feminist ethnography. In Elizabeth St. Pierre & Wanda Pillow (Eds.), *Working the ruins: Feminist poststructural theory and methods in education* (pp. 284–311). New York: Routledge.

Legacy of Kain, The. (2000). Retrieved May 2, 2003, from http://www.legacyofkain.com/

Lemke, Jay L. (1995). *Textual politics: Discourse and social dynamics.* London: Taylor & Francis.

Levidow, Les, & Robins, Kevin. (Eds.). (1989). *Cyborg worlds: The military information society.* London: Free Association Books.

Life on the Internet. (1997). PBS Online. Retrieved April 26, 2003, from http://www.pbs.org/internet/index.html

Lummis, Trevor. (1987). *Listening to history: The authenticity of oral evidence.* London: Hutchinson.

Lynch, Patrick D., & Charleston, Mike. (1990). The emergence of American Indian leadership in education. *Journal of American Indian Education, 29*(2). Retrieved May 26, 2003, from http://jaie.asu.edu/v29/V29S2eme.htm

McBeth, Sally. (1993). Myths of objectivity and the collaborative process in life history research. In Caroline B. Brettell (Ed.), *When they read what we write: The politics of ethnography* (pp. 145–162). Westport, CT: Bergin & Garvey.

Mead, Margaret. (1970). *Culture and commitment: The new relationships between the generations in the 1970s.* Garden City, NY: Doubleday.

Meares, Carol A., & Sargent, John F. (1999). *The digital workforce: Building infotech skills at the speed of innovation.* A Report of the U.S. Department of Commerce. Washington, DC: Office of Technology Policy.

Merit's history: Three decades of growth, innovation, and achievement at Michigan's leading ISP. (1998). An article reprinted from Library Hi Tech (Vol. 16, No. 1). Retrieved May 26, 2003, from http://www.merit.edu

Moran, Charles. (1999). Access: The A-word in technology studies. In Gail E. Hawisher & Cynthia L. Selfe (Eds.), *Passions, pedagogies, and 21st century technologies* (pp. 205–220). Logan: Utah State University Press.

Moris, Francisco A. (1996). Semiconductors: The building blocks of the information revolution. *Monthly Labor Review, 119*(8), 6–17.

Myers, Miles. (1996). *Changing our minds: Negotiating English and literacy.* Urbana, IL: National Council of Teachers of English.

NASA. Retrieved May 16, 2003, from http://www.nasa.gov

National Center for Educational Statistics. (1980). *The Condition of Education 1980* (NCES 80-400). Washington, DC: U.S. Department of Education.

National Center for Educational Statistics. (1995). *Digest of education statistics 1995* (NCES 96-133). Retrieved April 21, 2003, from http://nces.ed.gov/pubsold/D95

National Center for Educational Statistics. (2000, May). *Digest of education statistics 1999.* Retrieved May 26, 2003, from http://nces.ed.gov/pubs2001/digest/foreword.asp

National Council of Teachers of Mathematics. (2000). *Principles and standards for school mathematics.* Retrieved November 24, 2003, from http://standards.nctm.org/

Native American History Timeline. (n.d.). Retrieved November 23, 2003, from http://www.intervarsitynw.org/us%20Native%20American%20Timeline.doc

Native Americans and the digital divide. (1999, October 14). *The Digital Beat, 1*(17), Benton Foundation Web site. Retrieved April 17, 2003, from http://www.benton.org/DigitalBeat/db101499.html

New London Group, The. (1996). A pedagogy of multiliteracies: Designing social futures. *Harvard Educational Review, 66*(1), 60–92.

1900s, The: American news and lifestyle headlines from 1900–1999 . . . plus a century of sound. (1999–2002). Retrieved April 16, 2003, at the Tripod Web site from http://archer2000.tripod.com/index.html

Noble, Douglas D. (1989). Mental materiel: The militarization of learning and intelligence. In Leo Levidow & Kevin Robins (Eds.), *Cyborg worlds: The military information society* (pp. 13–41). London: Free Association Books.

Olson, C. Paul. (1987). Who computes? In David Livingston (Ed.), *Critical pedagogy and cultural power* (pp. 179–204). South Hadley, MA: Bergin & Garvey.

Ovando, Carlos J. (2001). Beyond 'blaming' the victim': Successful schools for Latino students. *Educational Researcher, 30,* 29–31, 39.

Path of the women's rights movement, 1848–1999, The. (1997–2002). Retrieved April 16, 2003, from http://www.legacy98.org/timeline.html

PBS life on the Internet. (1997). Web site of the Public Broadcasting System. Retrieved May 26, 2003, from http://www.pbs.org/internet/

Polsson, Ken. (1995–2001). *Chronology of events in the history of microcomputers.* Retrieved April 16, 2003, from http://www.islandnet.com/~kpolsson/comphist/

Prior, Paul. (1998). *Writing/disciplinarity: A sociohistoric account of literate activity in the academy.* Mahwah, NJ: Lawrence Erlbaum Associates.

Reinharz, Shulamit. (1992). *Feminist methods in social research.* New York: Oxford University Press.

Richardson, Laurel. (2000). Skirting a pleated text: De-disciplining an academic life. In Elizabeth St. Pierre & Wanda Pillow (Eds.), *Working the ruins: Feminist poststructural theory and methods in education* (pp. 153–163). New York: Routledge.

Rodriguez, Richard. (1982). *Hunger of memory: The education of Richard Rodriguez.* Boston: Godine.

Rose, Mike. (1989). *Lives on the boundary: The struggles and achievements of America's underprepared.* New York: Free Press.

Rudolph, Frederick. (1972). *The American college and university: A history.* New York: Vintage Books.

Russell, David. (1991). *Writing in the academic disciplines, 1870–1990: A curricular history* (Rev. ed.). Carbondale: Southern Illinois University Press.

Ryder, Norman B. (1965). The cohort as a concept in the study of social change. *American Sociological Review, 30,* 843–861.

Schell, Eileen E. (1998). *Gypsy academics and mother-teachers: Gender, contingent labor, and writing instruction.* Portsmouth, NH: Boynton/Cook.

Schell, Eileen E., & Stock, Patricia Lambert. (2001). *Moving a mountain: Transforming the role of contingent faculty in composition studies and higher education.* Urbana, IL: National Council of Teachers of English.

Schoen, Donald. (1983). *The reflexive practitioner.* New York: Basic Books.

Segal, Mady Wechsler. (1999). Military culture and military families. In Mary Fainsod Katzenstein & Judy Reppy (Eds.), *Beyond zero tolerance: Discrimination in military culture* (pp. 251–261). New York: Rowman & Littlefield.

Selfe, Cynthia. (1999). *Technology and literacy in the twenty-first century: The importance of paying attention.* Carbondale: Southern Illinois University Press.

Selfe, Cynthia L., & Hawisher, Gail E. (2002). A historical look at electronic literacy: Implications for the education of technical communicators. *Journal of Business and Technical Communication, 16*(3), 231–276.

Shorris, Earl. (1992). *Latinos: A biography of the people.* New York: Norton.

Sides, Charles H. (1984). *How to write papers about computer technology.* Philadelphia: ISI Press.

Smith, Jessie Carney, & Horton, Carrell Peterson. (Eds.). (1995). *Historical statistics of Black America: Agriculture to labor & employment.* Detroit: Gale Research, Inc.

Soul Reaver. (2000). Retrieved May 2, 2003, from http://www.eidosinteractive.com/gss/legacy/legacyofkain/main.html

Spillers, Hortense J. (1991). Who cuts the border: Some readings on 'America.' In Hortense Spillers (Ed.), *Comparative American identities* (pp. 1–25). New York: Routledge.

St. Pierre, Elizabeth, & Pillow, Wanda. (Eds.). (2000). *Working the ruins: Feminist poststructural theory and methods in education.* New York: Routledge.

Standards for the English language arts. (1996). Newark, DE, and Urbana, IL: International Reading Association and the National Council of Teachers of English.

Standards projects. (1999). *National Educational Technology Standards for Students.* Retrieved May 16, 2003, from http://www.iste.org/standards/index.cfm

Stimpson, Catharine R., with Cobb, Nina Kressner. (1986). *Women's studies in the United States.* New York: Ford Foundation.

Street, Brian V. (1995). *Social literacies: Critical approaches to literacy in development, ethnography, and education.* London: Longman.

Stuckey, Elspeth. (1991). *The violence of literacy.* Portsmouth, NH: Boynton Cook/Heinemann.

Suárez-Orozco, Marcelo M., & Páez, Mariela M. (Eds.). (2002). *Latinos: Remaking America.* Berkeley: University of California Press.

Sullivan, Patricia, & Dautermann, Jennie. (Eds.). (1996). *Electronic literacies in the workplace: Technologies of writing.* Urbana, IL: National Council of Teachers of English.

Survey shows widespread enthusiasm for technology. (1999). NPR/Kaiser/Kennedy School Technology Survey. Retrieved May 12, 2003, from http://www.npr.org/programs/specials/poll/technology/

Technology counts '99: Building the digital curriculum. (1999, September 23). *Education Week on the Web.* The Web site of Milken Exchange. Retrieved April 21, 2003, from http://www.edweek.org/sreports/tc99/

Thompson, Paul. R. (1988). *The voice of the past: Oral history.* Oxford, UK: Oxford University Press.

Thurston, Catherine. (1994). Computer-assisted instruction. In *Encyclopedia of English studies and language arts of the National Council of Teachers of English* (pp. 250–252). New York: National Council of Teachers of English.

Timeline of Computing History. (1996). Computer innovative technology for computer professionals. Retrieved November 24, 2003, at IEEE Web site at http://www.computer.org/computer/timeline/

Tyner, Kathleen. (1998). *Literacy in a digital world: Teaching and learning in the age of information.* Mahwah, NJ: Lawrence Erlbaum Associates.

U.S. Census Bureau. (2001). U.S. Hispanic population: 2000. Retrieved April 17, 2003, from http://www.census.gov/population/socdemo/hispanic/p20-535/gifshow/sld001.htm

U.S. Department of Commerce. (February 2002). *A Nation Online: How Americans are expanding their use of the Internet.* Retrieved February 24, 2003, from http://www.ntia.doc.gov/ntiahome/dn/index.html

U.S. Department of Labor. (1999). *Futurework: Trends and challenges for work in the 21st century.* Washington, DC: Author.

U.S. Department of Labor. (1999). *Report on the American workforce.* Retrieved April 16, 2003, from http://www.bls.gov/opub/rtaw/rtawhome.htm

U.S. Department of Labor. (n.d.). Title IX, education amendments of 1972. Retrieved May 15, 2003, from http://www.dol.gov/oasam/regs/statutes/titleix.htm

Villanueva, Victor, Jr. (1993). *Bootstraps: From an American academic of color.* Urbana, IL: National Council of Teachers of English.

Visweswaran, Kamala. (1994). *Fictions of feminist ethnography.* Minneapolis: University of Minnesota Press.

Warnke, Jacqueline. (1996). Computer manufacturing: Change and competition. *Monthly Labor Review, 119*(8), 18–29.

Wei, Christina Chang, & Horn, Laura. (2002, May). Persistence and attainment of beginning students with Pell Grants. Retrieved April 12, 2003, from http://nces.ed.gov/das/epubs/2002169/

Weiss, Edmund H. (1985). *How to write a usable user manual.* Philadelphia: ISI Press.

White, Daniel. (1998). *Postmodern ecology: Communication, evolution, and play.* Albany, NY: SUNY Press.

White, Jan V. (1982). *Editing by design: A guide to effective word-and-picture communication for editors and designers.* New York: R.R. Bowker Company.

White, Stephen. (1996–2001). A brief history of computing. Retrieved April 16, 2003, from http://www.ox.compsoc.net/~swhite/timeline.html

Whittier, Nancy. (1995). *Feminist generations: The persistence of the radical women's movement.* Philadelphia: Temple University Press.

Wysocki, Anne Frances, & Johnson-Eilola, Johndan. (1999). Blinded by the letter: Why are we using literacy as a metaphor for everything else? In Gail E. Hawisher & Cynthia L. Selfe (Eds.), *Passions, pedagogies, and 21st century technologies* (pp. 349–368). Logan: Utah State University Press.

Zakon, Robert H. (1993–2003). *Hobbes' Internet timeline, v6.0.* Retrieved April 21, 2003, at the Web site of the Internet Society at http://info.isoc.org/internet/history/

Zinn, Howard. (1998). *The twentieth century: A people's history.* New York: HarperPerennial.

Author Index

Subject Index